Subjects
and Aliens

HISTORIES OF NATIONALITY,
LAW AND BELONGING IN
AUSTRALIA AND NEW ZEALAND

Subjects and Aliens

HISTORIES OF NATIONALITY,
LAW AND BELONGING IN
AUSTRALIA AND NEW ZEALAND

**EDITED BY KATE BAGNALL
AND PETER PRINCE**

Australian
National
University

ANU PRESS

Australian
National
University

ANU PRESS

Published by ANU Press
The Australian National University
Canberra ACT 2600, Australia
Email: anupress@anu.edu.au

Available to download for free at press.anu.edu.au

ISBN (print): 9781760465858
ISBN (online): 9781760465865

WorldCat (print): 1390723283
WorldCat (online): 1390723081

DOI: 10.22459/SA.2023

Cover design and layout by ANU Press. Cover photograph: Stereograph – Chinese procession and Queen's arch, Federation celebrations, 1901, Museums Victoria.

This book is published under the aegis of the Humanities and Creative Arts editorial board of ANU Press.

Contents

List of Figures

Acknowledgements

This book evolved from a symposium on the history of nationality and citizenship in Australia and New Zealand convened by Kate Bagnall at the University of Wollongong in 2017 and supported by the Centre for Colonial and Settler Studies. Kate is very grateful to the scholars who presented their work at the Subjects and Aliens symposium, including those who were ultimately unable to prepare their research for publication in this volume. Kim Rubenstein presented the keynote lecture at the 2017 symposium. We thank Kim for her intellectual contribution and leadership in the field of citizenship, and her ongoing interest and support for this project.

We express further thanks to those who assisted with the symposium and this collection, not least Lauren Samuelsson at the University of Wollongong and our copyeditor, Rani Kerin. We also thank the ANU Press team, and the ANU Press publication subsidy committee for their support and enthusiasm for publishing this book.

Research for the volume has been assisted by an Australian Research Council (ARC) Discovery Early Career Researcher Award (Kate Bagnall, DE160100027 'Chinese Seeking Citizenship in Australia, New Zealand and Canada, 1860–1920'), a Royal Society of New Zealand Marsden Fast-Start Grant (Jane McCabe), two ARC Discovery Project Awards (Margaret Allen, DP0452778 'Links across Empire, India and Australia, 1880–1925' and DP170104310 'Beyond Empire: Transnational Religious Networks and Liberal Cosmopolitanisms') and an Australian Government Research Training Program Scholarship (Emma Bellino).

Preface

Kim Rubenstein

What a delight to be asked to write the preface to this substantial collection, one that captures the energy and richness of a University of Wollongong 2017 workshop[1] that I so well remember. This resulting book is a tribute to its editors and contributors. Their commitment and perseverance over five years has produced an excellent, evergreen analysis and makes important research accessible to citizenship and membership scholars in Australia, New Zealand and beyond – not to mention the greater community.

The collection highlights the prescience of bringing Australian and New Zealand scholars together to focus on citizenship scholarship and its central importance to community and political coherence. As this collection goes to press, the prime minister of Australia, Anthony Albanese, has flagged giving New Zealanders a faster pathway to citizenship and even aligning voting entitlements between the two countries. Australians who are permanent residents and who have lived in New Zealand for more than a year can vote in New Zealand elections.[2] The Australian Parliament's Joint Standing Committee on Electoral Matters has been asked to consider the rights of New Zealand citizens in Australia – working here, being part of the community, paying taxes and otherwise contributing.

---

1   The symposium was convened by Kate Bagnall as part of her DECRA fellowship. It was organised through the Colonial and Settler Studies Network and supported by the Feminist Research Network, all at the University of Wollongong.
2   See 'Are You Eligible to Enrol and Vote?', Electoral Commission, accessed 2 March 2023, vote.nz/enrolling/get-ready-to-enrol/are-you-eligible-to-enrol-and-vote/; Section 74, Electoral Act 1993 (NZ), legislation.govt.nz/act/public/1993/0087/latest/DLM308827.html.

Already, some scholars have voiced publicly their scepticism about the constitutionality of such a move.[3] They reference the democracy founding sections (7 and 24) of the Australian Constitution, warning that 'the people' referred to may not include New Zealanders. If so, then extending voting rights to them may be unconstitutional.

But, when delivering the opening lecture at the 2017 symposium – and setting the scene for constitutional engagement around nationality, law and belonging – I explained that at the time of Federation, 'the people' were not Australian citizens, there was no such concept. Indeed, during the constitutional convention debates, the framers resisted any attempt to define and delineate Australian citizenship as a key membership status. These were debates in which New Zealand representatives participated, although ultimately determining not to become part of the Commonwealth.

New Zealanders, and all other dominion members of the British Empire, held the same membership status in 1901 as Australian residents did at that time – they were all British subjects. So, in 1901, when the Commonwealth of Australia was established, New Zealanders residing in Australia held identical rights of membership as other Commonwealth residents – for British subject status was the fullest form of membership. That said, those New Zealanders and other British subjects at the time held stronger forms of membership than Indigenous Australians, who, while formally British subjects, were not extended full British subject rights. This discussion is just one of many indicating the ongoing value of diving into the historical foundations of nationality, law and belonging in Australia and New Zealand and laying them bare in this monograph.

To their credit, the editors go further – explaining in their first chapter how *Subjects and Aliens* gathers scholarship investigating legal and social histories of nationality and citizenship in Australia and Aotearoa New Zealand, at the same time as highlighting the intersections of gender, race and ethnicity with nationality and citizenship.

---

3   Tom McIlroy, 'Giving Kiwis Voting Rights in Australia Constitutionally "Risky"', *Australian Financial Review*, 27 October 2022, www.afr.com/politics/federal/giving-kiwis-voting-rights-in-australia-unsafe-2022 1027-p5btel.

'Citizenship', and its equivalent term 'nationality'[4] – so central to political ideals and organisation since the days of the Athenian lawgiver Solon, embossed by the Enlightenment and modern democratic theory,[5] enlarged by T. H. Marshall's broader socioeconomic gloss in the 1950s[6] and further commodified in a globalised world[7] – has, nonetheless, never been more nebulous, contested, ambulatory, fractured and abused than now. While citizenship 'has no definition that is fixed for all time … [i]t has always been at stake in struggles and the object of transformations'.[8]

It is, therefore, timely that this collection challenges ideas of who historically 'belonged' in Australia and New Zealand and highlights how citizenship rights in the two countries have been inconsistent and contested. By examining histories of law and policy surrounding nationality and citizenship rights in Australasia through the lived experience of individuals, families and communities negotiating their lives as British subjects or 'aliens' – those without British subject status – we can see that the ongoing contestation has remarkable foundations.

With the focus of the collection directed to the first half of the twentieth century, up to the introduction of Australian and New Zealand citizenship in 1949 and to the earlier colonial period, we gain valuable insights into the current pressing issues of our time: who belongs, what does belonging mean, and how secure is that membership when the democratic foundations to our system of government are so unclear and fragile?

---

4   Both terms refer to the full legal status of membership of the nation-state; 'citizenship' is more often used in a domestic legal context and 'nationality' in the international law context.
5   See Paul Barry Clarke, *Citizenship* (London: Pluto Press, 1994).
6   T. H. Marshall, *Citizenship and Social Class: And Other Essays* (New York: Cambridge University Press, 1950).
7   Aihwa Ong, *Flexible Citizenship: The Cultural Logic of Transnationality* (Durham, North Carolina: Duke University Press, 1999), doi.org/10.7202/704267ar.
8   Etienne Balibar, 'Propositions on Citizenship', *Ethics* 98, no. 4 (1988): 723, doi.org/10.1086/293001.

1

Australia's 'Alien Races' Meet New Zealand's 'Race Aliens'

Peter Prince and Kate Bagnall

Introduction

A sense of belonging is a fundamental human emotion. It can be reinforced by nationhood – witness the pride of those who go through modern citizenship ceremonies. Or it can be undermined by laws and restrictions created by nation-states. As late as 1971 in Western Australia, for example, Aboriginal people had to apply for 'certificates of citizenship' – on land their ancestors had belonged to for over 60,000 years – to escape racist control over where they lived, worked and who they could marry. Their citizenship 'dog tags' were not a source of pride. Such contradictions in who 'belonged' to the nation, in law and in practice, are at the heart of this book.

Subjects and Aliens brings together scholarship exploring legal and social histories of nationality and citizenship in Australia and Aotearoa New Zealand, with a particular focus on the intersections of gender, race and ethnicity with nationality and citizenship. The collection aims to challenge ideas of who historically 'belonged' in Australia and New Zealand and consider how citizenship rights in the two countries have been inconsistent and contested. To do so, the collection examines histories of law and policy surrounding nationality and citizenship rights in Australasia and considers the lived experience of individuals, families and communities as they negotiated their lives as British subjects or 'aliens' (in a legal sense, as non-British subjects). The temporal focus of the collection is the first half of the

1

twentieth century, up to the introduction of Australian and New Zealand citizenship in 1949,[1] with reference to the earlier colonial period and to significant continuing resonances today.

The volume further speaks to the growing national discussion in the two countries about the shameful, as well as the worthy, elements of our British colonial history and its aftermath. This has been spurred on in Australia's case by the 2017 *Uluru Statement from the Heart* and the campaign for constitutional enshrinement of a First Nations Voice. As Richard Hil explains:

> Yes, we're at an inflection point. The illusion of *Pax Britannica* is just that. The time for a historical reckoning has arrived. Truth told; it's been there for centuries. The gruesome facts of colonial violence and the heroism of past and ongoing Indigenous resistance can no longer be denied. The Voice to Parliament, based on one of the most important and moving documents of recent times, the Uluru Statement of the Heart, has far more historical [resonance] than any number of drumbeats.[2]

While not so singularly focused as, for example, the 2022 *Acts of Reckoning* edition of the *Griffith Review*,[3] this volume seeks to confront the problematic history of belonging in Australia and New Zealand. In that sense, it is not merely a descriptive history. Instead many of the chapters could be described as 'normative' or expressing a value judgment as to what should be. In particular, we draw attention to what we consider a persistent breach of the rule of law, namely the failure of white authorities to follow their own imposed rules about legal belonging, and the right to equal citizenship and protection that should have flowed from this.

A theme running through the collection is the effect of 'race' on belonging. In both countries, race was more important than the law in relation to who 'belonged' or was 'one of us'. As Prince argues in Chapter 7, Papuans born as Australian citizens before Papua New Guinea gained independence in 1975 were excluded from the mainland for reasons linked directly to the White Australia policy. Restrictions on non-European New Zealanders entering

---

1   The legal status of 'Australian citizen' was created by the *Nationality and Citizenship Act 1948* (Cth) (No. 83 of 1948), which commenced on 26 January 1949. The legal status of 'New Zealand citizen' was created by the *British Nationality and New Zealand Citizenship Act 1948* (NZ) (No. 15 of 1948), which came into effect on 1 January 1949.

2   Richard Hil, 'The Drumbeat of History Sounds for the Monarchy', *Pearls and Irritations*, 2 October 2022, johnmenadue.com/the-drumbeat-of-history-sounds-for-the-monarchy/.

3   Ashley Hay and Teela Reid, eds, *Griffith Review 76: Acts of Reckoning* (Text Publishing, 2022), www.griffithreview.com/editions/acts-of-reckoning/.

Australia ended only in 1973.[4] It was not until 1975 that Australia enacted its *Racial Discrimination Act* (Cth) outlawing discrimination on the basis of ethnicity. Similar legislation had commenced in New Zealand only a few years before.[5]

The historical examples in this book are about belonging in the face of exclusion and discrimination. But in Australia, remarkably, 'belonging' remains a contested constitutional and legal concept more than 120 years after Federation. Delegates to the 1890s constitutional conventions refused to define who 'belonged', focusing on racial rather than legal criteria for national membership. Future High Court chief justice Isaac Isaacs said conferral of 'citizenship' on any subject of the Queen resident in the new Commonwealth would 'deprive Parliament of the power of excluding Chinese, Lascars, or Hindoos who happened to be British subjects'.[6] This omission still causes angst today, leaving Australia to determine constitutional membership by the opposite: who is not an 'alien'. That word remains the most powerful in the Australian Constitution – its meaning is 'very important in determining who is an Australian'.[7] But the way the racial use of 'alien' – as a derogatory label for non-Europeans – infected the law in colonial and post-Federation Australia is little understood. That makes the type of history in this volume all the more important. However, as Chapter 7 contends, the High Court has to date managed only a flawed history of belonging in Australia.

For its part, New Zealand has no single constitutional document, and it removed the archaic term 'alien' from official use in its *Citizenship Act 1977*. So New Zealand has been spared Australia's litigation in recent decades over who 'belongs' and what can be done to those unfortunate enough to be labelled as 'aliens' or as not belonging.[8] Yet the intergenerational trauma of a prejudiced historical approach to 'belonging' remains evident in both countries.

---

4   Ian Hoskins, *Australia & the Pacific* (Sydney: NewSouth Publishing, 2021), 343.
5   Ibid. The legislation in both countries implemented the 1969 *United Nations Convention on the Elimination of All Forms of Racial Discrimination*.
6   *Official Record of the Debates of the Australasian Federal Convention*, Melbourne, 3 March 1898, 1788. For an account of the citizenship proposal at the conventions, see Kim Rubenstein, *Australian Citizenship Law*, 2nd ed. (Pyrmont, NSW: Thomson Reuters, 2017), ch. 2.
7   Rubenstein, *Australian Citizenship Law*, 361.
8   See, most recently, *Commonwealth v. AJL20* [2021] HCA 21; *Chetcuti v. Commonwealth of Australia* [2021] HCA 25; *Alexander v. Minister for Home Affairs* [2022] HCA 19. See also Chapter 7 (this volume). As Chief Justice Gleeson noted in his dissenting judgment in *Al-Kateb* (2004) 219 CLR 562 at 577, a failed asylum seeker (i.e. an 'alien') can be kept in immigration detention indefinitely 'regardless of personal circumstances, regardless of whether he or she is a danger to the community, and regardless of whether he or she might abscond'.

Displacing Indigenous Law

This collection is concerned with the development, interpretation and application of British law, imposed on people and land already governed by Indigenous laws. In Australia's case:

> Given that there were more than 250 First Nations in Australia and the Torres Strait in 1788 the successful imposition of English law is anomalous and inconsistent with other parts of the British Empire where existing local law was recognised ... The British arrived on a continent inhabited for thousands of years by cultures with a deeply embedded sense of law and correct behaviour.[9]

In terms of belonging, 'everyone in Aboriginal society knew their identity and place within their kinship system and from an early age were taught their legal obligations to others'.[10]

In New Zealand:

> When Europeans first sighted these lands in 1642, *Aotearoa* comprised many prosperous Māori tribal nations with an operative system of law based on kinship, seasonal economic activity that valued fish, shellfish, birds, wood and greenstone, and closely managed territorial relationships.[11]

In Australia and New Zealand, non-European as well as European settlers occupied lands belonging to First Nations peoples, made all the worse in Australia by the lack of even the (disputed) agreement-making in New Zealand's 1840 Treaty of Waitangi. Under the third article of the Waitangi treaty (in the English version), Queen Victoria imparted to 'the Natives of New Zealand ... all the Rights and Privileges of British Subjects'. However, as Jacinta Ruru and Jacobi Kohu-Morris observe, while this should have given Māori nations undisturbed possession of their lands, estates, forests, fisheries and other properties, in reality, 'the British honoured neither the Māori nor the English version' of the treaty.[12]

---

9   Sarah McKibbin, Libby Connors and Marcus Harmes, *A Legal History for Australia* (Oxford: Hart, 2021), 214, doi.org/10.5040/9781509939602.

10   Ibid., 216.

11   Jacinta Ruru and Jacobi Kohu-Morris, '"Maranga Ake Ai" The Heroics of Constitutionalising *Te Tiriti O Waitangi*/The Treaty of Waitangi in *Aotearoa* New Zealand', *Federal Law Review* 48, no. 4 (2020): 556, 558, doi.org/10.1177/0067205x20955105.

12   Ibid.

The Language of Belonging

Key terms of belonging have multiple meanings, in particular, they have racial and legal meanings. 'Nationality', for example, refers to an ethnic group forming part of one or more political nations, as well as to the status of belonging to a particular nation. The word 'alien' – apart from its science fiction use – also has a non-legal meaning ('a person belonging to another family or race, a stranger') as well as a legal meaning ('One who is a subject of another country than that in which he resides. A resident foreign in origin and not naturalised').[13] The ambiguity of such words made them useful tools for racial exclusion in nineteenth- and twentieth-century Australasia. For example, as explained later in this chapter, the perception that South Sea Islanders were 'aliens' in a racial sense allowed the High Court of Australia in 1906 to authorise their forcible removal under the 'aliens power' in the Constitution even though many were British subjects and not 'aliens' at all under the law.

'Citizenship' is another term with multiple meanings, although with less racial connotation. As Kim Rubenstein explains, the formal notion of 'citizenship' is 'primarily concerned with the legal status of individuals within a community'. In contrast, 'citizenship' in a non-legal sense involves 'the collection of rights, duties and opportunities for participation which define the extent of socio-political membership within a community'.[14] Helen Irving notes that, as the Australian colonies moved towards Federation, there was much discussion of 'citizenship' in this informal sense:

> In the 1890s, the word 'citizen' appears again and again, in speeches, in the press, in the rules and charters of organisations, and in debates about political entitlement. We find the rhetoric of citizenship attached in particular to the federation movement.[15]

But, in terms of legal status, as Guy Aitken and Robert Orr note:

> The *Constitution* does not contain any reference to Australian citizenship. Indeed, at the advent of federation in 1901, and for a long time after that, there was no such concept. All persons in Australia were either British subjects or aliens.[16]

---

13 *Oxford English Dictionary* (Oxford: Clarendon Press, 1989).

14 Rubenstein, *Australian Citizenship Law*, 6–7.

15 Helen Irving, 'Citizenship before 1949', in *Individual, Community, Nation: Fifty Years of Australian Citizenship*, ed. Kim Rubenstein (Melbourne: Australian Scholarly Publishing, 2000), 9, 10.

16 Guy Aitken and Robert Orr, *Sawer's The Australian Constitution*, 3rd ed. (Canberra: Australian Government Solicitor, 2002), 48.

Until citizenship was formally created in New Zealand and Australia by legislation in 1949, the nationality of their 'citizens' was solely that of 'British subject'. Importantly, this legal status was shared with inhabitants of other British possessions. Any natural-born or naturalised inhabitant of the various British colonies and dominions across the world – whatever their racial background and whether they were in Africa, Asia, the Pacific Islands or Australasia – shared the imperial nationality of 'British subject', with common allegiance to the King or Queen of England. As Justice Higgins said in the 1908 Australian High Court case *Potter v. Minahan*:

> All the King's subjects are members of one great society, bound by the one tie of allegiance to the one Sovereign, even as children hanging onto the ropes of a New Zealand swing. The top of the pole is the point of the union: *Calvin's Case*.[17]

In *Calvin's Case* (1608), the revered champion of the rule of law, Sir Edward Coke, laid down the guiding principle for legal membership of the British Empire for the next three and a half centuries, namely: 'they that are born under the obedience, power, faith, ligealty, or ligeance of the King, are natural subjects, *and no aliens*'.[18]

While there were many other factors that, in practice, determined if a person became a member of the Australian or New Zealand communities, it followed that the only formal legal test under imposed British law until after World War II was whether a person was a 'British subject' or an 'alien'. If someone was a British subject, they could not, under the law applying in the two countries, be a legal outsider or 'alien'. This distinction was, however, routinely ignored by key figures in Australia and New Zealand, who described and treated non-European settlers as 'aliens' even if they were legally British subjects, undermining the very rule of law upon which the society was founded.

---

17   (1908) 7 CLR 277, 320–1.
18   *Calvin v. Smith* or the *Case of the Postnati* ('*Calvin's Case*') (1608) 7 Coke Report 1a, 5b; 77 Eng. Rep. 377, 383. Emphasis added. For the facts and analysis of *Calvin's Case*, see Keechang Kim, 'Calvin's Case (1608) and the Law of Alien Status', *Journal of Legal History* 17, no. 2 (1996): 155; Polly J. Price, 'Natural Law and Birthright Citizenship in *Calvin's Case* (1608)', *Yale Journal of Law & the Humanities* 9, no. 1, art. 2. (1997): 73.

Belonging and Race

Australia and New Zealand played a prominent role in global racial discrimination in the nineteenth and twentieth centuries. In 1921, the British Foreign Office observed that the issue:

> primarily concerns the following countries: Japan, China, British India, United States of America … Canada, Australia, New Zealand, South Africa. The first three countries demand the right of free immigration and freedom from discrimination disabilities for their nationals in the territories of the last five countries. The question can be regarded from an economic or from a political point of view, but in essence it is a racial one.[19]

An enduring theme in white colonisation has been the confusion of race with nationality and allegiance. As Sophie Couchman (Chapter 2) explains, during World War I government officials in Australia wrongly thought men 'not substantially of European origin or descent' would not fight for their country, assuming they lacked allegiance despite being locally born with British subject legal status. Likewise, in Chapter 4, Margaret Allen's discussion of the remarkable Indian statesman V. S. S. Sastri's visit to Australia in 1922 shows that racial difference was more important for white Australians than common nationality and allegiance as British subjects. At the 1891 National Australasian Convention, Chairman of the Constitutional Drafting Committee Sir Samuel Griffith first proposed what became the notorious 'races' power in section 51(xxvi) of the Australian Constitution, declaring:

> The intention of the clause is that if any state by any means gets a number of an alien race into its population, the matter shall not be dealt with by the state, but the Commonwealth will take the matter into its own hands … What I have had more particularly in my own mind was the immigration of coolies from British India, or any eastern people subject to civilised powers.[20]

Notwithstanding his leading role in drafting the Constitution, Griffith had no hesitation in labelling British Indians as an 'alien race', even though they were legally British subjects. A generation later, Sastri encountered similar

---

19 Public Record Office, Foreign Office, United Kingdom, 371/6684, 10 October 1921, cited in Paul Gordon Lauren, *Power and Prejudice: The Politics and Diplomacy of Racial Discrimination* (Boulder: Westview, 1988), 103.
20 *Official Report of the Australasian Convention Debates*, Sydney, 3 April 1891, 701, 703.

prejudice against Indian people. Despite his standing in the British Empire and his visit as an official guest of the Commonwealth, Sastri's extensive tour of the Australian states resulted in little relaxation of domestic racial restrictions against Indian Australians.

In Australia, key political and legal figures used the term 'alien races' as a derogatory label for Chinese and other non-European inhabitants, despite knowing many were British subjects and not 'aliens' under the law. In 1888, the premier of Victoria, Duncan Gillies, reported to the Imperial Parliament that the Chinese were 'not only an alien race, but remain aliens',[21] explaining that 'naturalised British subjects are still Chinese and are as objectionable as if they were to come from the centre of China'.[22] This racial use of 'alien' spilled over into legal usage, infecting even John Quick and Robert Garran's iconic 1901 commentary on the new Australian Constitution.[23] After Federation, the misuse of 'alien' at the Commonwealth level reinforced the discriminatory use of the word by the Australian states.[24] In Queensland, in particular, the racial meaning of the word was so embedded that it became the law, in place of the correct legal meaning. This culminated after World War I in numerous prosecutions of 'coloured aliens', with little or no regard as to whether those brought before the courts were British subjects or not.[25]

In New Zealand from 1898 until 1954, annual government yearbooks and census records included the population category 'race aliens'. As New Zealand's 1912 yearbook explained: 'Persons of other than European descent are classified in the immigration returns as "race aliens".'[26] In other words, these were New Zealand residents deemed not to belong solely because of their racial background. Inhabitants from British India, Hong Kong, Fiji and other British possessions were labelled in this way even though they legally belonged as British subjects. Even New Zealanders of

---

21 *Daily Telegraph*, 17 April 1888, cited in Ian Welch, 'Alien Son: The Life and Times of Cheok Hong Cheong, 1851–1928' (PhD thesis, The Australian National University, 2003), 237–38.
22 Victoria, *Parliamentary Debates*, Legislative Assembly, 6 December 1888, 2357, cited in Marilyn Lake, 'Chinese Colonists Assert Their "Common Human Rights": Cosmopolitanism as Subject and Method of History', *Journal of World History* 21, no. 3 (2010): 375, 385, doi.org/10.1353/jwh.2010.0011.
23 See Peter Prince, 'Aliens in Their Own Land. "Alien" and the Rule of Law in Colonial and Post-Federation Australia' (PhD thesis, The Australian National University, 2015), 153ff, openresearch-repository.anu.edu.au/handle/1885/101778.
24 Ibid., ch. 4.
25 Ibid., chs 6 and 7.
26 Statistics New Zealand, 'The New Zealand Official Year-Book, 1912', accessed 30 January 2022, www3.stats.govt.nz/New_Zealand_Official_Yearbooks/1912/NZOYB_1912.html?_ga=2.166736184.787224941.1628550701-1851378558.1628476897#idsect1_1_27390.

part-Māori descent were classified as 'race aliens'. This was inconsistent with New Zealand's own law. The *British Nationality and Status of Aliens (in New Zealand) Act 1923* confirmed the longstanding common law position that an alien 'means a person who is not a British subject'.[27] There was no explanation in the yearbooks that, regardless of their non-European heritage, many 'race aliens' were British subjects and not legal 'aliens'. To the contrary: some yearbooks even included a table listing former inhabitants of 'British possessions' as 'race aliens'.[28] The 1920 yearbook noted that:

> Of the race aliens arriving in New Zealand a large proportion are Chinese, some of whom, however, have been formerly resident in the Dominion. Hindus and other natives of India are also of late years arriving in considerable numbers.[29]

Similarly, in the 1941 yearbook, New Zealand's government statistician stated that:

> The principal race aliens with whom New Zealand is concerned are Chinese, Indians, and Syrians, and the first two are shown separately from other race aliens … At the census of 24th March, 1936, the numbers of the principal alien races in New Zealand (inclusive of persons of mixed blood) were: Chinese, 2,899; Syrian, 1,235; and Indian, 1,157.[30]

Under New Zealand law, inhabitants from the provinces of 'British India' were British subjects.[31] The same was true of Chinese settlers from British possessions in Asia.[32] In addition, people born in New Zealand itself, regardless of ethnic origin (such as most, if not all, of the 'persons of mixed

---

27   First Schedule, Part III, section 27(1).

28   Statistics New Zealand, 'The New Zealand Official Year-Book, 1920', accessed 2 March 2023, www3.stats.govt.nz/New_Zealand_Official_Yearbooks/1920/NZOYB_1920.html?_ga=2.166738360. 787224941.1628550701-1851378558.1628476897#idsect1_1_4064.

29   Ibid. Emphasis added.

30   Statistics New Zealand, 'The New Zealand Official Year-Book, 1941', accessed 2 March 2023, www3.stats.govt.nz/New_Zealand_Official_Yearbooks/1941/NZOYB_1941.html#idsect1_1_13860. Emphasis added.

31   The British Raj was divided into the states of 'British India', directly ruled by the United Kingdom, and the 'Indian Native States', ruled by their own princes under the supervision of the British Crown. The latter 'did not form part of the Dominions of the Crown at any time prior to the commencement of the *Indian Independence Act 1947*'. Clive Parry, *Nationality and Citizenship Laws of the Commonwealth and Republic of Ireland* (London: Stevens & Sons, 1957), 836–37. As Parry says in relation to India, 'a possible view is that the inhabitants of some States were as such British subjects though those of others were not' (841–42).

32   British possessions in Asia with significant ethnic Chinese populations in the nineteenth and early twentieth centuries included Hong Kong, the Straits Settlements (Penang, Malacca and Singapore), Labuan and the Malay States.

blood') were also legal subjects. But, for New Zealand, as in Australia, race and ethnicity were more important than law when categorising the national population. Communities with a non-European ethnic background were branded 'the Other', outsiders, race aliens who did not belong, irrespective of their actual legal status. With its roots in the racial exclusion imposed in the latter half of the nineteenth century, this was a common theme in English settler nations ('white men's countries'). As Mae M. Ngai says about the United States in the 1920s:

> the legal racialization of these ethnic groups' national origin cast them as permanently foreign and unassimilable to the nation ... [and] these racial formations produced 'alien citizens' ... For Chinese and other Asians, alien citizenship was the invariable consequence of racial exclusion from immigration and naturalised citizenship ... While not strictly a legal term, the concept underwrote both formal and informal structures of racial discrimination and was at the core of major, official race policies.[33]

Beyond those of non-European heritage, non-British European communities could also face exclusionary measures. Jane McCabe describes in Chapter 3, for example, how both Chinese settlers and their New Zealand–born descendants who established market gardens on Otago's Taieri Plain, and Dalmatian communities toiling in the Hokianga kauri gum-digging industry, had to navigate legal restrictions that privileged ethnically British families.

One factor in the continuing idea that non-Europeans in Australia and New Zealand, particularly those of Chinese heritage, were 'aliens' was the removal of the right to become a British subject through naturalisation. Australia's first federal *Naturalization Act*, enacted in 1903, prohibited the naturalisation of any person who was 'an aboriginal native of Asia, Africa, or the Islands of the Pacific, excepting New Zealand'.[34] This law codified and broadened a policy in place across the Australasian colonies before Australian Federation whereby Chinese settlers were denied the right to naturalise. New South Wales prohibited Chinese naturalisation by law in 1861, repealed this in 1867, and then reinstated it again in 1888, while other colonies perhaps more opaquely made an administrative decision to no longer grant naturalisation to ethnic Chinese from the late 1880s

---

33   Mae M. Ngai, *Impossible Subjects. Illegal Aliens and the Making of Modern America* (Princeton: Princeton University Press, 2014), 8, doi.org/10.1515/9781400850235.
34   Section 5, *Naturalization Act 1903* (No. 11 of 1903).

onwards. New Zealand unsuccessfully attempted to introduce legislation to prohibit Chinese naturalisation in 1896, ultimately accomplishing this through a decision of Cabinet in 1908.[35] It was not until the 1950s that non-European immigrants in Australia, and Chinese immigrants in New Zealand, were once again able to be naturalised. For half a century, therefore, many long-term residents were denied citizenship rights, while the rights of those naturalised or born as British subjects in Australia and New Zealand or elsewhere in the British Empire were eroded through racist policies and administrative decision-making.

Reckoning with Our History

In 2009 Miranda Johnson asked:

> Why are historians the underdogs in the current legal regime in Australia … When compared, for instance, with the central role that historians in New Zealand's Waitangi Tribunal have played, some of whom have sat as tribunal members, the comparatively weaker influence of historians on the Australian legal scene seems even more striking.[36]

Chapter 7 contends that in the decade or more since this statement there has been little progress in the Australian High Court's preparedness to properly take account of the historical context in an area of major Commonwealth power – the practically unrestrained ability to make laws with respect to 'aliens' in section 51(xix) of the Australian Constitution. The chapter argues that the legacy of the law from the White Australia period lives on in decisions in Australian courts. A man born in Malta who arrived in Australia in 1948 as a small boy with equal membership status as a 'British subject' – that is, before 'Australian citizenship' even existed in a formal sense – lost his appeal against deportation in 2021 because the High Court ruled that he had always been an 'alien' who never legally belonged in the country he had lived in for over seven decades.[37] His banishment was in addition to serving a long prison sentence for a serious crime. A similar

---

35   Kate Bagnall, 'Circulations of Belonging: Chinese British Subjects in Australasia, 1880–1920', in *The Making and Remaking of Australasia: Mobility, Texts and 'Southern Circulations'*, ed. Tony Ballantyne (London: Bloomsbury Academic, 2022).

36   Miranda Johnson, 'Review of Ann Curthoys, Ann Genovese and Alexander Reilly's *Rights and Redemption: History, Law and Indigenous People*', *History Australia* 6, no. 1 (2009): 25.1, 25.2, doi.org/10.2104/ha090025.

37   *Chetcuti v. Commonwealth of Australia* [2021] HCA 25.

case in 2018 authorised the expulsion of another Australian originally from Malta, also deemed an 'alien' by the High Court despite making Australia his home for over 60 years.[38] Within every community there are those who implicitly renounce the accepted values of a peaceful and ordered society by committing crimes. Society punishes them, but they are not regarded as being outside the community or not belonging simply because they commit such actions. New Zealand was the nation most affected by Australia's 'reverse transportation' policy (modified but not abandoned in 2022 by the new Albanese Labor government),[39] which stripped inhabitants without formal citizenship of their residency rights, expelling them to their places of birth where they might lack any ties and did not belong in any practical sense.

The idea that some people do not belong in Australia today because of their crimes and are undeserving of the benefits of citizenship – including the right to stay in the country – parallels the deep-rooted prejudice in New Zealand and Australia that non-Europeans did not belong because of their ethnicity and were not entitled to the same protection from the Crown as white inhabitants. The treatment of South Sea Islander communities in both countries provides a good example.

In 2021, the New Zealand Government apologised to the country's Pasifika community for the 'dawn raids' in the 1970s when police and immigration officials targeted families with Samoan or other South Sea Islander heritage as visa overstayers on the basis of their racial background. Many Pasifika people were already New Zealand citizens and belonged legally. Others were no more liable to overstay their visas than arrivals from the United States or the United Kingdom, but they were far more likely to be arrested and deported.[40] Prime Minister Jacinda Ardern said New Zealand's 'immigration laws of the time were enforced in a discriminatory manner ... Pacific peoples were specifically targeted and racially profiled when these activities were

---

38 *Falzon v. Minister for Immigration and Border Protection* [2018] HCA 2.
39 In July 2022, the prime minister of Australia, Anthony Albanese, in a joint press conference with his New Zealand counterpart Jacinda Ardern, signalled a shift in Australia's policy of deporting non-citizen convicted criminals, stating 'where you have a circumstance where someone has lived their entire life, effectively, in Australia with no connection whatsoever to New Zealand, then commonsense should apply'. As the *Guardian* reported, this was 'a foreign policy win for Ardern, who has been pushing for years to end the deportations of those with tenuous links to New Zealand'. See Tess McClure and Paul Karp, 'Anthony Albanese Offers New Zealanders Fresh Approach on Voting Rights in Australia and Deportation Policy', *Guardian*, 8 July 2022, www.theguardian.com/australia-news/2022/jul/08/anthony-albanese-offers-new-zealanders-fresh-approach-on-voting-rights-in-australia-and-deportation-policy.
40 Ben McKay, 'New Zealand Pledges Pacific Healing from Apology', *Canberra Times*, 1 August 2021, www.canberratimes.com.au/story/7365944/nz-pledges-pacific-healing-from-apology/.

carried out'. She acknowledged 'the enduring hurt … caused to those who were directly affected … as well as the lasting impact these events have had on subsequent generations'.[41] As she said:

> The dawn raids period is a defining one in New Zealand's history …
> To this day Pacific communities face prejudices and stereotypes …
> an apology can never reduce what happened, or undo the decades of
> disadvantage experienced as a result, but it can contribute to healing
> for Pacific peoples.[42]

The Australian example shows the importance of acknowledging the type of history examined in this volume. In *Robtelmes v. Brenan* (1906), Australia's newly established High Court said Australia's entire South Sea Islander community were 'indisputably aliens' who did not belong and could forcibly be deported.[43] The High Court's reasoning in *Robtelmes* is still cited today in support of the Commonwealth's sweeping power over 'aliens' under the Constitution.[44] But the significance of the case as a violation of the rule of law has yet to be appreciated.

As explained above, under legal principles unchanged since *Calvin's Case*, nationality and alien status had nothing to do with the colour of a person's skin. Contrary to law, the High Court in 1906 held that all Islanders were 'aliens' because of their race. As Australia's first national census showed, two-thirds of the country's Islander community legally belonged as British subjects and were not 'aliens' under the law.[45] Moreover, each of the

---

41   Te Rina Triponel, 'PM Jacinda Ardern Delivers Formal Apology on Dawn Raids at Auckland Town Hall', *New Zealand Herald*, 1 August 2021, www.nzherald.co.nz/nz/pm-jacinda-ardern-delivers-formal-apology-on-dawn-raids-at-auckland-town-hall/5QDI3T3VV4KM5ZCOOQQ4AEUT2I/.

42   AAP, 'Jacinda Ardern to Apologise for 1970s 'Dawn Raids' on Pacific Community', *Guardian*, 14 June 2021, www.theguardian.com/world/2021/jun/14/jacinda-ardern-to-apologise-for-1970s-dawn-raids-on-pacific-community. Ardern's remorse on behalf of New Zealand went beyond mere words, shown by her actions both in wearing a hijab after the Christchurch massacres, and, more recently, with the apology to Pasifika people donning the cloak as part of the *ifoga*, a traditional Samoan reconciliation or forgiveness protocol.

43   *Robtelmes v. Brenan* (1906) 4 CLR 395 (2 October 1906). See Peter Prince and Eve Lester, 'The High Court and Respect for Australian South Sea Islanders', *AUSPUBLAW*, 24 February 2021, www.auspublaw.org/blog/2021/02/the-high-court-and-respect-for-australian-south-sea-islanders; Peter Prince and Eve Lester, 'The God of the "God Powers": The Gaps between History and Law', in *Griffith Review 76: Acts of Reckoning*, edited by Ashley Hay and Teela Reid (Text Publishing, 2022), www.griffithreview.com/articles/the-god-of-the-god-powers/.

44   *Chu Keng Lim v. MILGEA* (1992) 176 CLR 1, 26; *Ruddock v. Vardalis* (2001) 110 FCR 491 (Tampa case); *Al-Kateb v. Godwin* (2004) 219 CLR 562; *Plaintiff M76/2013* (2013) 251 CLR 322; *Falzon v. Minister for Immigration and Border Protection* [2018] HCA 2 at [92]; *Commonwealth v. AJL20* [2021] HCA 21 at [21]; *Alexander v. Minister for Home Affairs* [2022] HCA 19, at [138], [150], [208].

45   Commonwealth Census Bureau, *Census of the Commonwealth of Australia 3rd April, 1911* (1917), vol. 1, part 1, Statistician's Report, 227–28.

High Court justices had a disqualifying conflict of interest in the matter before them, not acknowledged or declared at the time. Edmund Barton (as Australia's first prime minister) and Richard O'Connor (as leader of the government in the Senate) secured passage through the new Australian Parliament of the *Pacific Island Labourers Act 1901*, providing for expulsion of the Islander community. Introducing the Bill, Barton highlighted Samuel Griffith's support as premier of Queensland for abolition of Islander labour. A driving force of Griffith's political life had indeed been removal of Islander labour from Queensland.[46]

Extraordinarily, it took until 2020 for the court's racialisation of the term 'alien' in *Robtelmes* to be acknowledged. In the landmark 'Aboriginal belonging' case *Love & Thoms*, Justice Edelman of the current High Court said it had been 'persuasively argued' that the 1906 case 'implicitly applied criteria based upon racial perceptions'.[47] In *Chetcuti* (2021), Edelman again referred to the 'racially based approach' in *Robtelmes*, saying the decision 'was reached by application of the concept of alienage through a racial lens, irrespective of considerations of British subjecthood'.[48] However, he did not say that the racial branding of Australian Islanders in 1906, with its calamitous consequences for the Islander community, was unlawful. Moreover, the current High Court chief justice, Susan Kiefel, says the *Robtelmes* decision remains authoritative,[49] supporting almost unlimited Commonwealth power over individuals, including the ability to exclude, expel and detain indefinitely without trial.[50]

As Ann Curthoys, Ann Genovese and Alexander Reilly argue in their important study of law and history in Australia:

> the longer the law has relied on a version of the past and the legal norms that have developed around that version, the more disruptive it is to reinterpret the past and to establish new norms. In this sense, the methods of history are antithetical to legal resolution, and historians deal in the type of facts that the law would prefer to leave undisturbed.[51]

---

46 Peter Prince, '"Australia's Most Inhumane Mass Deportation Abuse": *Robtelmes v. Brenan* and Expulsion of the Alien Islanders', *Law & History* 5, no. 1 (2018): 117.
47 *Love & Thoms* (2020) 397 ALR 597 at 698–99.
48 *Chetcuti v. Commonwealth of Australia* [2021] HCA 25 at [63].
49 Hon Susan Kiefel AC, 'Legacies of Sir Samuel Griffith', *Sir Samuel Griffith Lecture*, Griffith University, Brisbane, 17 November 2020.
50 *Commonwealth of Australia v. AJL20* [2021] HCA 21.
51 Ann Curthoys, Ann Genovese and Alexander Reilly, *Rights and Redemption: History, Law, and Indigenous People* (Sydney: UNSW Press, 2008).

One tangible sign of Australia's willingness to confront the racialised socio-legal context of the White Australia era would be for the High Court to engage substantively with the cases and laws from that period that made possible the great suffering of Islanders and other non-European inhabitants.

As the *Robtelmes* case shows, it is important to recognise the different ways in which the language of national belonging is used. The shameful case of Australia's most famous Indigenous artist, Arrernte man Albert Namatjira, discussed in Chapter 7, is another example. The white Australian community – including the responsible Commonwealth minister – believed Namatjira was 'made a citizen' in 1957 when, after a public campaign, his name was not included in a list of 15,000 Aboriginal people in the Northern Territory deemed to be 'wards' requiring 'protection' by the government. Contemporary academic commentary has repeated this view.[52]

When applying a non-legal meaning of 'citizenship' as a 'bundle of rights' (freedom of movement, the right to vote, serve on a jury, decide where to live, work, choose friends, partners, etc.), it may be appropriate to say Namatjira was 'made a citizen' when no longer, in theory, subject to oppressive control by white officials. But, from 1788 under imposed British law, Aboriginal Australians had full membership status, first as 'British subjects' and then, from 26 January 1949, also as legal 'Australian citizens'.[53] A lack of focus in historical commentary on formal nationality means past lawmakers have not been held to account for their failure to respect the legal status of First Nations peoples and other non-Europeans under British law, and the denial of the rights of citizenship and protection that should have accompanied that status. As Namatjira's story shows, the lives of Indigenous Australians were controlled until well after World War II, denying them full 'citizenship' in a practical sense despite their formal legal equality.

As well as race or ethnicity, other factors, including national origin, gender, religion and perceived differences in standard of living, affected perceptions of belonging and citizenship in Australia and New Zealand. Emma Bellino's chapter shows how a combination of gender and racial discrimination affected the belonging of Australian women. Australia's *Nationality Act 1920* copied 1914 Imperial legislation,[54] declaring that 'the wife of an alien

---

52   Julie T. Wells and Michael F. Christie, 'Namatjira and the Burden of Citizenship', *Australian Historical Studies* 31 (2000), 110, 120, doi.org/10.1080/10314610008596118.
53   Under the *Nationality and Citizenship Act 1948*.
54   *British Nationality and Status of Aliens Act 1914*.

shall be deemed to be an alien'.[55] Australian women who married men of foreign nationality lost their British subject status and became 'aliens' under the law, without the right to vote.[56] In terms of public perception, this loss particularly affected ethnic Chinese and other non-European Australian women because, as Bellino notes, white Australian women continued to be considered 'Australian' regardless of the nationality of their husbands.

In 1923, New Zealand also introduced a 'marital denaturalisation' law.[57] Michael King calls this 'an example of xenophobia made legal', noting that 'Miriam Soljak, a New Zealander of Irish descent who had married a Dalmatian immigrant, spent most of her adult life fighting for the repeal of this legislation'.[58] As Helen Irving says, in 1934, New Zealand 'was the first to adopt a scheme for the restoration of rights to maritally denaturalised women'.[59] Australia followed suit in 1936. But these reforms merely allowed women who married foreign nationals to regain 'the rights of British subjects' and not legal British subject status itself. As Bellino explains in Chapter 5, maritally denaturalised women in Australia who regained British subject rights were still subject to the humiliation of compulsory 'alien' registration in World War II. It was only after the war that Australia and New Zealand, along with other British dominions, repealed their conditional marital nationality laws,[60] giving women their own independent nationality.[61]

Conclusion

This collection is part of a renewed scholarly interest in the history of nationality and citizenship in Australia and New Zealand. A number of substantial book-length studies on Australian citizenship emerged around the time of the centenary of Australian Federation in 2001, when historians and legal researchers, and the national community more broadly, turned

55 Section 18.
56 Under section 39 of the *Commonwealth Electoral Act 1918*, only 'natural-born, or naturalized subjects of the King' could enrol to vote.
57 *British Nationality and Status of Aliens (in New Zealand) Act 1923*, First Schedule, Part III, section 10.
58 Michael King, *The Penguin History of New Zealand* (Penguin Books, 2003), 367. For further discussion of Miriam Soljak's case, see Harriet Mercer, 'Gender and the Myth of a White Zealand, 1866–1928', *New Zealand Journal of History* 52, no. 2 (2018): 23.
59 Helen Irving, *Citizenship, Alienage, and the Modern Constitutional State: A Gendered History* (New York: Cambridge University Press, 2016), 177, doi.org/10.1017/CBO9781107588011.
60 Ibid., 161.
61 Ibid., 367.

their attention to the nation's democratic foundations and legacies.[62] However, New Zealand's less contested citizenship history did not receive the same consideration at the time of its centenary of dominion status in 2008.[63] Since then, historians and legal scholars, including those published in this collection, have turned their attention more directly to the lived experience of subjects and citizens, as well as those who were 'aliens' under the law, and to the intersections of nationality and citizenship with race and gender.[64] While much of this work continues to take a national perspective, comparative and transnational approaches have much to offer our understanding of the legal and social histories of nationality and citizenship rights.[65]

We hope this book enlivens the reader's interest in histories of the varied and remarkable communities – Indigenous, immigrant and settler – that contributed to the fabric of Australian and New Zealand society in the nineteenth and twentieth centuries. For those not of British heritage, this was often in the face of racially based social and institutional prejudice

---

62   See Alastair Davidson, *From Subject to Citizen: Australian Citizenship in the Twentieth Century* (Cambridge University Press, 1997), doi.org/10.1017/CBO9780511518232; John Chesterman and Brian Galligan, *Citizens without Rights: Aborigines and Australian Citizenship* (Cambridge University Press, 1997), doi.org/10.1017/CBO9780511518249; David Dutton, *One of Us? A Century of Australian Citizenship* (Sydney: UNSW Press, 2002); Kim Rubenstein, *Australian Citizenship Law in Context* (Sydney: Lawbook, 2002).

63   On the history of New Zealand citizenship, see, however, J.C. Beaglehole, 'The Development of New Zealand Nationality', *Cahiers d'Histoire Mondiale: Journal of World History* 2, no. (1954): 106; Paul Spoonley, 'Aliens and Citizens in New Zealand', in *Citizenship in a Global World. Migration, Minorities and Citizenship*, ed. A. Kondo (London: Palgrave Macmillan, 2001), 158, doi.org/10.1057/9780333993880_9; K. McMillan, 'Developing Citizens: Subjects, Aliens and Citizens in New Zealand since 1840', in *Tangata: The Changing Ethnic Contours of New Zealand*, ed. P. Spoonley, C. Macpherson and D. Pearson (Southbank: Thomson, 2004), 267; K. McMillan and A. Hood, 'Report on Citizenship Law: New Zealand', EUDO Citizenship Observatory, *Country Report*, RSCAS/EUDO-CIT-CR 2016/9, hdl.handle.net/1814/42648.

64   See, for example, Rachel Bright, 'Rethinking Gender, Citizenship, and War: Female Enemy Aliens in Australia during World War I', *Immigrants & Minorities* 40, no. 1–2 (2022): 13, doi.org/10.1080/02619288.2021.1977126; Andonis Piperoglou, 'Migrant Acculturation Via Naturalisation: Comparing Syrian and Greek Applications for Naturalisation in White Australia', *Immigrants & Minorities* 40, no. 1–2 (2022): 59, doi.org/10.1080/02619288.2021.1974405; Harriet Mercer, 'Gender and the Myth of a White Zealand, 1866–1928', *New Zealand Journal of History* 52, no. 2 (2018): 23; Emma Bellino, 'Married Women's Nationality and the White Australia Policy, 1920–1948', *Law & History* 7, no. 1 (2020): 166; Peter Prince, 'The "Chinese" Always Belonged', *History Australia* 15, no. 3 (2018): 475, doi.org/10.1080/14490854.2018.1485463; Kate Bagnall, '*Potter v. Minahan*: Chinese Australians, the Law and Belonging in White Australia', *History Australia* 15, no. 3 (2018): 458, doi.org/10.1080/14490854.2018.1485503.

65   See, for example, Helen Irving, *Citizenship, Alienage, and the Modern Constitutional State*; Helen Irving, *Allegiance, Citizenship and the Law* (Cheltenham: Edward Elgar Publishing, 2022), doi.org/10.4337/9781839102547; Jatinder Mann, *Redefining Citizenship in Australia, Canada, and Aotearoa New Zealand* (New York: Peter Lang, 2019), doi.org/10.3726/b15770.

that denied their belonging in the national community. But belong they did, as readers will find as they make their way through this collection. Together the chapters explore how laws that governed nationality and citizenship rights were devised by politicians, administered by bureaucrats, interpreted by the courts and understood by the people. Many non-European residents had full membership status under white law as 'British subjects' and so were 'us' in law, while others were denied the possibility of becoming 'us' due to racist policies. These facts, particularly the treatment of legal members of the national community as 'outsiders', 'aliens' or 'the Other' by white authorities, are central to the histories of both countries, yet much work remains to improve our national memories. As well as formally recognising First Nations peoples as the original custodians, we need to acknowledge that non-British immigrant settlers have as much right as British settler groups to belong and be seen as 'one of us' in both New Zealand and Australia.

2

'Not Substantially of European Origin or Descent': How Race Came to Shape Australian Enlistment during World War I

Sophie Couchman

Introduction

On 19 November 1914, Senator Thomas Bakhap spoke out in parliament about how insulting it was that those born in Australia but 'not substantially of European origin or descent' (NSEOD) were 'exempt' from service during World War I (WWI).[1] He was speaking from the heart. Bakhap's paternity was not recorded, but he was brought up by a Chinese stepfather and embraced the language and culture of his adoptive father as his own.[2] He knew it was possible to be a so-called 'coloured' Australian and share in a sense of Australian national pride:

> Irrespective of the fact that certain people may be native born Australians, may have been educated in Australia, may perhaps have lived all their lives here, and may be willing to serve in our Military

1   Commonwealth of Australia, Parliamentary Debates, Senate, 19 November 1914, 772 (Senator Bakhap), historichansard.net/senate/1914/19141119_senate_6_75/#subdebate-11-0-s1.
2   Hilary L. Rubinstein, 'Bakhap, Thomas Jerome Kingston (1866–1923)', *The Biographical Dictionary of the Australian Senate*, vol. 1, 1901–1929 (Melbourne: Melbourne University Press, 2000), 252; Adrienne Petty, 'Deconstructing the Chinese Sojourner: Case Studies of Early Chinese Migrants to Tasmania' (PhD thesis, University of Tasmania, 2009), 117–40.

Forces, they are exempted from duties other than those of a non-combatant nature in a most insulting fashion, and they are told, legislatively, that they may perhaps be taken to the battlefield very much as the Spartans took their helots.[3]

Bakhap accused the government of hypocrisy for sending troops on ships crewed by 'Asiatics' and yet barring them from service except in a non-combat capacity. His objections fell on deaf ears. No-one engaged with his argument and his comments were declared out of order, as the debate concerned amendments to unrelated sections of the Commonwealth *Defence Act 1903*.

Bakhap was speaking five years too late to have any impact on the clauses of the Defence Act to which he was referring, as these had been introduced in 1909 and 1910. Nor did he fully appreciate that the 'native born Australians' to whom he referred were British subjects and that, in barring their enlistment, the government was curtailing the legal rights and obligations of its own subjects. He was also wrong about it being the Defence Act that determined enlistment in Australia's expeditionary forces in WWI; it was actually military orders issued after the start of the war. This chapter is about why these two commonly held misunderstandings are important.

Like Bakhap, historians continue to attribute the racial bar on enlistment during WWI to the Defence Act or, more specifically, to a clause added in 1910 that exempted those NSEOD from compulsory service in Australia's defence forces 'in times of war'.[4] Some have argued that there was some 'ambiguity' as to whether, by being exempt, these men were also barred from volunteering in Australia's expeditionary forces, but this distinction

---

3   Commonwealth of Australia, *Parliamentary Debates*, Senate, 19 November 1914, 772 (Senator Bakhap).

4   Richard Broome, *Aboriginal Victorians: A History since 1800* (Sydney: Allen & Unwin, 2005), 201; Peter Stanley, '"He Was Black, He Was a White Man, and a Dinkum Aussie": Race and Empire in Revisiting the Anzac Legend', in *Race, Empire and First World War Writing*, ed. Santanu Das (Cambridge: Cambridge University Press, 2011), 221, doi.org/10.1017/cbo9780511973659.012; Morag Loh, 'Fighting Uphill: Australians of Chinese Descent and the Defence Forces, 1899–1951', in *Chinese in Australia and New Zealand: A Multidisciplinary Approach*, ed. Jan Ryan (New Delhi: New Age International, 1995), 61; Philippa Scarlett, 'Aboriginal Service in the First World War: Identity, Recognition and the Problem of Mateship', *Aboriginal History* 39 (2015): 54, doi.org/10.22459/ah.39. 2015.08. Also see exhibitions and websites: 'Chinese Anzacs: Chinese Australians and World War One', exhibition, Chinese Museum, Melbourne (14 July 2014 – 31 July 2015); 'Black Diggers', exhibition, Arts Centre, Melbourne (20 April – 17 May 2015); 'George and Herbert Kong Meng', Australian War Memorial (AWM), last updated 19 January 2021, www.awm.gov.au/learn/schools/resources/anzac-diversity/chinese-anzacs/george-meng.

is not noted as being significant.[5] The 1910 Defence Act exemption, and an earlier one introduced in 1909 for compulsory military training, were certainly pivotal, marking the first time that participation in Australia's military forces was legislatively constrained by race. As Morag Loh observed, the 'legislation which established independent armed services also institutionalised racism within them'.[6]

These exemptions did not, however, set enlistment criteria into Australia's two expeditionary forces during WWI – the Australian Naval and Military Expeditionary Force (AN&MEF) and the 1st Australian Imperial Force (AIF) – except in a few isolated instances.[7] As stipulated in the Defence Act, when Australian forces operated outside the Commonwealth, enlistment had to be voluntary.[8] One cannot be exempt from something that is voluntary unless the meaning of 'exempt' is distorted from something 'free from an obligation or liability imposed on others'[9] into something that is a 'a barrier or restriction to an action'. In assuming, and not seriously questioning, that the Defence Act set enlistment criteria, scholars have missed the fact that it was a military order, not introduced until after the first contingent of AIF soldiers had been sent overseas, that introduced the racial bar. Shifting attitudes and approaches to the participation of those NSEOD in Australia's military forces have also been obscured by the assumption that this racial bar was static and unchanging.

---

5   Rod Pratt, 'Queensland's Aborigines in the First AIF', *Sabretache: The Journal of the Military Historical Society of Australia* 31, no. 1 (1990): 20; Timothy C. Winegard, 'A Case Study of Indigenous Brothers in Arms during the First World War', *Australian Army Journal* 6, no. 1 (2009): 34; Noah Riseman, 'Enduring Silences, Enduring Prejudices: Australian Aboriginal Participation in the First World War', in *Endurance and the First World War: Experiences and Legacies in New Zealand and Australia*, ed. David Monger, Katie Pickles and Sarah Murray (Newcastle upon Tyne: Cambridge Scholars Publishing, 2014), 179.

6   Morag Loh, *Dinky-Di: The Contributions of Chinese Immigrants and Australians of Chinese Descent to Australia's Defence Forces and War Efforts 1899–1988* (Canberra: Office of Multicultural Affairs, 1989), 22.

7   There were four circumstances in which the 1909 and 1910 exemption clauses added to the *Defence Act 1903* applied to enlistment during WWI: i) compulsory training of cadets, which continued intermittently throughout the war; ii) recruitment of the few troops who served within the Australian Commonwealth; iii) initial AIF recruitment whereby military district commandants were instructed to draw roughly half of their recruits from men who had served in the militia or had war service; and iv) during the governor-general's call-up on 29 September 1916. National Archives of Australia (hereafter NAA): A2657, vol. 2, letter to minister of defence from Brigadier-General W. T. Bridges, 8 August 1914; AWM, 27, 301/13, circular to commandants all Military Districts from W. T. Bridges, commanding AIF, 11 August 1914; A. G. Butler, *Official History of the Australian Army Medical Services in the War of 1914–1918, Volume I Gallipoli, Palestine and New Guinea*, 2nd ed. (Melbourne: Australian War Memorial, 1938), 17–19; Australia, Department of Defence, *Report upon the Department of Defence: From the First of July, 1914, until the Thirtieth of June, 1917*, Part 1 (Melbourne: Albert J. Mullett, 1917), 87–8; C. E. W. Bean, *Official History of Australia in the War of 1914–1918* (Sydney: Angus & Robertson, 1921), 37.

8   Defence Act, Part III, section 49.

9   Definition of 'exempt', *The Australian Concise Oxford Dictionary*, ed. J. M. Hughes, P. A. Michell and W. S. Ramson, 2nd ed. (Melbourne: Oxford University Press, 1995), 390.

Exemptions in the Defence Act and the military orders that barred and then loosened restrictions on the enlistment of those NSEOD constrained the legal and moral rights and obligations of Australia's subjects based on their race. For many, this racism is simply another strand in the tapestry of the White Australia policy. However, this overlooks the deception and complexity of how people of colour have been discriminated against in Australia. It does not help us understand how it was that significant numbers of men who were NSEOD did enlist and serve during WWI.[10] Moreover, it overlooks the gradual process whereby something written into legislation in 1909 and 1910 as an exemption came to be used as a bar during WWI. Through an examination of legislation, military orders and individual cases, this chapter reveals how legislation and regulations were applied in practice, often via bureaucratic decisions made behind closed doors, and sparked by specific cases as people NSEOD encountered these mechanisms. It shines a light on how British subjects in Australia came to be treated differently according to their race as part of this process. It was not an accident that Bakhap misunderstood the processes that excluded those NSEOD. As we shall see they were deliberately kept obscure.

Despite legislation and military orders covering anyone deemed NSEOD, scholarship has tended to focus on individual racial groups rather than examining such peoples' experiences as a whole, although Timothy Winegard has compared the involvement of First Nations peoples across the British dominions to show the reluctance of all countries, to differing degrees, to embrace their enlistment.[11] The lack of engagement between historians of Aboriginal history and military history observed by Joan Beaumont and Allison Cadzow is mirrored within Chinese Australian history.[12] After First Nations peoples, Chinese Australians were the next largest group who might be defined as NSEOD. They were followed, although to a much lesser extent, by descendants of 'non-European races' such as 'Hindus',

---

10   Philippa Scarlett, *Aboriginal and Torres Strait Islander Volunteers for the AIF: The Indigenous Response to World War One*, 4th ed. (Macquarie, ACT: Indigenous Histories, 2018); 'Chinese Anzacs', Victorian Collections, accessed 6 March 2023, victoriancollections.net.au/stories/chinese-anzacs.

11   Timothy Charles Winegard, *Indigenous Peoples of the British Dominions and the First World War* (New York: Cambridge University Press, 2012), doi.org/10.1017/cbo9781139057387.

12   Joan Beaumont and Allison Cadzow, 'Serving Our Country', in *Serving Our Country: Indigenous Australians, War, Defence and Citizenship*, ed. Joan Beaumont and Allison Cadzow (Sydney: NewSouth Publishing, 2018), 4. Discrimination against Chinese Australians during WWI is surprisingly absent from most general Chinese Australian texts with the exception of the work of Loh and Rolls. Morag Loh, *Sojourners and Settlers: Chinese in Victoria 1848–1985* (Melbourne: Barradene Press, 1985); Eric Rolls, *Citizens: Continuing the Epic Story of China's Centuries-Old Relationship with Australia* (Brisbane: University of Queensland Press, 1996).

'African Negroes' and 'Polynesians' (which included 'Papuans', 'Māoris' and 'Fijians').[13] Research into the involvement of these other groups is still in its infancy, mostly providing accounts of the lives and service of the men who enlisted.[14] Bringing together the experiences of men of different backgrounds during WWI helps give us a more complete picture of how legislation, regulations and military orders operated in practice.

There are deep and significant differences in racial attitudes towards different groups understood to be 'NSEOD', and this is particularly noticeable for First Nations peoples and immigrant groups. The lives of Aboriginal and Torres Strait Islander peoples and the legislative frameworks that surrounded them were shaped by a history of violent dispossession and ongoing processes of colonial oppression that were different to immigrant groups who, while not racially 'white', were themselves also colonisers.[15] Views about hierarchies of race shaped how 'evolved' each of these groups were believed to be.

The argument that Australian citizenship did not automatically ensure equal civil rights within the military is well known within Aboriginal historical scholarship, and Joan Beaumont has also explored how the bar on women's participation in military service shaped the nature of their citizenship.[16] While understood, this history is less well articulated within Chinese Australian scholarship, which tends to focus on the racially discriminatory nature of legislation for people born in China rather than how the rights of their Australian-born descendants were curtailed. Important exceptions to this are works by Kate Bagnall, who explores how fluid understandings of race

---

13 These are the classifications used in the Commonwealth Census for the most numerous 'half-caste' 'non-European races'. 'Census of the Commonwealth of Australia, 1911', Bureau of Census and Statistics, 3 April 1911, 16, www.abs.gov.au/AUSSTATS/abs@.nsf/DetailsPage/2112.01911?OpenDocument.

14 Dzavid Haveric, 'ANZAC Muslims: An Untold Story', *Australian Journal of Islamic Studies* 3, no. 3 (2018): 78, doi.org/10.55831/ajis.v3i3.147; Katy Nebhan, 'The Afghan Anzac? A Story of Loyalties and Legends among Australian Muslims', in *Loyalties*, ed. Victoria Mason (Western Australia: API Network, 2007), 155; Rodney Noonan, 'Adelaide's Indian Enlistees in the First AIF', *South Australian Genealogist*, May 2007. An exception is *Law in War* by Catherine Bond, however, she also assumes that the Defence Act determines enlistment. Catherine Bond, *Law in War: Freedom and Restriction in Everyday Life in Australia during the Great War* (Sydney: NewSouth Publishing, 2020).

15 Helen Irving, *To Constitute a Nation: A Cultural History of Australia's Constitution* (Cambridge: Cambridge University Press, 1999), 114.

16 Siobhan McDonnell and Mick Dodson, 'Race, Citizenship and Military Service', in *Serving Our Country: Indigenous Australians, War, Defence and Citizenship*, ed. Joan Beaumont and Allison Cadzow (Sydney: NewSouth Publishing, 2018), 23–52; Joan Beaumont, 'Australian Citizenship and the Two World Wars', *Australian Journal of Politics and History* 53, no. 2 (2007): 171, doi.org/10.1111/j.1467-8497.2007.00452.x; John Chesterman and Brian Galligan, *Citizens without Rights: Aborigines and Australian Citizenship* (Cambridge: Cambridge University Press, 1997), doi.org/10.1017/CBO9780511518249.

shaped the experiences of Australian-born Chinese and mixed-race Chinese Australians travelling under the Commonwealth *Immigration Restriction Act 1901*, and Peter Prince, who has shown how the term 'alien' was deliberately given racial meanings and illegally applied so that the rights of 'coloured' British subjects were curtailed.[17] Chinese immigrants were increasingly denied access to naturalisation in different colonies from the 1880s and eventually at the federal level under the 1903 *Naturalization Act*, in part to curtail perceived immigration fraud.[18] One of the reasons why citizenship was not defined and incorporated into the Australian Constitution was to prevent full participation of Chinese and Australian-born Chinese people in Australia as citizens.[19] The full implications of this, such as access to pensions and other benefits, have only been broadly touched on, with racism, rather than denial of equal civil rights, used as an explanation. Military service is one of the key elements of citizenship; however, the ways in which the Defence Act and military orders curtailed the rights of those NSEOD as British subjects and full legal members of the Australian community has not been emphasised outside Aboriginal historical scholarship.

Australia's armed forces were established within a context of racial paranoia and the construction, through legislation and political nation-building, of a White Australia.[20] Prior to the introduction of compulsory military training in 1909, Australia relied on Britain for its military defence. However, in the first decade of Australia's Federation, politicians became increasingly concerned about military threats from Asia – from China and, after their defeat of Russia in 1905, especially from Japan – a fear, as Helen Irving argues, that was 'more metaphorical than based in reality'.[21] Britain was also building closer economic and military ties with Japan and politicians feared Britain's desire to maintain the economic success of its empire might

17   See for example: Kate Bagnall, '*Potter v. Minahan*: Chinese Australians, the Law and Belonging in White Australia', *History Australia* 15, no. 3 (2018): 458, doi.org/10.1080/14490854.2018.1485503; Peter Prince, 'Aliens in Their Own Land. "Alien" and the Rule of Law in Colonial and Post-Federation Australia' (PhD thesis, The Australian National University, 2015), openresearch-repository.anu.edu.au/handle/1885/101778.
18   Charles Price, *The Great White Walls Are Built: Restrictive Immigration to North America and Australasia 1836–1888* (Canberra: Australian National University Press, 1974), 194–98.
19   Kim Rubenstein, 'The Influence of Chinese Immigration on Australian Citizenship', in *After the Rush: Regulation, Participation, and Chinese Communities in Australia 1860–1940*, ed. Sophie Couchman, John Fitzgerald and Paul Macgregor (Melbourne: Otherland Press, 2004), 21.
20   Peter Cochrane, *Best We Forget: The War for White Australia, 1914–18* (Melbourne: The Text Publishing Company, 2018), 116–17; Leslie Lloyd Robson, *The First A.I.F. A Study of Its Recruitment 1914–1918* (Melbourne: Melbourne University Press, 1970), 12–14.
21   Irving, *To Constitute a Nation*, 109.

leave Australia vulnerable if it was threatened by an Asian power. In pushing for compulsory universal training in 1909, Minister for Defence Joseph Cook argued:

> We have set up a White Australian ideal … But we are dealing for maintenance [of it] with a country of the world that is unable to close its doors to the coloured labour of the world as we do. We are depending on a nation that opens its doors wide to the world.[22]

Australia's politicians imagined that White Australia would need to protect itself from attack from its Asiatic neighbours as part of a war between the races. They also believed that Australia's so-called coloured population would not wish to serve in a defence force designed to protect White Australia. Embedded in this attitude was a belief that members of military armies should reflect the citizenry of the country.[23] For a newly federated Australia that dreamed of being 'white', that meant a white defence force.

However, Australia's politicians were wrong – not only about who Australia would be fighting but also about who would want to fight on Australia's behalf. How Australia was imagined was contested even when views about White Australia were at their strongest.[24]

Exemptions to Military Service and the Defence Act 1903

While the construction of a White Australia bound Australia's colonies together at its Federation in 1901, the original Commonwealth Defence Act passed in 1903 contained no racial bars or exclusions on military participation (see Table 2.1). It consolidated earlier colonial laws to establish a small federal defence force to support Britain's forces in defending Australia.[25] Under the Act, all men who were British subjects of a particular

---

22   Commonwealth of Australia, *Parliamentary Debates*, House of Representatives, 21 September 1909, 3613 (Joseph Cook, minister for defence). See generally Neville Meaney, *Australia and World Crisis, 1914–1923* (Sydney: Sydney University Press, 2009).

23   Hugh Smith, 'Minorities and the Australian Army', in *A Century of Service: 100 Years of the Australian Army*, ed. Peter Dennis and Jeffrey Grey (Canberra: Army History Unit, Department of Defence, 2001), 129–30.

24   On Chinese Australian views of Australian Federation, see John Fitzgerald, 'Visions of Australian Federation – the View from the Chinese Press Gallery', in *The Overseas Chinese in Australasia: History, Settlement and Interactions: Proceedings from the Symposium Held in Taipei, 6–7 January 2001*, ed. Henry Chan, Ann Curthoys and Nora Chiang (Taipei: IGAS, 2001), 102.

25   Robson, *The First A.I.F.*, 10.

age could be called upon to serve. These men could be British subjects by birth (natural-born) or by naturalisation. Each of Australia's colonies had separate naturalisation laws until the Commonwealth Naturalization Act 1903. Being born or naturalised within the British Empire, including in places like Hong Kong and British Malaya, also made one a British subject. However, naturalisation was not necessarily recognised. And, as we shall see, distinctions between an individual's naturalisation status, their birthplace and their race were often blurred.

Under the principal Defence Act, those whose religious doctrines forbad them to 'bear arms or perform military service' were exempt and the governor-general could, by regulation, also exempt others from military service.[26] This appreciation that some of Australia's subjects should be allowed to be exempt from compulsory military service was something carried over from the earlier, and ultimately abandoned, 1901 Defence Bill (see Table 2.1). This Bill did not contain any racial language and clearly stated that an 'exemption *shall not prevent any person from serving*, if he desires it and is not disabled by bodily infirmity'.[27] This wording was not used in the 1903 Defence Act, but it was still up to the individual to claim the exemption.[28] Exemptions were imagined as a special privilege an individual could apply for rather than an exclusion imposed on them.

While there might not have been a racial bar written into the Defence Act in 1903 or the associated regulations, Dick McDonald's case shows how men could still face racial discrimination in its application.

Table 2.1: Exemptions to military service in Defence Bills and Acts, 1901–10

Defence Bill/Act	Note	Exemptions
1901 Defence Bill, section 4	Ultimately abandoned	• 'Ministers of religion of all denominations' • 'Gaolers, warders of gaols' • 'Officers, keepers, and warders of all public lunatic asylums' • 'Persons disabled by bodily infirmity' • 'The only son of a widow, being her only support'
1903 Defence Act, section 61(1)	Principal Act	• 'The Governor-General may, by Regulation, declare what persons shall be exempt' • 'Persons whom the doctrines of their religion forbid them to bear arms or perform military service'

26 Defence Act, Part IV, section 61(1).
27 Defence Bill 1901, section 4 (iii). Emphasis added.
28 Defence Act, Part IV, section 61(2).

Defence Bill/Act	Note	Exemptions
1909 Defence Act, section 138	Addition to the Principal Act; established Citizen's Force and compulsory military training	• 'Those who have been reported by the prescribed medical authorities as unfit' • 'Those who are NSEOD' (does not extend to non-combatant duties) • 'School teachers who have qualified at a school of naval or military instruction, or other prescribed course as Instructors or Officers of the Junior or Senior Cadets' • 'Members of the Permanent Naval or Military Forces'
Section 140	Addition	• 'Governor-General may, by proclamation … exempt from the training mentioned in Part XII of this Act in time of peace all persons residing within any area specified in the proclamation'
Section 141	Addition	• 'No person may serve in the Cadets or in the Defence Force who [has] been convicted of any disgraceful or infamous crime or be of notoriously bad character'
1910 Defence Act, section 61	Replaced section 61 of the Principal Act; introduced compulsory service in times of war	• 'Persons reported by the prescribed medical authorities as unfit for any naval or military service' (does not extend to non-combatant duties) • 'Members and officers of the Parliament of the Commonwealth or of a State' (does not extend to non-combatant duties) • 'Judges of Federal or State Courts' • 'Police, stipendiary or special magistrates of the Commonwealth or State' • 'Ministers of Religion' • 'Persons employed in the police or prison services of the Commonwealth or State' • 'Persons employed in lighthouses' • 'Persons employed as medical practitioners or nurses in public hospitals' • 'Persons who are NSEOD' (judged by prescribed medical authorities, does not extend to non-combatant duties) • 'Persons who satisfy the prescribed authority that their conscientious beliefs do not allow them to bear arms' • 'Persons engaged in any employment specified by the Regulations or by Proclamation'
Section 138	Addition	• 'Persons who are students at a Theological College as defined by the Regulations' (exempt from compulsory military training)
Section 140A	Addition	• 'The Governor-General may by Proclamation grant a temporary exemption for a period not exceeding one year to – (a) persons who reside outside the areas in which training is carried out; and (b) persons who reside at so great a distance from the places appointed for training that compulsory attendance at the training would involve great hardships'

Dick McDonald, 1906–8

Dick McDonald, whose father was 'European' and mother was 'Aboriginal', attempted to enlist in the Commonwealth Military Forces in 1906.[29] In 1908, after being refused for the second time, he spoke with, then wrote to, his local Australian Labor Party (ALP) member, Danish-born Niels Rasmus Wilson Nielsen. Dick wanted to know if he was eligible to enlist because he had not been told why he had been refused. He explained: 'I did not ask why. But I think it is colour.'[30] If Dick McDonald was rejected because of his race (this was never made clear), his letter illustrates the inconsistency with which race could be interpreted and applied:

> they have one men [*sic*] in the company who is a coloured man he is what they call a fair half-cast and then there is one man in the senior cadets here who is darker than I and I find it very hard to think that I'm debared [*sic*] from enlisting.[31]

Perhaps race was not always a consideration, or skin colour was not the only factor considered, when making enlistment decisions?

Regardless, the final advice from the Department of Defence was that 'legally there is no objection to anyone being enlisted whose father is a European and whose mother is an aboriginal native of the Commonwealth'.[32] However, an important corollary was added to this decision: 'The question of acceptance of any man in a regiment rests with the commanding officer.'[33] Dick ended up serving in the 37th Infantry Band at Kiama. Technically, he served in the military by playing in the band in a non-combatant capacity (as specified under soon-to-be-passed amendments to the Defence Act).[34]

Although Dick McDonald was barred from full participation, the decision-making was inconsistent. We know that other Aboriginal men, as well as some Australian-born Chinese men, succeeded in serving in colonial and

---

29 NAA: A2023, A38/7/58.
30 Ibid.
31 Ibid.
32 Ibid.
33 Ibid.
34 NAA: B2455, McDonald R.

early federal military units.[35] And, while prevented from full enlistment prior to WWI, Dick successfully enlisted in the 1st AIF as part of the Waratah recruiting march in December 1915.[36]

1909 and 1910 Amendments to the Defence Act

A year after Dick McDonald wrote to Nielsen, amendments to the Defence Act (passed in 1909) introduced compulsory military training for boys and men. Exemptions were granted to particular groups, including those NSEOD. The governor-general could also exempt people from particular geographic areas and could withdraw exemptions (see Table 2.1). It was now 'medical authorities' who judged whether an individual qualified for an exemption, although the burden of proof still fell on the person claiming the exemption. In other words, an exemption was still considered something that people NSEOD could apply for rather than something that was imposed on them. Exemptions did not cover non-combatant duties. Other exempted groups were not minorities subject to discrimination and all were treated differently to those convicted of 'any disgraceful or infamous crime' or 'of notoriously bad character', who were not permitted to serve at all. These exemptions were not written to be punitive.

They were, however, part of a growing raft of legislation implemented in the early decades of the twentieth century aimed at building a White Australia. These amendments can be viewed as part of a trend whereby Australian legislators, wary of criticism and interference from the British Government, became more circumspect with how they chose to racially discriminate against non-white groups within legislation. British concerns about maintaining smooth relations with Japan, China and India meant that the Australian Government had to be careful to not overtly discriminate against 'coloured' groups, particularly those within the British Empire.[37] The Immigration Restriction Act 1901 marked a significant early example

---

35   John Maynard, 'The South African "Boer War"', in *Serving Our Country: Indigenous Australians, War, Defence and Citizenship*, ed. Joan Beaumont and Allison Cadzow (Sydney: NewSouth Publishing, 2018), 53; Loh, *Dinky-Di*, 14–15; NAA: B2455, Kong Meng George, Kong Meng Herbert, Langtip Ernest Walter, Langtip Bertie Allan.

36   Scarlett, 'Aboriginal Service in the First World War', 138; NAA: B2455, McDonald R.

37   Gwenda Tavan, *The Long, Slow Death of White Australia* (Melbourne: Scribe Publications, 2005), 10. For further examples see Prince, 'Aliens in Their Own Land', 211–46.

of this. Under pressure from the British Government, the text of the Act did not use racial language in its definition of a 'prohibited immigrant' and instead used a dictation test.[38] Officials were instructed to give the test to 'coloured' arrivals in a language not spoken by the entrant.[39] Although the British Government did not challenge the racial exemptions introduced into the Defence Act, had they, Australia could have argued that people NSEOD had a choice as to whether to be exempt or not. Racial discrimination occurred in the application of the Act, not in the Act itself.

Those NSEOD were also among those exempt from compulsory service within the Commonwealth during times of war after amendments to the Defence Act were passed in 1910 (see Table 2.1). Again, these exemptions did not extend to activities of a non-combat nature. And, again, other exempt persons were not from groups usually subject to discrimination. There was considerable parliamentary debate about whether conscientious objectors would be eligible for exemption under these amendments but no discussion about people NSEOD. In wording these amendments to the Defence Act, politicians imagined they would have to restrict the number of people claiming exemptions from compulsory training or service. Exemptions were, therefore, a boon granted to people, not something imposed on them. This changed, however, when the laws were put into practice.

Charlie Chung Quong, 1911

In 1911, as a natural-born British subject, Charlie Chung Quong turned up to compulsory cadet training as required under the 1909 amendments to the Defence Act; however, as someone NSEOD, he was told that he would be given administrative duties – not combat training.[40] Rather than something requested by Charlie, the exemption clause was imposed on him. Charlie stopped attending training – accounts vary as to why. As a result, his superiors took him to the Children's Court. They wanted to make an example of him. He was fined £5. Mr Howit, a benefactor of the Chung Quong family, pleaded the boy's case to the Department of Defence, arguing that the family could not afford the fine and that Charlie needed to work to support his family. The department remitted Charlie's fine. The department also decided that it was now 'advisable' that boys who were NSEOD would

---

38   *Immigration Restriction Act 1901* (Cth), section 8.
39   NAA: A1, 1903/3997; A. C. Palfreeman, *The Administration of the White Australia Policy* (Melbourne: Melbourne University Press, 1967), 81–4.
40   NAA: MP84/1, 439/3/145.

not be called up for training – not even in a non-combatant capacity as allowed for under the Act. District commandants were duly notified of this decision in August 1912.

Anecdotal reports show officials were inconsistent in how they interpreted this. While some Australian-born boys with Chinese ancestry were barred because of their heritage, others participated in cadets. Sam Tong Way from Ballarat and Frank Chinn from Melbourne described the hurt and humiliation they felt when they were prevented from training as cadets.[41] When WWI was declared, Sam Tong Way persisted and eventually succeeded in enlisting, alongside his brother Hedley, but Frank Chinn chose not to try, wishing to avoid further humiliation.[42] Conversely, Harry Hoyling and Herbert Henry Goon, both of Chinese descent, served as senior cadets for three years and three and a half years, respectively.[43] Yet, in barring even a few boys from training as cadets for being NSEOD, military bureaucrats established an important precedent: they turned a voluntary exemption from compulsory participation into an exclusion or bar to participation.

Wider Adoption of the Phrase 'NSEOD' as a Bar to Participation

After the phrase 'not substantially of European origin or descent' appeared in the Defence Act, it was then applied to other aspects of military and naval operations and was increasingly used as a bar to full participation in military life.[44] Amendments to the Defence Act in 1910 had also established military training colleges – the Royal Military College at Duntroon in 1911 and a naval college in 1913.[45] Both introduced regulations that barred those NSEOD from enrolling.[46] Brigadier General William Throsby Bridges, who established the college at Duntroon, was involved in drafting the 1909 and 1910 amendments and was charged with the creation of the AIF. Bridges also drove the introduction of the regulation that barred the enrolment of those NSEOD into Duntroon. This was in response to the attempted enrolment of Abdul Hamid Wade (1900–1982) in 1913. Bridges sought

---

41   Loh, 'Fighting Uphill', 60.
42   Ibid., 60; NAA: B2455, Tong Way Samuel John.
43   NAA: B884, Q187318; NAA: B2455, Goon H. H.
44   See e.g. the defence department's regulation that soldiers with wives who were NSEOD would not be taken onto the marriage roll. 'Racial Purity', *Daily Post* (Hobart), 26 February 1912, 4.
45   Defence Act, Part XIII, section 147 (as amended 1910); *Naval Defence Act 1910*, section 18.
46   Loh, *Dinky-Di*, 22.

legal advice from Robert Garran, Australia's first federal attorney-general who had also been involved in drafting the Australian Constitution and played a primary role in drafting Australia's federal laws from 1901 until his retirement in 1932.[47]

Abdul Hamid Wade, 1913

Abdul Hamid Wade was born in Australia. His mother, Emily, was Dublin born and his father, also Abdul, was a naturalised British subject (1902). Abdul senior was born in Afghanistan when it was a British protectorate and had lived in Australia for over 30 years.[48] Abdul senior wrote to the minister of defence in March 1913 asking whether his son was eligible to enrol as a cadet.[49] The department acknowledged receipt of the letter in April and contacted Bridges, commandant of the college, for advice. The college rushed through changes to the regulations related to cadet entry criteria so that the department could state in reply to Abdul senior that 'the Regulations do not permit of the admission of your son'.[50] No further explanation was provided.

Behind the scenes we see that Bridges sought to change enlistment regulations so that 'only persons of pure European descent' could be admitted. He also incorrectly advised the department that if Abdul Hamid was born before his father was naturalised, then he was not a 'natural born British subject' under the Defence Act:

> As a matter of policy, I think only persons of pure European descent should be admitted as cadets and if the Regulation quoted does not secure this, then it should be amended without delay.[51]

When the department contacted Robert Garran, secretary of the Attorney-General's Department, for advice, he corrected Bridges and explained that, being born in Australia, Abdul Hamid was a natural-born British subject regardless of his father's naturalisation status. Further, he pointed out that a regulation based on the concept of 'pure European descent' would:

47 Bond, *Law in War*, 15–16.
48 Christine Stevens, 'Wade, Abdul (1866–1928)', *Australian Dictionary of Biography*, National Centre of Biography, 2005, adb.anu.edu.au/biography/wade-abdul-13230/text7395.
49 This case was also discussed by Coulthard-Clark and Huggonson. See C. D. Coulthard-Clark, *A Heritage of Spirit: A Biography of Major-General Sir William Throsby Bridges* (Melbourne: Melbourne University Press, 1979), 96; David Huggonson, 'The Dark Diggers of the AIF', *Australian Quarterly* 61, no. 3 (1989): 352, doi.org/10.2307/20635547.
50 NAA: MP84/1, 1862/5/983.
51 NAA: MP84/1, 1862/5/983.

raise considerable difficulties – and would, if strictly interpreted, involve complete investigation in ancestry for an indefinite number of generations. E.g. a Maori great-grandmother, or a remote North American Redskin ancestor, would debar a candidate who to all appearance was a full-blooded European.[52]

So, rather than adopt Bridges's more restrictive wording, the amendments to the regulations followed Garran's recommendations and used the weaker phrase 'not substantially of European origin or descent' to introduce a racial bar to enrolment at Duntroon.[53] Garran observed that:

> However precise the rules as to eligibility were made, there will always be cases where a candidate, though eligible as a matter of law, is undesirable as a matter of policy.[54]

And this is what happened, the legislation operating in a way that achieved Bridges's objective to keep Duntroon 'white'.[55]

On Garran's recommendation, a deliberate decision was made not to provide Abdul senior with a reason for the department's refusal. The department simply stated that 'Regulations' barred his son from admission. A year and a half later, well into WWI, Abdul senior told the *Daily Telegraph* that his son's application to Duntroon was refused 'on the grounds of his father's nationality', even though his son was an 'Australian native'.[56] The article was republished in at least three other newspapers but Abdul senior's incorrect attribution of his son's rejection to 'nationality' rather than 'race' was never corrected or questioned. As Peter Prince has shown, this blurring of race and nationality has had serious ongoing repercussions today.[57]

---

52   NAA: MP84/1, 1862/5/983.
53   Royal Military College of Australia Regulations 1913. These regulations were amended by 'Statutory Rules 1913, No. 147', Federal Register of Legislation, www.legislation.gov.au/Details/C1913L00147.
54   NAA: MP84/1, 1862/5/983.
55   A scan of the lists of Duntroon cadet names suggests that it was not until well into the twentieth century that any NSEOD were accepted into the college. NAA: A10160; C. D. Coulthard-Clark, *Duntroon, the Royal Military College of Australia, 1911–1986* (Sydney: Allen & Unwin, 1986), 283–329.
56   'The Colour Line', *Daily Telegraph* (Sydney), 5 February 1915, 7.
57   Peter Prince, 'Australia's Most Inhumane Mass Deportation Abuse: *Robtelmes v Brenan* and Expulsion of the Alien Islanders', *Law & History* 5, no. 1 (2018): 117–45.

Military Orders and the Racial Bar to Enlistment

By the start of WWI, the application of the NSEOD exemption clause in the Defence Act carried none of the nuance it might have had in 1901 or even 1910. That those NSEOD, despite being British subjects, were barred from enlisting in Australia's expeditionary forces was no longer remarkable. On 16 October 1914, nearly a month after the start of the war, Colonel E. T. Wallack issued a military order to the 2nd Military District (New South Wales) that: 'Only British subjects substantially of European origin or descent are to be accepted for service with the expeditionary forces.'[58] Three days later, the *Sydney Morning Herald* reported that 'in the future only British subjects substantially of European origin or descent are to be accepted for service with the expeditionary forces', confirming that this was a new regulation and a change in enlistment practice.[59] More surprising than the bar itself was the delay in its introduction. This is perhaps best understood as bureaucratic oversight – a delay in realising that, despite what policymakers imagined, those NSEOD not only wanted to enlist but also were actually being enlisted in Australia's expeditionary forces.

Although military orders and regulations were developed within the authority of the Defence Act, their use gave defence officials flexibility, as they could be modified as needed without requiring parliamentary approval and there were also differences in how they were implemented across military districts. On 8 May 1917, after three years of heavy losses, low enlistment rates and one failed attempt to introduce conscription, another military order was issued to the 2nd Military District that 'half-castes' could enlist provided the examining medical officers were satisfied that 'one of the parents is of European origin'.[60] The wording of these military orders varied across military districts. During WWI, Australia was divided into military districts broadly corresponding to each state and territory. Each district issued separate military orders, although, unfortunately, not all have survived. AIF District Standing Orders in 1916 for the 3rd Military District

---

58 AWM: Military Forces of the Commonwealth, 2nd Military District, District Order 124, 16 October 1914.

59 'Recruiting', *Sydney Morning Herald*, 19 October 1914, 8.

60 AWM: 2nd Military District, District Order 54, 8 May 1917, paragraph 6(1) (citing D.C.R. 187/1/2364). Australian Government, *Index to Military Orders*, 1917, Part 1, January to June, Military Order 200(2) Enlistment of Half-castes. This military order references 'Circular 113, 1917'. Thanks to Philippa Scarlett for assisting me to locate the original military order at the AWM.

(Victoria) stated: 'Men not "substantially of European origin" or descent are not to be enlisted'—but without reference to British subjecthood.[61] An instruction booklet for enlisting officers published in Brisbane the same year stated: 'Aboriginals, half-castes, or men with Asiatic blood are not to be enlisted. This applies to all coloured men.'[62] Finally, when restrictions were loosened, the Western Australian Recruitment Committee decided to ignore them; however, men NSEOD did still successfully enlist in Western Australia.[63]

George Kong Meng's complaint against his rejection from the AIF on the basis of being 'NSEOD' represented a significant challenge to the military order barring the enlistment of those NSEOD. It received the most publicity of any objection to the bar at the time and remains one of the most-cited examples today.[64] It is considered particularly significant because, at the time George was rejected for service, his brother was already serving on the front. The crucial point missed is that his brother, Herbert, enlisted on 1 September 1914, a month and a half *before* the military order that barred the enlistment of those NSEOD.

George Kong Meng, 1916

In September 1915, George Kong Meng tried to enlist but was rejected with no reason provided in surviving documentation.[65] At over 38 years old, George was only eligible to enlist once age restrictions were relaxed in June 1915, making men up to 45 years eligible. After being rejected a second time on 14 January 1916 (no official documentation on this attempt survives), he wrote an angry letter to Melbourne's *Argus* and *Age* newspapers. He explained how, without being asked his ancestry, he had been rejected and given a certificate stating he was 'not substantially of European origin' signed by the medical officer.[66] George was a British subject born in Victoria to a Tasmanian-born mother of British ancestry and a Chinese-Malay father, born in Penang under British colonial rule.

---

61   NAA: A1194, 20.41/6634, Australian Military Forces, 3rd Military District, District Standing Orders, Australian Imperial Force, 1916.
62   Australian War Memorial, *Instructions for the Guidance of Enlisting Officers at Approved Military Recruiting Depôts* (Brisbane: Government Printer, 1916).
63   Huggonson, 'The Dark Diggers of the AIF', 353.
64   This case was first discussed by Morag Loh in 1989. Loh, *Dinky-Di*, 22–3.
65   NAA: B2455, Kong Meng George.
66   'Recruiting Stupidity', *Argus* (Melbourne), 24 January 1916, 11; 'A Rejected Recruit', *Age* (Melbourne), 24 January 1916, 10.

His father was arguably the wealthiest Chinese merchant in the nineteenth century and was well known and highly respected within Victoria. In the letter, George argued that he was a natural-born British subject with parents who were also British subjects, that he had six years training with the 'old Victorian Mounted Rifles, and 8th Australian Light Horse Regiment', that his brother was already serving and, finally, that England and France were using 'coloured troops' so why not Australia?

His case put considerable public pressure on the Department of Defence's decision. We know that letters were written to the department about his case over the next few months: for example, letters were received from E. Stewart of Prahran in February, Mr Garrett of Longwood in April and Joseph Cook MP (leader of the federal opposition) in June. Unfortunately, no details of their arguments or the government's response have survived archival culling.[67] George Kong Meng's letter was also widely discussed and reproduced in other Victorian newspapers.[68] The only positions that did not call for a reassessment of the decision were taken by newspapers in Sydney and Perth that did not engage with the merits of the case.[69] Responses in Victorian newspapers, where George and his family were known, were supportive, and commentary pointed out various contradictions and inconsistencies in how the Department of Defence was dealing with race, nationality and enlistment. Those supporting George felt that being born in, and growing up in, Australia made him a suitable military candidate and a loyal subject, regardless of his racial background. Melbourne's *Punch*, better known for its racist cartoons, was surprisingly forthright in its support for George:

> The system that bars George Kong Meng from serving his country at the front certainly shrieks for immediate revision. Mr. Kong Meng is of Chinese blood, but he is of Australian birth, is married to an Australian, and all his interests are Australian. He is denied the privilege of fighting for his native country because his father was an oriental. This is preposterous.[70]

---

67   NAA: B540, 144/1. Thank you to Jodie Boyd for alerting me to this series. On the culling of WWI case files, see Anne-Marie Conde, 'A Societal Provenance Analysis of the First World War Service Records Held at the National Archives of Australia', *Archives and Manuscripts* 48, no. 2 (2020): 142–56, doi.org/10.1080/01576895.2020.1754259.
68   Newspapers that reported on the incident included: *Euroa Advertiser, Casterton Free Press and Glenelg Shire Advertiser, Punch* (Melbourne), *Omeo Standard and Mining Gazette, Violet Town Sentinel, Murchison Advertiser and Murchison, Toolamba, Mooroopna and Dargalong Express.*
69   'Personal Items', *Bulletin*, 10 February 1916, 14; 'A "White Australian" Recruit', *Westralian Worker* (Perth), 25 February 1916, 4.
70   ['Elusive Popularity'], *Punch* (Melbourne), 3 February 1916, 6. Also republished in the *Euroa Advertiser.*

Questioning the high number of enlistment rejections, the *Argus* suggested that there was 'no good and sufficient reason' why George Kong Meng should not serve with 'his fellow Australians' and was critical of the medical officer who acted 'without tact and without proper inquiry as to Mr Meng's nationality'.[71] The article urged the minister for defence to review the matter. The *Euroa Advertiser* was convinced that George had been 'inadvertently' turned down and 'felt sure' that he would 'receive immediate notification of acceptance of his services as soon as the official enquiries have been made'.[72] The *Euroa Gazette* similarly felt that his enlistment would be assured 'when proper inquiries have been made'.[73] One correspondent used George's case to show the inconsistency of government policy when it came to those with German ancestry.[74] Writing from Sydney, another quipped, 'try Sydney', as Arthur Quong Tart, the Sydney-born son of the late Quong Tart and his Lancashire-born wife Margaret, had succeeded in enlisting there.[75]

Despite the high level of public support, numerous calls for review and the range of arguments posed, the Department of Defence doubled down on its decision. The minister simply restated that 'the rule in force was that recruits for the Australian Imperial Force must be substantially of European origin'.[76] The only explanation as to why George's brother had succeeded in enlisting was that there had been a 'lack of co-ordination between departments'.[77] Barry Mackinnon, chairman of the State Parliamentary Recruiting Committee, acknowledged that while some men NSEOD had successfully enlisted, they 'desire[d] no more': 'Those of Asiatic origin, though born in Australia, will not be eligible.'[78] This was a distortion of the actual rule that stated that if you were 'substantially of European origin' you were eligible. While some rejected men did eventually succeed in enlisting, George Kong Meng was not one of them.[79]

---

71   ['Tuesday, January 25, 1916'], *Argus* (Melbourne), 25 January 1916, 6–7.
72   'An Error of Judgment', *Euroa Advertiser* (Vic.), 28 January 1916, 2.
73   *Euroa Gazette* (Vic.), 1 February 1916, 2.
74   'Germans in the Public Service', *Argus* (Melbourne), 28 January 1916, 7.
75   G. Macadam, 'Recruiting Stupidity', *Argus* (Melbourne), 31 January 1916, 8.
76   'A Rejected Recruit', *Age* (Melbourne), 25 January 1916, 8.
77   'Enlistment of Aliens', *Argus* (Melbourne), 5 February 1916, 17. Also republished in the *Australasian*.
78   Ibid.
79   'Other Volunteers', *Euroa Gazette* (Vic.), 23 November 1915, 4; 'Other Volunteers', *Euroa Gazette* (Vic.), 6 November 1917, 5.

While commentators observed that George's brother Herbert (1866–1954) had succeeded in enlisting, they missed the fact that he had enlisted prior to the military order barring the enlistment of those NSEOD.[80] They also overlooked the fact that Herbert had lied about his age; he lowered it by 10 years, claiming he was 38 and thus eligible to enlist.[81] Even more significant was the fact that 11 days after George was rejected for service and two days after his letter was printed, not just one but four of Chin Langtip's Australian-born sons (from Port Albert) successfully enlisted in Melbourne.[82] Ernest Walter Langtip's application form has a handwritten note stating that he was 'of substantial European origin', even though only one of his parents was of 'European origin'. All have annotations stating that their applications had been 're-examined' at the Melbourne depot, having passed medical assessments locally. Unfortunately, George Kong Meng's 1916 enlistment documentation no longer survives so we are not able to compare the steps he went through in Melbourne to assess differences in administrative process. Inconsistent enlistment decisions like this were commonplace during WWI, an inevitable outcome of the nature of the system established to bar those NSEOD from enlisting – a system largely closed to scrutiny, poorly defined and described, and open to subjective decision-making.

George Kong Meng's letter was the most significant public challenge to the bar to enlistment of those NSEOD but there were others. Newspaper editors and members of the public disagreed with and questioned the racial bar in other situations too, and were supported by sympathetic readers. Other cases considered unjust included the rejections of William Frederick Pow of Glen Valley in May 1915;[83] Mansfield-born Thomas Brooks of French and West Indian ancestry in July 1915;[84] and Charles Lionel Fooke, who had a Cantonese-born father and English mother, in January 1916. Charles Fooke successfully enlisted and passed the follow-up medical examination in Melbourne only to be rejected after being casually questioned by an officer at the barracks.[85] These cases, each of which was reported in the press, provide insight into the disconnect between the position of members of the public and the Department of Defence. The public supported the

---

80   NAA: B2455, Kong Meng, Herbert.
81   Victorian birth registration, 9420/1866.
82   NAA: B2455, Langtip Ernest Walter, Langtip Bertie Allan, Langtip Henry, Langtip Leslie Oliver.
83   'Rejected Soldiers', *Omeo Standard and Mining Gazette*, 9 May 1916, 3.
84   'Rejecting Recruits', *Truth (Melbourne)*, 17 July 1915, 1 (city edition).
85   'The Colour Line in Recruiting', *Casterton Free Press and Glenelg Shire Advertiser*, 31 January 1916, 4.

enlistment of these men – even if their often racialised language suggested that they did not view them as equals. Newspaper articles show a sustained questioning of the applicability of the racial bar on the enlistment of 'half-castes' throughout the war, calls for more flexibility in its interpretation, and sympathy and support for the men rejected. However, there is no evidence that the Department of Defence altered its official position in response to any of these calls. Nor did the department offer any public clarification about how it was interpreting the bar.

At the end of August 1915, Senator Thomas Bakhap once again addressed the Senate, this time during question time, calling for the removal 'at the first opportunity' of the 'reference to men of Australian birth but of Asiatic extraction' from the Defence Act.[86] The minister for defence, Senator George Pearce, responded that the Act 'contains no such reference' to 'persons of Asiatic extraction' only to 'persons of European nationalities'. Pearce closed the discussion by stating: 'I do not think it either wise or expedient that I should make any further statement on the matter.'[87] Newspapers reported the interaction but there was no public commentary on it. It is unfortunate that Bakhap did not read the Defence Act more closely and reflect more deeply on the difference between subjecthood and race because his argument had a sound basis. But Pearce's response was incorrect too. The Act did not reference 'European nationality' but its opposite. His comment, whether deliberate or not, obfuscated the important distinction between nationality and race. We know from indexes to Department of Defence correspondence files that the department investigated Bakhap's question further, but the results of this investigation have been lost.[88]

Conclusion

In September 1916, as part of public discussions related to the government's attempt to introduce conscription, Reg H. Meaburn, a regular correspondent to the *Mercury* in Hobart, argued that 'all Chinese and other Asiatics naturalised in the Commonwealth should be liable to serve when called upon'. He suggested that this was something Senator Bakhap should be

---

86 Commonwealth of Australia, *Parliamentary Debates*, Senate, 25 August 1915, 6044–45 (Thomas Bakhap), historichansard.net/senate/1915/19150825_senate_6_78/#subdebate-11-0-s0.
87 Ibid., (George Pearce).
88 AIF correspondence files were heavily culled after the war. NAA: B540, 144/1/ – Part 1.

looking into.[89] 'Naturalisation', Meaburn observed, 'has its duties as well as its privileges'. His comments touch on the overarching argument of this chapter: that, in barring the participation of those NSEOD in military service during WWI, the Australian Government created a third category of people, those who were British subjects in law but, because they were not white, were considered to lack allegiance to Australia and were treated as 'aliens' despite their birth rights or naturalisation status.[90]

In response to Meaburn, someone calling themselves 'TASMAN' wrote that naturalised British subjects who were 'Asiatic' were treated differently and were barred from enlistment under the Defence Act.[91] Meaburn, in turn, replied that if it was only a matter of changing the Defence Act 'then it is quite time it was altered', suggesting that the Chinese community could appeal to the Australian Parliament to have it changed.[92] Neither Bakhap, the Chinese Australian community in Tasmania nor Chinese Australians elsewhere took up this suggestion. This is noteworthy given that Chinese Australian communities mobilised against discriminatory legislation in many other circumstances. This serves as a reminder that not all Australians who were NSEOD would have wanted to enlist.

When drawing up Australia's defence legislation in the early twentieth century, politicians and government bureaucrats assumed that Aboriginal Australians and other 'coloured' Australians would not want to enlist because they had been excluded from an Australia imagined as a white nation. The Australian Government imagined that Australia would be defending itself against an Asian enemy and that it would be the white citizens within this newly forged nation that would rise up to defend it. This was not so. We know Australia's First Peoples and those with Chinese, Indian and Syrian ancestry all sought to enlist during WWI and that many succeeded. Tracing changes in the Defence Act, we see that Australia's defence forces were not initially constructed with racial constraints but that this changed over time. White Australians of British and European (ironically, largely German) ancestry were to be included; excluded were those NSEOD – that is, Aboriginal Australians and those with Chinese ancestry, as well as those with Indian, Japanese, Syrian and Polynesian or other South Sea Islander ancestry.

---

89   Reg. H. Meaburn, 'Naturalised Aliens', *Mercury* (Hobart), 7 September 1916, 7.
90   For a discussion on how 'coloured' Australians, despite their status as British subjects, were classified as 'aliens' in law and practice, see Prince, 'Aliens in Their Own Land'; Prince, 'Australia's Most Inhumane'.
91   Tasman, 'Naturalised Aliens', *Mercury* (Hobart), 9 September 1916, 9.
92   Reg. H. Meaburn, 'Naturalised Aliens', *Mercury* (Hobart), 14 September 1916, 7.

Exemptions to compulsory military training and service in the Defence Act of 1909/1910, including racial ones, were written into legislation as a boon, a choice. Was the fledgling Australian Government being magnanimous and giving those NSEOD the opportunity to excuse themselves from participating in White Australia? If so, they failed to recognise that their imagined White Australia was not shared by all, and that non-white Australians would nevertheless want to defend their own imagined Australia – one that included them. It is more likely that the Australian Government intended to bar those NSEOD from Australia's defence forces but needed a discreet way to hide this fact from the British Government, which was intent on maintaining its empire and building its relationships with Asia, particularly Japan.

In the end, the war Australia had been preparing for was a European one, outside the Commonwealth, and so it was not Australia's defence forces that were used but two expeditionary forces (the AIF and the AN&MEF). Enlistment was voluntary and enlistment criteria were set out in a series of evolving military orders. As Peter Stanley has observed, while the orderly volumes of regulations, military and standing orders might suggest that the AIF worked like a machine, the reality was far from it – it was 'more like a plant, needing constant tending and pruning'.[93]

On 16 October 1914, after the first contingent of soldiers was sent to the war, a military order was issued that barred those NSEOD from enlisting with the expeditionary forces. Sporadically throughout the war, examples of men refused enlistment because of their race were criticised in newspapers as unjust. The inconsistencies and contradictions of Department of Defence decisions were highlighted, but the department did not shift its stance until May 1917. In the face of plummeting enlistment rates, and before a second attempt to introduce conscription in December 1917, restrictions were eased and Aboriginal people of mixed descent were permitted to enlist.

Little archival evidence survives to help us unravel what the government's specific intentions were. Through a close reading of changes to the Defence Act, military orders and instructions, and analysis of pivotal cases, we can see how an exemption that started as voluntary came to be employed as an exclusion or bar to participation. The cases examined here shed light on how lived experiences shaped administrative policy and decision-making,

---

93   Peter Stanley, *Bad Characters: Sex, Crime, Mutiny, Murder and the Australian Imperial Force* (Sydney: Allen & Unwin, 2010), 20–21.

contributing to a hardened stance. By the start of WWI, many people, including Senator Thomas Bakhap, assumed that exemption clauses within the Defence Act determined enlistment. The Department of Defence did nothing to dispel this notion. In discussions about enlistment in newspapers, government correspondence and parliamentary debates, concepts of race and nationality were often used interchangeably. The difference between these concepts was not well understood, or perhaps even deliberately misunderstood, as nobody tried to publicly correct or clarify errors. When people questioned the racial bar on enlistment, they were largely ignored. This may well have been a deliberate ploy on the part of the government to ensure that laws and regulations were fluid and open to interpretation so that officials could make subjective decisions with little oversight and behind closed doors. In doing so, the Australian Government was able to obscure the fact that they had created a category of people who were British subjects in law but, because of their race, were not given equal rights.

3

Freedom and Freehold: Intergenerational Land Ownership by Chinese and Dalmatian Farming Families in New Zealand

Jane McCabe

Introduction

For some decades, in New Zealand and Australia, academic and community historians have promulgated the belief – or at least implicitly worked on the assumption – that one of the benefits of naturalisation was the right to own land. Consequently, it has been understood that the ban on naturalisation for Chinese peoples in New Zealand, from 1908 to 1951, prevented land ownership, unless an individual was already naturalised. This belief has been reinforced by evidence that most Chinese market gardeners leased land, rather than owning it outright. This in turn has been woven into a narrative of resilience, since many of the Chinese families who established successful market gardens arrived in the era of non-naturalisation. These families often went on to purchase land post-1951, once naturalisation was again possible, reinforcing the belief that the two were directly related.

More recently, scholars have suggested that, in terms of *legal* restriction, only in the years 1942–45 were non-naturalised Chinese peoples in New Zealand barred from purchasing land.[1] While this attenuates the extent of this discriminatory measure, it is notable how late this brief ban was, given that many other restrictions had been removed by this time.[2] Further, there is much anecdotal evidence that land purchase was restricted in informal ways, such as refusal to sell land to Chinese peoples, and these social mechanisms can be much more difficult to address than legal discrimination.[3] A third point related to this corrective about land purchase by non-naturalised peoples is whether individuals and families *believed* that their ability to own land was negated by their 'alien' status, due either to local information or that shared across national boundaries via the transnational family networks that were common in the first half of the twentieth century. In other words, if an individual in Queensland, for example, was prevented from owning land because they were barred from naturalising, it seems plausible that a relative or associate in New Zealand might have assumed the same to be true for them.

James Ng's third volume of *Windows on a Chinese Past* (1999) is likely to be the most authoritative source on this complex matter. In this detailed work, Ng cited a list (compiled by Nigel Murphy for the Chinese Association) of all the legal consequences of non-naturalisation – every Act that brought in restrictions during the period of non-naturalisation – for Chinese people in New Zealand.[4] This myriad of legal restrictions ranged from disallowing ownership of ships or aircraft to voting or serving on local bodies and other

---

1   Joanna Boileau, *Chinese Market Gardening in Australia and New Zealand* (Cham, Switzerland: Palgrave Macmillan, 2017), 136, doi.org/10.1007/978-3-319-51871-8; Ruth Lam and Lily Lee, *Sons of the Soil: Chinese Market Gardeners in New Zealand* (Pukekohe, NZ: Dominion Federation for New Zealand Chinese Commercial Growers, 2012), 17, 529.

2   Discriminatory measures in New Zealand were gradually reduced from the mid-1930s through to the end of World War II, for example, Chinese women were granted permits to join their husbands in New Zealand, Chinese peoples were allowed to access old age pensions and other social security services, and the poll tax was waived from 1934 and repealed in 1944. Paul Spoonley and Richard Bedford, *Welcome to Our World? Immigration and the Reshaping of New Zealand* (Auckland: Dunmore Publishing Ltd, 2012), 103–4.

3   Miles Fairburn raised related issues in an article questioning whether research into the causative factors of discrimination against the Chinese had considered the potential gap between 'legal and institutional expressions' of prejudice versus 'quotidian expressions'. Miles Fairburn, 'What Best Explains the Discrimination against the Chinese in New Zealand, 1860s–1950s?', *Journal of New Zealand Studies* 2&3 (2004): 66, doi.org/10.26686/jnzs.v0i2/3.90.

4   James Ng, *Windows on a Chinese Past*, vol. 3 (Dunedin: Otago Heritage Books, 1999), 152.

boards, through to receiving pensions and other social services. However, uncertainty remained concerning 'the Chinese purchase of agricultural land'. As Ng explained:

> Many of us can *vaguely recall our parents saying* that Chinese were unable to purchase agricultural land, although they were able to buy shops. The chief benefit of my grandfather being naturalised in 1905 was *said to be* his legal ability to buy land for his kin who were market gardeners in Gore and Ashburton. A World War 1 regulation barred Chinese aliens from land transactions unless they were first issued with a licence. This regulation was extended in 1922. In World War 2, the Aliens Land Purchase Regulations, 1942, barred Chinese aliens from ownership of land and remained in force until 1945.[5]

In this chapter, I seek to bring further clarity (and, admittedly, further complexity) to this discussion by examining rural land ownership and intergenerational transmission by non-British families in two disparate regions of New Zealand: Chinese market gardeners on the Taieri Plain in the southern province of Otago, and Dalmatian gum diggers turned farmers and wine growers in Hokianga in the Far North. These communities were part of a major research project I conducted on farming families and inheritance.[6] An important feature of my methodology was to broaden the term 'farming family' – which, in New Zealand, is commonly understood to refer to Pākehā agriculturalists – to include families of Māori and non-British ancestry, as well as horticulturalists, since they faced the same issues with family inheritance. 'Mainstream' farming families were also included so as to enable analysis across the spectrum of families of different classes, religions, cultures and ethnicities that made up these particular rural communities. The overall argument of the project is that the familial trade in land – buying and selling, leasing and inheriting – is central to rural community formation. During the course of the research it became clear that this trade is one that blurs the boundaries between family, extended family and community. Neighbours, for example, can become more like kin over generations of farming, and marriage between families over many generations has created complex community-wide connections.

---

5   Ibid. Emphasis added.
6   The Royal Society of New Zealand Marsden Fast-Start project (2017–20) was entitled 'Splitting up the Farm? A Cross-Cultural Study of Land and Inheritance in Aotearoa, 1870–1970'. I am currently writing a monograph, *Family Land: Inheritance, Culture and the Family Farm*, for Auckland University Press.

It is from this 'bundle of relationships' approach to rural communities that I put the spotlight in this chapter on non-British farming families and consider the effect of naturalisation on their efforts to build-up landholdings.[7] While the pattern of Chinese emigration to places like Australia and New Zealand will be familiar to most readers, the Dalmatian story warrants further introduction. In the late nineteenth century, Dalmatian men from an area south of Split (now part of Croatia), comprising a narrow coastal strip and a number of islands, travelled to the Far North of New Zealand to engage in digging for kauri gum – deposits of resin from ancient forests that experienced a 'boom' similar to that of gold.[8] These men were escaping political and economic hardship, and, like Chinese families, a practice developed whereby some sons sought opportunities overseas. The resulting chain migration saw the establishment of a community that continues to self-identify as 'Dalmatian', despite political events that might have dislodged this terminology.[9] One of the main contrasts to the Chinese experience in New Zealand was a high degree of intermarriage with Māori women in the Far North, leading to the existence of a mixed community known locally as 'Māori-Dallies'.[10] Marriage to local women can, of course, be connected to geographical divergence too: it would be a much longer journey for Dalmatian men to make regular trips home to wives, as Chinese men often did.

Bringing Dalmatian families into comparison and contrast with Chinese farmers in the south has a number of benefits. In both cases, land ownership in the initial phase was attempted by single men (either unmarried or with wives and children at home). This placed them at a disadvantage in an era in which there was growing concern about the prevalence of single men in rural districts and the need for families to form the moral nucleus of a 'new' society. Both also faced the distressing scenario of an initially positive reception followed by a period of strong 'anti' rhetoric, based on racist ideas about work habits, competitive and collective behaviour, and fears of an 'influx', all of which underpinned the use of naturalisation as a means of

7   I take Erik Wolf's phrase and its meaning for historical purposes from Tony Ballantyne's citation in the opening of *Orientalism and Race: Aryanism and the Webs of Empire* (New York: Palgrave Macmillan, 2002), 1, doi.org/10.1057/9780230508071_1.

8   For a map of the region see 'Origin of Dalmatians Emigrating to New Zealand before 1949', *Te Ara, Encyclopedia of New Zealand*, accessed 6 March 2023, teara.govt.nz/en/map/262/origin-of-dalmatians-emigrating-to-new-zealand-before-1949.

9   For example, see Dalmatian Cultural Society website, accessed 6 March 2023, www.dalmatian.org.nz/.

10   See Senka Bozic-Vrbancic, *Tarara: Croats and Māori in New Zealand: Memory, Belonging, Identity* (Dunedin: Otago University Press, 2008).

restricting opportunity and the desire/ability to settle in New Zealand.[11] These demographic and political forces saw Chinese and Dalmatian men forming connections that can be described as kin-based rather than directly familial: working with others from the same home village, for example.[12] This collective activity extended to land ownership, occupation and use, and so adds an important dimension to our understanding of familial inheritance, which, for these non-British communities, was founded on kin-based 'trading' within their own communities and was only later followed by integration into wider rural land exchange and transmission down a family line that conformed to the mainstream ideal of the family farm.

Land and the Law: State Regimes, Local Cultures

The aspiration to own freehold land was a key feature of a developing national imaginary in New Zealand from the mid to late nineteenth century. The 1860s–70s were pivotal decades in which Enlightenment ideals about broadening access to civic participation, land ownership and enfranchisement were being negotiated in new imperial spaces. The question facing those intent on implementing 'reforms' in the colonies was how far these rights might be extended beyond the British male elite – since there were not only class but also racial and gendered barriers to full participation in political and social life. In New Zealand, land was a particularly contentious issue: the 1860s saw prolonged conflict between the state and iwi (Māori tribe) in various parts of the North Island (known as the New Zealand Wars), which culminated in the punitive confiscation of large swathes of land from Māori deemed to have fought against the Crown. Meanwhile, in the South Island, where almost all Indigenous land was alienated in the 1840s, most land suitable for farming had been tied up by a political, moneyed elite that had seized the opportunity to take up large pastoral runs. Various factions in government debated the 'land question' seemingly endlessly based on opposite views about its distribution.

---

11 Spoonley and Bedford, *Welcome to Our World*, 37–38.
12 As Senka Bozic-Vrbancic noted of the Dalmatian men in the Far North, 'one after another … they would come to camps … boys from Podgora in one camp, those from Vrgorac in another, some from Zrnovo in yet another, or sometimes all together'. Bozic-Vrbancic, *Tarara*, 67.

After two decades of debate, the Liberal government of the 1890s gained a mandate to implement a two-pronged strategy for redistributing land into the hands of the small family enterprises: (a) breaking up the large landholdings of early British arrivals and (b) embarking on a long project to acquire the several million acres of the North Island that remained in *papatupu* (customary) Māori ownership for resale or lease to British families.[13] A series of legislative measures and schemes were devised to enable family farmers to get onto this land with minimal capital outlay, and to impinge on the ability of the wealthy to accrue large landholdings in the first place. In the process, the ideal of the small 'yeoman' farmer took firm root in New Zealand – more so than in any other part of the British Empire – and persisted right through the twentieth century and, arguably, to the present day.[14]

Immigration and naturalisation laws, which developed alongside this liberalisation of land law, can be understood as a mechanism to regulate new admissions to the widening middle class – the result of opportunistic individuals rapidly gaining not only wealth but also political influence through land speculation. Immigration was vital to supply the labour to make the land productive (clearing bush, draining swamps, building fences) but there was a persistent shortage of farm labourers and manual workers that could not be filled by British migrants. This meant that any purist rhetoric of excluding non-British peoples was regularly set aside, and workers who may not have been 'desirable' but were nonetheless acceptable were allowed to cross the border. However, once across the border, persistent efforts were made to regulate 'second tier' immigrants in order to privilege British families (and British values) in forming the nucleus around which rural and urban communities grew.[15]

In the early colonial period, naturalisation law was a key mechanism for controlling non-British peoples once inside the borders through its connection to property rights. Prior to 1866, non-British subjects in New Zealand could not own or inherit property; however, they could gain this right

---

13   See two key works: Tom Brooking, *Lands for the People? The Highland Clearances and the Colonisation of New Zealand: A Biography of John McKenzie* (Dunedin: University of Otago Press, 1996); Tom Brooking, '"Busting up" the Greatest Estate of All: Liberal Māori Land Policy, 1891–1911', *New Zealand Journal of History* 26, no. 1 (1992): 78–98.

14   Tom Brooking, 'Yeotopia Found … but? The Yeoman Ideal That Underpinned New Zealand Agricultural Practice into the Early 21st Century, with American and Australian Comparisons', *Agricultural History* 93, no. 1 (2019): 68–101, doi.org/10.3098/ah.2019.093.1.068.

15   I made this argument in relation to Anglo-Indian adolescents resettled in New Zealand as domestic servants and farm labourers in Jane McCabe, 'Working the Permit System: Anglo-Indian Immigration to New Zealand, 1920–1940', *New Zealand Journal of History* 48, no. 2 (2014): 27–49.

by becoming naturalised. Although it required an act of Parliament for each 'batch' to achieve this, there were few restrictions on becoming naturalised in this era.[16] In 1866, the *Aliens Act* formalised a process for applying for naturalisation. At the same time, land ownership and naturalisation became detached, at least in the eyes of the law. One did not have to be naturalised to legally own and transmit or transfer the ownership of land. As naturalisation ceased to be a means of controlling land ownership, land *tenure* became central to the 'land question' and was increasingly used as a means for the government to regulate landholdings. 'Special settlement' schemes were devised as a means for getting British families onto land recently acquired from local iwi by the Crown. Land was leased to families who lacked the capital to purchase it outright, freeing up any resources they did have (and often providing additional funds) for 'breaking in' the land: clearing scrub, draining swamps, fencing, and developing crops and stock.[17] Those leases ranged in term from 30 years to the so-named 'perpetual' leases (999 years) that were effectively freehold.

While there were no stated restrictions as to who could take up land in these schemes, the regulations were, of course, culturally biased towards British families. But the emphasis here needs to be placed on both parts of that phase – 'British' and 'families'. There was a racial/cultural bias and also a class/social one. Settlement schemes stated that preference would be given to *married* men, and, while families with less means were targeted, values of respectability and hard work were built into the regulations.[18] Officials selected families to take up blocks of land; they were then monitored, their progress and productivity was tracked and the state retained the right to remove the lease.[19] Being awarded a block of land did not come with the future right to freehold nor the right to transfer the lease to the next generation. Thus, the related ideals of freehold land ownership and of keeping the farm in the family were restricted for families of *all* ancestries and origins.

---

16 'Nationality', *Te Ara, Encyclopedia of New Zealand*, accessed 6 March 2023, teara.govt.nz/en/1966/nationality-and-naturalisation.

17 See W. R. Jourdain, *Land Legislation and Settlement in New Zealand* (Wellington: Department of Lands and Survey, 1925), 22–37, for a summary of the various land acts and regulations for these closer settlement schemes from the 1860s to the 1890s.

18 This stipulation reflected concerns about the prevalence of itinerant single male labourers in early colonial New Zealand. Miles Fairburn's 'atomisation' thesis is the most well known, though much debated, work here. See Miles Fairburn, *The Ideal Society and its Enemies: The Foundations of Modern New Zealand Society 1850–1900* (Auckland: Auckland University Press, 1989).

19 This discretionary power of officials to implement policy echoes my argument in McCabe, 'Working the Permit System', 27–49.

Having said that, the ground was undoubtedly tilted in favour of British families. My research into these settlement schemes in Northland shows that British families played an active role in pressuring the government to acquire Māori land outright for the purposes of making it available for British families to purchase freehold. Indeed, a key aim of my land/inheritance study was to explore the extent to which colonial families were actors in the process of land alienation (rather than just beneficiaries), and, beyond that, to examine their participation in the rural land trade, within and between families, over generations. What has been surprising is the extent to which leasing has figured in this local trade. Previously, land ownership has been understood as having moved through a clear progression from *papatupu*, to Crown land, to freehold Pākehā ownership. Once one reconceptualises the almost mythical idea of familial inheritance of the farm as a community land trade, the potential for looking across ethnic and legal boundaries – a genuinely inclusive community study – is opened up. And, by looking at freehold *and* leasehold land, the intricate relationships that underpin this trade are revealed. It then becomes possible to paint a more accurate picture of everyday life for non-British landholders in rural communities; to consider the subtle workings of discrimination and integration; and to recognise concomitant economic, legal, social and familial dynamics.

To consider the way these state-level policies and laws played out locally, a brief sketch of my two study districts is necessary. Taieri and Hokianga (see Figure 3.1) are not only physically but also socially distant from each other, occupying opposite positions in the national ideal of intergenerational farm ownership. In Hokianga, the achievement of this ideal was hampered by geographical features that made much of the area ill-suited to modern farming, and by the complex historical processes referred to above that saw large areas of *papatupu* land converted into Māori title, then purchased by the Crown with the desired outcome of moving the land into freehold British ownership. However, much land remained in Māori title or Crown ownership and was subject to various state schemes. As a consequence, land ownership in Hokianga has been fragmentary and land tenure insecure – conditions that work against the aspiration of 'keeping it in the family'. In contrast, on the Taieri, land alienation from the local Kāi Tahu iwi to the Crown was swift. This largely swampy plain was part of the large Otakou purchase in 1844.[20] Apart from a small reserve, it was quickly converted into freehold farms owned by predominantly Scots families.

20 For details of this purchase and its effects on the local Kāi Tahu community, see Angela Wanhalla, 'Transgressing Boundaries: A History of the Mixed Descent Families of Maitapapa, Taieri, 1830–1940' (PhD thesis, University of Canterbury, 2004), ch. 3.

1. Mongonui
2. Hokianga
3. Bay of Islands
4. Whangarei
5. Hobson
6. Rodney
7. Waitemata
8. Eden
9. Manukau
10. Coromandel
11. Thames
12. Piako
13. Waikato
14. Waipa
15. Raglan
16. Kawhia
17. Taranaki
18. Patea
19. Tauranga
20. Whakatane
21. Cook
22. Wairoa
23. Hawkes Bay
24. Wanganui
25. West Taupo
26. East Taupo
27. Rangitikei
28. Manawatu
29. Waipawa
30. Hutt
31. Wairarapa West
32. Wairarapa East

33. Sounds
34. Marlborough
35. Kaikoura
36. Waimea
37. Collingwood
38. Buller
39. Inangahua
40. Amuri
41. Cheviot
42. Grey
43. Ashley

44. Selwyn
45. Akaroa
46. Ashburton
47. Geraldine
48. Waimate
49. Westland
50. Waitaki
51. Waikouaiti
52. Maniototo
53. Vincent
54. Lake
55. Peninsula
56. Taieri
57. Bruce
58. Clutha
59. Tuapeka
60. Southland
61. Wallace
62. Fiord
63. Stewart Island

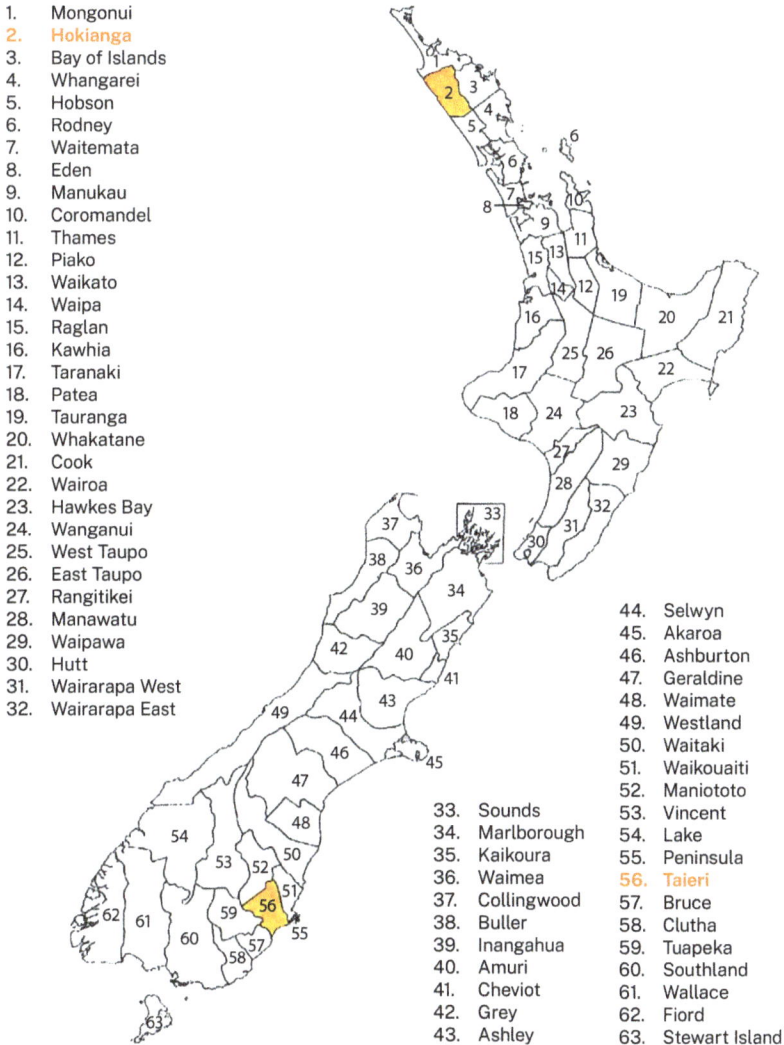

Figure 3.1: Taieri and Hokianga in an 1876 map of NZ counties.

Source: Rebecca Lenihan, *From Alba to Aotearoa* (Dunedin: Otago University Press, 2015), 12.

Complicating these apparently dichotomous dynamics, however, were the activities of non-British, non-Māori landholding families in both districts. On the Taieri, it was Chinese descendants of goldminers who established the market gardens – and intergenerational family enterprises – that provided food for the growing colonial city of Dunedin. In Hokianga, Dalmatian men who came to New Zealand to labour for a different extractive industry boom, that of kauri gum, also looked to purchase land and set up family businesses once the gum ran out. Like the Chinese, they faced discriminatory measures that aimed to limit their immigration, their working and social lives, and the opportunity to own land. But a closer look reveals much about the processes of socialisation that saw both communities navigate legal restrictions, form binding relationships in their respective rural districts and build landholdings that can be viewed as part of extended/transnational family wealth. The effect of global forces upon these communities in New Zealand must also be acknowledged, as they shaped different trajectories of land ownership and transmission for each. In the sections below, I am mindful of the operation of multiple imaginaries – home/away, local, national, and transnational – that shaped the way non-British families grew their landholdings.

Chinese Land Ownership in Otago

My study of farming families and inheritance examined Chinese ownership of land for market gardening on the Taieri Plain, a rural district 30 kilometres west of the city of Dunedin, where a number of family businesses were established from the 1920s. The origins of the Chinese presence in Otago lies several generations earlier, in 1865, when a small party of Chinese miners was invited by the provincial government to travel from Victoria to work the goldmines gradually being abandoned by European miners. This began a chain migration that would see over 5,000 Chinese arrive in Otago over the next 20 years.[21] While most of these men travelled through the city of Dunedin and across the Taieri Plain directly to the goldfields of Central Otago, many others stopped on the way, establishing businesses to capitalise on the opportunities that the goldrush and a developing colony offered. As they did elsewhere, Chinese men established laundries, grocers and market gardens in what is now the centre of Dunedin city. The first market garden was set up in 1867, and, by 1880, the Chinese were regarded as having a monopoly on the vegetable trade in Dunedin.[22] The missionary Alexander Don's 'roll of Chinese', an extraordinary collection of data

---

21   See Manying Ip, 'Chinese New Zealanders: Old Settlers and New Immigrants', in *Immigrants and National Identity in New Zealand: One People, Two Peoples, Many Peoples?*, ed. Stuart Greif (Palmerston North: Dunmore Press, 1995); Malcolm McKinnon, *Immigrants and Citizens: New Zealanders and Asian Immigration in Historical Context* (Wellington: Institute of Policy Studies, Victoria University of Wellington, 1996), 23–25.
22   'Chinese Market Gardening', *Otago Witness*, Issue 1383, 1 June 1878.

relating to the Chinese population in Otago at the turn of the twentieth century, shows that 159 (of 347) Chinese men in Dunedin were employed in market gardening.[23]

This was also the era when gold began to run out, and more Chinese sought new avenues for income through market gardening – as labourers for Chinese employers, and by establishing their own gardens. At the same time, Dunedin city was growing, and land used for market gardening in the flat areas in the south of the city was gradually reclaimed for residential and other developments.[24] The Ding family story typifies the pattern of movement that saw market gardens incrementally shifting from Dunedin to the Taieri (and areas north of Dunedin) in the 1920s and 1930s.[25] Ding Chun arrived in Dunedin in 1908. In 1917, he leased land in Forbury, in South Dunedin, for market gardening. The land was reclaimed as an educational reserve in the 1920s (it would later become the site of Kings High School) and the family took over a plot of land in Kaikorai Valley, on the outskirts of the city, from the Sew Hoys, a well-known family who had established gardens there. By this time, Ding Chun's son, born in China, had joined his father in New Zealand. They only stayed a short time in Kaikorai Valley, due to the poor soil quality, before taking up land in North Taieri.[26] But the soil there was also found to be ill-suited to vegetable growing – very dry, with a shingle base. It was from there that the Ding family made a more permanent shift to Outram, in West Taieri, in the 1930s. The soil and conditions were good. The Dings and a number of other Chinese families established long-term, intergenerational family market gardens in this area that persist to the present day.

These multiple steps towards settlement in Outram suggest regular encounters with legal and social structures in order to occupy and use land, which I will return to shortly. But first it is useful to outline the national and global context within which the Taieri land story occurred – one of increasing social and political anxieties about the growth of a non-British presence in New Zealand, expressed most overtly in restrictive immigration rules that targeted Chinese migrants.[27] Quotas, reading tests and a hefty poll tax made Chinese men's entry and re-entry into New Zealand difficult

23   Lam and Lee, *Sons of the Soil*, 41.
24   *Chinese Market Gardening*, 140; Lam and Lee, *Sons of the Soil*, 41–42.
25   Lam and Lee give many examples of families who followed this trajectory. See Lam and Lee, *Sons of the Soil*, ch. 2.
26   Interview with Charlie Ding, Wellington, 18 April 2019; Lam and Lee, *Sons of the Soil*, 43–44.
27   McKinnon, *Immigrants and Citizens*, 26–31.

and ruled out bringing their wives with them. The pattern that developed as a result – for those who did reasonably well – was a highly mobile, transnational one: remitting money to family in China, travelling home to marry but returning to New Zealand without their wives, continuing to build a living and sending money home.[28] This transnational life persisted over generations as men took sons who were old enough back with them to New Zealand to assist with small businesses. The pointedly restrictive actions of the New Zealand Government only began to turn a corner in 1939 when the Japanese invasion of China led to a number of wives of Chinese men resident in New Zealand being permitted to cross the border temporarily, and then permanently.[29]

From their immersed community perspective, Lily Lee and Ruth Lam's 2012 *Sons of the Soil* reveals many stories of intergenerational land ownership among Chinese families in New Zealand.[30] Joanna Boileau's more recent monograph enlarges the frame by looking at Chinese market gardeners in Australia and New Zealand, and she too pays specific attention to land tenure.[31] Both works make some clear claims about patterns and regulations of land ownership, supported by official records and community sources. Boileau, citing *Sons of the Soil*, affirms that the only time that Chinese were not allowed to buy land in New Zealand was during World War II, between 1942 and 1945.[32] But, as she also states, prior to this ban, the majority of Chinese market gardeners had leased their plots anyway. Boileau, and Lee and Lam, attribute the prevalence of leasing to a combination of factors on both sides of this colonial encounter. On the one hand, Chinese were 'restricted from owning land by a complex web of institutional racism', and 'European landowners may have been reluctant to sell their land to Chinese, although they would consider leasing it for short periods'; on the other hand, most market gardeners were 'single men, mobile, and lacked the capital to invest in land'.[33] Thus, Boileau states, Chinese market gardeners were 'not part of the agrarian ideal' that brought British migrants to settler

---

28   There is a considerable body of scholarship on the development of these transnational Chinese families in this era. Lam and Lee's *Sons of the Soil* presents many family biographies that beautifully illustrate how they operated over multiple generations to the present day.

29   Manying Ip, 'Old Settlers and New Immigrants'.

30   Lam and Lee, *Sons of the Soil*.

31   Boileau, *Chinese Market Gardening*.

32   Ibid., 136.

33   Ibid.

colonies like New Zealand and Australia, and it was not until the postwar era that evidence has been found of Chinese families regarding leasehold land as a stepping stone to purchasing land outright.[34]

This question of aspirations affects intergenerational land ownership in a number of ways. One of the reasons I undertook a study of farming families was because the family model of ownership is currently under threat in New Zealand. This is not the first time that the rural sector has faced a significant challenge. The difference now is a developing sense among (Pākehā) farming families that the *desire* to pass land onto the next generation is waning, due to (a) the increasing requirement to take on high levels of debt and (b) the burden of paperwork associated with new environmental regulations. While the desire of offspring to take over the family farm has been waning for many decades, if the aspiration of parents to pass it down also disappears, the family model of farm ownership will face a greater challenge than ever before. Aspiration is also directly tied to land tenure. As already stated, my study has revealed the prevalence of leasehold in Taieri and Hokianga. If one does not have freehold ownership of a property, how can one aspire – let alone achieve – intergenerational ownership? There are, of course, different types of leases, and some of these can be transferred down the generations. But many cannot. As historian James Ng has said about the Chinese community and their local aspirations: 'the wish follows the capability'.[35]

To set the Chinese market gardens into this historic set of aspirations, we can gather from Boileau, and Lee and Lam, that because Chinese men were deterred from bringing family to New Zealand, they continued to regard the colony primarily as a place of opportunity – a place to make money to send home.[36] Therefore, any profit was invested in the soil, in the production of crops or else sent home. According to Boileau, these priorities not only attenuated the desire to purchase land but also the investment of any extra monies into accommodation, as evidenced by the poor state of their lodgings. These men, intent on working and making a profit, had no wives or elderly parents or young children resident in New Zealand for whom they needed to provide a comfortable home. In addition, any

---

34   Ibid. Boileau cites Lam and Lee, *Sons of the Soil* here, regarding a market gardener in Auckland in the 1970s.
35   James Ng, *Windows on a Chinese Past*.
36   There has been substantial scholarly debate in New Zealand and Australia about the extent to which Chinese migrants were 'sojourners' rather than settlers.

awareness of public opinion and increasingly restrictive immigration rules would understandably make them reticent about spending money on the one thing that could not be taken home: land.

Leasing suited a mobile and uncertain existence; it also enabled the forging of partnerships with other Chinese to work the land together. As exemplified in the Ding case, leases made one vulnerable to being told to leave; however, on the positive side, leases also facilitated the movement to better ground that was necessary as different soils were experimented with. The Ding trajectory away from the garden in South Dunedin initially led to them acquiring a plot of land from another Chinese family. But the move to the Taieri required forging relationships with non-Chinese farmers. It was at this point that broader social forces began to have purchase as a mechanism in the regulation of land ownership. Because Taieri land had been quickly alienated from local Kāi Tahu, control of the land market in this district, especially by the early twentieth century, was entirely in the hands of local families. This was in contrast to Hokianga where the state continued to play a significant role in the rural land trade, to which I will turn in the next section.

The operation of these social forces controlling land ownership and use were apparent from the first phase of Chinese gardening in Dunedin. An article in the *Otago Witness* in 1878 reported on a visit to several local gardens in order to ascertain 'the merits of the Mongolian system of growing vegetables'.[37] In the course of describing and assessing Chinese methods of gardening – both positive and negative – the author of the article expressed concern about the success of the Chinese gardeners at the expense of opportunities for British enterprise, and hinted at the role that the leasing of land played in this. A visit to Leung Foy's garden (the only Chinese gardener the author could find who spoke English) revealed that Foy leased five acres of flat land – 'deep, free loam' soil with a stream running through it – from a Mr Anderson. After describing in detail the intensive manual labour and watering techniques by which Foy and other Chinese extracted maximum production of vegetables (but not necessarily flavour or nutrients) from the land, the article drew to a close with expressions of anxiety about the potential spread of this monopolising behaviour. The concern was that profits were being sent out of the country, and also that 'we hear that some of them are now leasing rich flat soil ... for countrymen who are yet to arrive'.[38] The unstated suggestion or inference was that Chinese efforts

---

37 'Chinese Market Gardening', *Otago Witness*, Issue 1383, 1 June 1878.
38 Ibid.

should be thwarted by not leasing or selling land to them in the first place. However, the growing city quickly became dependent on the vegetables produced by the Chinese; therefore, presumably, the land taken up by early Chinese gardeners and traded within the community was tolerated – at least until the city's expansion led to reclaiming it.[39]

The move to the Taieri again required breaking new ground. As outlined earlier, the Ding family leased land in South Dunedin, Kaikorai Valley and North Taieri, before settling in Outram in the 1930s. I interviewed Charlie Ding, the third and final generation of this family to farm on the Taieri, about the family landholdings. The Dings leased the land – about 60 acres – from the Dows and the Robertsons, both well-known Taieri families. Charlie described their relationship with those families as very good. He and his brothers were the same age as the Robertson's boys; they all went to school together and remained friends until 'old, old age'.[40] The Ding family did well on this Outram property. Despite the land being leased, they built a number of cottages on it to house the workers they employed. This indicates they had rights to make substantial changes to the land and landscape. It also suggests a degree of security over their land tenure. When I suggested this to Charlie, he agreed, but also joked that the cottages could be moved. Regarding landholdings in the pre-Taieri period, Charlie was unsure about the nature of the leases, or whether there were official leases at all. The lack of records due to the prevalence of (a) leasing, which was often not recorded on land titles and (b) informal leasing, which generated no paperwork at all, is a major impediment to a close examination of Chinese land history in New Zealand.[41]

The Dings worked this Outram property for almost 20 years before their tenure came to a sudden halt. Right at the moment when they decided they wanted to purchase the land, both the Robertsons and the Dows faced family circumstances that saw them end their arrangements with the Ding family: in one case, the farmer died and his son wanted to sell to a different family; in the other, the farmer wanted to pass the land to his son to run as a dairy farm. So, although those relationships were very good, and their informal

---

39   According to James Ng's interview with Chew Cheung Ding, the family enjoyed mostly good social relations in Dunedin, and received generous assistance from the local (non-Chinese) community when their Forbury property was flooded in 1923. James Ng, *Windows on a Chinese Past*, 421.

40   Interview with Charlie Ding, Wellington, 18 April 2019.

41   This is in contrast to the situation in California, for example, where a large archive of lease records formed the basis of Sucheng Chan, *The Bitter-Sweet Soil* (Berkeley: University of California Press, 1989), a detailed examination of the landholdings and entrepreneurship of Chinese agriculturalists from 1860 to 1910.

method of leasing land had been unproblematic for nearly two decades, the Dings had no claim on the land. They were forced to pack up and fulfil their wish to purchase land by looking elsewhere on the Taieri. This did not prove difficult, no doubt owing to their settled place in the West Taieri farming community. Starting in the early 1950s, they purchased land from Pākehā farmers, beginning with 109 acres and adding another 250 acres in the 1960s – a substantial landholding by local standards.[42] When I asked Charlie about this new phase of purchasing land, he immediately attributed it to the political situation in China from 1949, and the desire to stay in New Zealand permanently. To his mind, that was the only explanation. When I suggested the resumption of naturalisation as a factor, he did not think this had had any effect, though he did state that it was difficult for Chinese to purchase land, and that the returned soldier settlement schemes had compounded these difficulties.[43]

While Charlie was, as it turns out, correct that naturalisation was not the only, or the legal reason, that land purchasing began post-1950, the bar on naturalisation certainly affected his family. Because the first generation of the Ding family – Chun Ding – arrived in 1908, he could not be naturalised.[44] And because his son, Chew Cheung Ding, born in China, arrived in 1920, he was unable to be naturalised either.[45] Like his father, Chew Cheung married in China and had several sons born there while continuing to work the property in Outram. Chew Cheung returned to China in 1936 to fetch his sons, which, owing to the war, took three years. His wife followed in 1940, and, in 1942, gave birth to another son, Charlie, my interviewee, the first of this Ding family to be born in New Zealand. Around the same time, after more than 30 years living apart, Chun Ding travelled to Hong Kong to look after his wife, returning to Outram with her in 1949. According to James Ng's account, it was only at this point that Chew Cheung felt able to direct his energy and his money into purchasing land, after supporting several branches of his family for many years and expending much time and travel to see them all reunited in Outram.[46]

---

42 Rural sections on the Taieri were originally surveyed at 50-acre lots. While these proved too small for a viable family farm, the local farm size came to average only 100–200 acres.
43 Interview with Charlie Ding, Wellington, 18 April 2019.
44 A police file for Ding Chun evidences his continued status as a 'registered alien' when he returned to New Zealand to live with his son in the late 1940s. Archives New Zealand Te Rua Mahara o te Kāwanatanga, Wellington, Ref: AAAC 504 Box 453 (R23997768).
45 Ding Chew Cheung, Certificate of arrival and payment of £100, 4 May 1920, Archives New Zealand Te Rua Mahara o te Kāwanatanga, Wellington, Ref: L24 3 (R23676751).
46 James Ng, *Windows on a Chinese Past*, 422.

In the course of looking for naturalisation and alien registration files for the Ding family at Archives New Zealand, I fortuitously came across a file that sheds further light on the question of land purchase. Mistakenly filed under the name 'Ding Chung' was an alien registration file for Ling Chung, a market gardener in Greytown, in the lower North Island, in the 1920s.[47] It contained a police report filed in 1942 by Constable Andrew McGregor noting that Ling Chung and his two brothers wished to purchase land for market gardening in Greytown. He noted that the land the brothers had been leasing for this purpose had recently been taken over by the government. Constable McGregor was writing in support of their wish to purchase land, noting that he had 'always found them to be good citizens, honest and hard-working'. A handwritten note stated that the application was granted.

This minor matter is significant for several reasons. First, it further demonstrates the precariousness of leasing (the government could simply take over land that had been leased over a long period). Second, it provides concrete evidence that it was possible for an unnaturalised person to purchase land (although it was probably necessary to have an established place and reputation in the local community). Third, and most usefully, as the transaction occurred in 1942 – in the period agreed upon by scholars as the only time in which Chinese were prohibited from purchasing land, it challenges any claim of blanket exclusion.[48]

Dalmatian Land Ownership in Northland

The pathway to land ownership for Dalmatian migrants in the Far North of New Zealand offers useful comparisons to the Chinese in the south. Dalmatian men arrived in New Zealand in the late nineteenth century in numbers almost equivalent to Chinese migrations to the goldfields: there were approximately 2,000 Dalmatian men in Northland at the turn of the century.[49] They arrived to take advantage of the gum extracted from the kauri

---

47   Ling Chung, Alien registration certificate, 1951, Archives New Zealand Te Rua Mahara o te Kāwanatanga, Wellington, Ref: AAAC 504 412/AL 37796 (R23817154).
48   The Aliens Land Purchase Regulations 1942 state that both the purchase and leasing or gifting land was restricted; however, they note that these activities could happen with the consent of the minister of justice (see nzlii.org/nz/legis/num_reg/alpr1942294/). A student publication in 1945 lists the number of farm purchases by 'aliens' under this Act as 65, totalling 3,657 acres. See 'Land Purchases', *The Spike or Victoria University College Review*, 1945, accessed 6 March 2023, nzetc.victoria.ac.nz/tm/scholarly/tei-VUW1945_Spik-t1-body-d15-d4.html.
49   Judith Bassett, 'Colonial Justice: The Treatment of Dalmatians in New Zealand during the First World War', *New Zealand Journal of History* 33, no. 2 (1999): 156.

tree, of which there were large forests in Northland.[50] Some may have arrived via goldrushes overseas and at Otago, but there were various other avenues by which news of the opportunity for gum-digging reached Dalmatia, initiating a chain migration. Over time, the response to these Dalmatian labourers took on a similar character to the Chinese in Otago. Early positive reports about their industriousness were soon replaced by concerns about an influx and fears that their collective behaviour (working together in gangs) and willingness to live in substandard conditions undercut British settlers engaged in the same work. They were labelled 'white Chinamen' among a host of other negative terms.[51] Like the Chinese in Otago, in the first wave of migration they were almost all single men. Many remitted money home and lived with others from their home villages, retaining aspects of their language and culture.[52]

Dalmatians were not directly targeted by immigration restrictions as the Chinese were, but they were subject to legal discrimination via the *Kauri Gum Industry Act 1898*, which established reserves for British subjects and required all others to have licences. Gradually, legal 'aliens' (non-subjects) were excluded from Crown gumfields.[53] Unnaturalised Dalmatians had to work on privately owned or Māori land to engage in gum-digging. This could be remedied by naturalisation, and, indeed, the restrictive measures led to a spike in applications: by 1914, half of the Dalmatian population in New Zealand were naturalised.[54] But delaying strategies were deployed to slow this process.[55] As a result, from the 1890s, Dalmatian men turned to other sources of making a living in New Zealand; for many, that was winegrowing and/or farming. As Judith Bassett demonstrates, all these activities were disrupted by the treatment of Dalmatians during World War I. Many New Zealanders believed that Dalmatians were Austrians, and thus thought they should be classified as 'enemy aliens' and not be allowed to enlist in the New Zealand forces. At the same time, there was concern that not enlisting would give them an advantage in their economic activities

---

50 Kauri gum had long been used by local Māori for a variety of purposes and became a sought after global commodity as a varnish from the 1860s. It is formed when resin leaks from the tree and hardens into lumps. These lumps fall to the ground and become submerged in swamps and bush. The 'diggers' searched for and retrieved these lumps – exhausting work in difficult conditions.

51 Bozic-Vrbancic, *Tarara*, 68–73.

52 Judith Bassett, 'Colonial Justice', 157.

53 Ibid.

54 Ibid.

55 'Work and War: 1890 to 1930', *Te Ara, Encyclopedia of New Zealand*, accessed 6 March 2023, teara. govt.nz/en/dalmatians/page-3.

(such as farming) while fit British men were overseas serving; the suggested resolution to this problem was that they should be put into camps and/or engaged in public works.[56]

Dalmatian men responded fiercely to allegations that they were enemies of New Zealand and allies of the Austro-Hungarian Empire. As Bassett outlines, they adopted a number of assertive and inventive means of protest and refusal against what they saw as illegal and unjust action against them.[57] This response can be read as an expression of their settled place in New Zealand, which was no doubt cemented by a history of marrying local women. In the initial period, when there were no Dalmatian women in New Zealand, rather than returning home and marrying, many Dalmatian men married Māori (and sometimes Pākehā) women. This early intermarriage has left a long legacy in Hokianga, where many locals have British, Māori and Dalmatian ancestry. This phase was followed by the era of so-called letter brides from the 1920s, which saw Dalmatian women entering into relationships by post and agreeing to marry before travelling to New Zealand to fulfil their promise. Together with the formation of cultural clubs and societies, this pre-figured a strengthening of a local Dalmatian identity.[58] Chain migration to New Zealand continued as political troubles at home stimulated waves of emigration out of what became Yugoslavia. Narratives of the community are structured by early gum-digging, letter brides and winemaking ventures that began in the Far North in the late nineteenth century and led to the establishment of a number of family businesses that persist today.[59]

Dalmatian family wine businesses would be one route into an examination of land ownership and inheritance for that community. However, while early winegrowing ventures did occur in Hokianga, it was further south, in west Auckland, that substantial vineyards and intergenerational enterprises were established. The land story in Hokianga for Dalmatians was a mix of farming, gum-digging and winemaking, usually undertaken by racially mixed families, and often involving land leased from the Crown in the settlement

---

56   Bassett, 'Colonial Justice', 157–59.
57   In 'Colonial Justice', Bassett explores this process from multiple perspectives, including public perceptions (and ignorance), official 'theatre' in administrative and legal processes, and the Dalmatian response.
58   Bozic-Vrbancic, *Tarara*, 140.
59   Adrienne Puckey, 'The Substance of the Shadow: Māori and Pākehā political Economic Relationships, 1860–1940' (PhD thesis, University of Auckland, 2006), 217.

schemes outlined earlier in this chapter.[60] Hokianga landownership does not feature strongly in the narrative of the Dalmatian community because it does not fit with a separate identity; instead, the Hokianga experience involved immersion in a regional culture, being accepted by Māori – and finding many points of cultural and social connection with local iwi – and being drawn into the ideal of hard work and self-sufficiency that modern family farming was built upon.

One of the first 'special settlement' schemes organised by the government in Northland was known as Puhata, at Herekino Harbour, just north of Hokianga, in 1887. Fifty-acre sections were offered for lease, with an initial term of 30 years, and subsequent leases for 21 years, without any right of acquiring freehold. The regulations, like others of the era, specified that the commissioner of Crown lands had absolute discretion over who the land was leased to and who the lessee could transfer it to. The lessee had no right to subdivide or sublet. Married men were preferred, and the land had to be occupied and improved by the lessee.[61] There were 125 applicants for the Puhata leases: 108 were taken up and 99 were occupied. Two years later, 79 farms were still occupied, but, by 1892, this had dropped to 25.[62] The settlement was regarded as a failure, as many were in the Far North, the landholdings being too small and too remote to sustain families through the required initial phase of clearing land and establishing the infrastructure necessary to connect farms to markets. The British men and families who had taken up the sections simply walked off the land, with little negative financial consequence since no initial outlay had been required.[63]

It was here in Puhata that Dalmatian men took up land abandoned by the British, pooling their landholdings to make farming more viable, and establishing what was the largest Dalmatian settlement in New Zealand at the time.[64] While there was no mention of naturalisation determining who

---

60   Hokianga has one of the highest proportions of Māori in New Zealand (in the latest census, 75 per cent of the population identified as Māori) and Māori retained numerical dominance in the area for many years after the arrival of Europeans. In 1924, for example, Hokianga was one of only two hospital districts in New Zealand that had more Māori than Europeans. 'Māori to European Ratio, 1924', *Te Ara, Encyclopedia of New Zealand*, accessed 6 March 2023, teara.govt.nz/en/document/31321/maori-to-european-ratio-1924.

61   'Public Notification', *Evening Bell*, 8 January 1887.

62   Winifred S. Davidson, 'The Settlement of Hokianga' (MA thesis, University of New Zealand, Auckland University College, 1948), 51–52.

63   That is not to say that this was an easy route for the families involved – many made arduous journeys from other parts of New Zealand to take up land in the Far North.

64   Petrie Family History, unpublished document supplied to the author by Hazel Petrie.

was able to take up the leases, it is clear that, in this scenario, the British were favoured in the initial selection, and non-British men (single men, rather than married, as was the stated preference) were allowed to take up land only after the British had rejected it – much like the latter stages of the goldrushes in Otago. Some of the Dalmatian men who took up sections in Puhata began planting vines. A Department of Agriculture report from 1896 stated that:

> at the Puhata Settlement, Herekino, a number of Austrian settlers are already beginning to profit by their industry and enterprise. A large area has been planted in vines and small cellars erected, which have been working well during the past year. An excellent wine was produced, and promises well for the future prospects of these useful settlers.[65]

However, the vines were susceptible to disease and the men continued to use gum-digging as a means of making a living. A government report in 1903 complained that the Puhata settlers spent too much time gum-digging rather than improving their sections.[66] The men responded that the landholdings were too small to make a living. Conditions improved over the next decade with the opening of a sawmill and a dairy factory, but this was the era when World War I saw Dalmatian men subjected to the discrimination and upheaval outlined above.

One of the men who took up land in Puhata was Tony Petrie (born Ante Petric), who arrived in New Zealand around 1900 aged 20.[67] He travelled to the Far North to join his brother Fabian, who had already been naturalised and taken up land at Puhata in 1898.

Tony and Fabian joined a partnership with two other Dalmatian men to create a landholding of 200 acres – four adjacent sections. Their burgeoning enterprise raised the ire of British settlers concerned about alcohol; this was the height of the temperance movement in New Zealand and there were specific concerns in the Far North about the effects of alcohol on Māori communities.[68] But, as it turned out, the venture was interrupted by a feud between a number of Dalmatian families that ended in a violent brawl, and resulted in Tony and Fabian being sentenced to several years imprisonment

---

65 Dick Scott, *Pioneers of New Zealand Wine* (Auckland: Reed New Zealand, 2002), 104, cited in Puckey, 'The Substance of the Shadow'.
66 Davidson, 'The Settlement of Hokianga', 52.
67 Petrie Family History.
68 See, for example, 'Adulterated Wine: Alleged Abuse in the North', *Evening Post,* 1 November 1911.

and hard labour. While it was a challenging time, both men took the opportunity to study in prison, and Tony later credited his incarceration with improving his English-language speaking ability. Upon his release, he relocated to Auckland and launched a varied business career, which saw him accrue several parcels of land, each over 1,000 acres, in different parts of the North Island.

A second case study is more deeply nested in the farming communities of Hokianga. Mijo Vujcich was born in Dalmatia in 1887 and emigrated to New Zealand in 1904.[69] He worked as a gum-digger in Hokianga and was naturalised in 1911. That year he took up land in a settlement scheme very similar to those of the 1880s. This one, known as Te Karae, had similar conditions to the earlier schemes, the main difference being that the lessons of the earlier period had been applied by increasing the section sizes to 300 acres. There was also a more complicated system of land tenure: leases were auctioned by the Crown, but the title had been awarded to (and remained with) local iwi. It seems likely that Vujcich's naturalisation was related to his application to take up land at Te Karae. He took up land in partnership with his brother; however, due to the land's unsuitability for farming, they only lasted a few years before purchasing land elsewhere in Hokianga. Mijo served in World War I and, while on leave in 1917, married Keiti Harris and became part of a large extended Māori family in the district. After the war he continued farming and also pursued winemaking and olive- and tobacco-growing.

Mijo's third daughter, Patricia, married Trevor White, whose English forebears had taken up land in a settlement scheme in Punakitere, south Hokianga. Patricia and Trevor's son, Paul White, was one of the interviewees for my study of inheritance and farming families. Paul embodies the complexity of family land histories in this district. On his Pākehā side he is descended from two English families who farmed for several generations after taking up land in the Punakitere settlement scheme. On his Dalmatian side he is directly connected to a history of discrimination against non-British settlers, who nevertheless also benefited from land alienated from Māori. He has researched and written separate family publications about these branches of his ancestry. Paul identifies most strongly with his Māori heritage and is an advocate for addressing the injustices of land alienated

69 Paul White, *The Vujcich Family from Dalmatia to Hokianga, New Zealand* (Rawene, New Zealand: Paul White, 2015). Viewed at Omapere Museum, Hokianga.

from local iwi.[70] His family history, which has seen land alienated from local iwi brought back into the fold through intermarriage, is not an unusual one in Hokianga. As he told me, his grandmother's Māori whānau were most pleased that she married into a family that had land in Te Karae, as they were part of the hapu (sub-tribe) that originally occupied it.

Conclusion

Hokianga is a complex site to conduct family/land research; however, it is one that brings to the fore questions about the extent to which diverse cultural groups, stitched into communities over time, can later be studied in isolation. In this chapter, I have focused on non-British families in two locations for the purpose of considering the consequences of naturalisation restrictions on intergenerational family farming. In the process, I have attempted to show the value of keeping other variables in the frame – perhaps at the cost of drawing any clear conclusion about naturalisation, but hopefully achieving a fuller understanding of how naturalisation restrictions affected the people they were aimed at.

In these two discrete examples, perhaps the most significant variable relating to family farming and naturalisation was intermarriage. Chinese men routinely had wives and children in China, meaning that when they brought sons to New Zealand to assist with – and eventually take over – the family business, those sons were not naturalised. This was in contrast to Dalmatian men, many of whom found their place in rural communities in the Far North by marrying into Māori and Pākehā families, the children contributing to the 'mixed' community, but at birth being 'natural-born' British subjects. This meant that any concerns over naturalisation were limited to the first generation of migrants, which was not the case for Chinese families, for whom the ban on naturalisation was an ongoing concern.[71] So, although I cannot say definitively that the ability to naturalise after 1951 explains the increase in land purchasing by Chinese families after that date, I do argue that it was part of the bundle of factors that saw market gardens on the Taieri take on a different character. In both districts, taking a relational, familial approach has usefully complicated and clarified the ways in which naturalisation was experienced and perceived by non-British family landholders.

---

70   Paul White was one of the team that negotiated and authored the settlement with the Crown for the Te Rawara iwi. *Te Rawara: Treaty Settlement Offer* (Te Rūnanga o Te Rawara, 2011).
71   The Act revoking naturalisation of German and Austrian peoples in 1917 may be an exception.

4

The 'Silver-Tongued Orator' Advocates for Australian Indians: Srinivasa Sastri's Tour of Australia in 1922

Margaret Allen

Introduction

On 1 June 1922, Srinivasa Sastri PC landed in Perth, Western Australia, to begin his tour of Australia. His brief was to persuade the Australian people and governments (federal and state) to accord 'full citizenship' to Indian residents. This meant enfranchisement for both state and federal elections, and the freedom to enter any occupation and to own property. During his tour he did not address the contentious issue of the White Australia policy. Sastri, an official guest of the Commonwealth, was greeted in Fremantle by the acting premier of Western Australia and by a representative of the Department of the Prime Minister who was to accompany him on his tour. This official recognition was rather ironic given the ferocity with which both federal and state governments sought to defend the White Australia project as a central plank of Australian policy and identity.

Sastri's ensuing tour, which was to encompass most states and last until 11 July, offered Australians and their elected representatives the opportunity to become more open towards the aspirations of Indians for social and civic equality within Australia. This brief arose from the 1921 Imperial Conference in London, a gathering of premiers of the British Empire with the British Government, where Sastri was a participant with the Indian delegation. It was agreed that his visit to Australia would be followed by similar visits to New Zealand and Canada; South Africa was the only white dominion to refuse to accept the mission.

As Sastri left India, his mission to the white dominions was endorsed by the viceroy, making him one of the first Indian diplomats and certainly the first to visit Australia.[1] During his six weeks journey he encountered Australians from all levels of society, addressed numerous meetings and met with state premiers and Cabinet ministers. He addressed the Australian Parliament in Melbourne, conferred with Prime Minister Billy Hughes and his Cabinet and spoke at a parliamentary dinner on 27 June. The tour and Sastri's speeches were reported extensively and, in general, in a positive manner in the press; yet, until very recently, his visit has received little scholarly attention.[2]

This chapter examines Sastri's tour and its significance and the level of its success in the light of contemporary struggles around race, colonialism and the campaign of Indians around the empire for imperial citizenship. While this story is very much an Australian one, it must also be told in the wider framework of transnational colonial and imperial histories. The chapter argues that, in many ways, this tour was an almost futile gesture and it only slowly led to some changes to the circumstances of Indians resident in Australia. The changes Sastri sought were relatively minor and related to the small and decreasing Indian community in Australia. The fact that any changes were slow and grudgingly granted exemplifies the power of the White Australia policy during this period. Prime Minister Hughes's apparent commitment to 'full citizenship' for Indians resident in Australia was rather illusory. Many of the changes needed were in the domain of state governments, which, like the federal government and general public, had a firm and stubborn commitment to the White Australia policy. Hughes believed that 'no Govt. (sic) could live for a day in Australia, if it tampered

---

1   Kama Maclean, *British India, White Australia: Overseas Indians, Intercolonial Relations and the Empire* (Sydney: UNSW Press, 2020), 145–6; Vineet Thakur, 'Liberal, Liminal and Lost: India's First Diplomats and the Narrative of Foreign Policy', *The Journal of Imperial and Commonwealth History* 45, no. 2 (2017): 1–47, doi.org/10.1080/03086534.2017.1294283; A. T. Yarwood, *Asian Migration to Australia* (Melbourne: Melbourne University Press, 1964), 137–40.

2   Maclean, *British India, White Australia*, 148ff; Vineet Thakur, *India's First Diplomat: V. S. Srinivasa Sastri and the Making of Liberal Internationalism* (Bristol: Bristol University Press, 2021), 105–21, doi. org/10.46692/9781529217698; Vineet Thakur, 'Colonial Subjects as Hegemonic Actors: V.S. Srinivasa Sastri's 1922 Public Diplomacy Tour of British Dominion Territories', in *The Frontiers of Public Diplomacy*, ed. Colin Alexander (London: Routledge, 2021), 78–95, doi.org/10.4324/9780429325120-5.

with a White Australia'.[3] Hughes's authority in the federal sphere was waning: he would lose office in February 1923 and, in any case, had no power over state governments' policies. While Sastri could raise issues relating to the small number of Indian residents, it was not possible for him to broach the larger issue of the restriction of Indian immigration to Australia.

Sastri was an excellent public speaker, logical and formidable in his delivery and able to appeal to the best instincts of his audiences. He attracted considerable attention in the press and large numbers attended the meetings he addressed. While some may have begun to question received notions about India and perhaps to widen their understanding of India's place in the world, an important element of his appeal was that he was different – an exotic curiosity. His Australian audiences were not accustomed to paying respect 'to a brown skin and a turban'.[4] He was an Indian who came from a different world and could speak in the King's English with great understanding of the British Empire and British culture. Some of the reports on him were, frankly, orientalist and his appeals for fair play could be sloughed off as part of the entertainment he provided.

There was a section of the press, largely representing the labour movement, that was deeply suspicious of Sastri's agenda and, despite protestations to the contrary, were convinced that he aimed to overturn the White Australia policy and thus undermine the Australian way of life. That any improvement to the conditions of Indians resident in Australia came after his visit must largely be laid at the feet of the resident Indians who agitated for it; the continued representations of other delegates visiting from India and the Government of India; and those few, more imperially minded, Australians who valued imperial connections over the narrow concerns of the White Australia policy and white solidarity within the empire.

The Circumstances Leading to Sastri's Tour of Australia

When Sastri arrived, he was the first Indian to come to Australia as a representative of the Government of India. Other Asian governments had previously sent representatives. Indeed, in 1887, the Chinese imperial

---

3   Margaret MacMillan, *Paris 1919: Six Months That Changed the World* (New York: Random House, 2001), 319.
4   A.G. Stephens, 'Indians in Australia', *Northern Champion* (Taree), 29 July 1922, 2.

commissioners visited,[5] in 1896 the Japanese Government established a consulate in Townsville and, in 1906, the Chinese commissioner, His Excellency the Prefect Hwang Hon Cheng, came to Australia as a representative of the Chinese Government to again investigate the position of the Chinese in Australia. Sastri came as representative of the British colonial government in India. His visit was, in a sense, symbolic of the changed position of India within the British Empire as the result of World War I. Indeed, 'India entered the emerging international system at the end of the First World War as a "quasi-international" actor, via the British Commonwealth'.[6]

That war had seen Britain heavily reliant on the manpower provided by India. India gave 552,000 combatants, 392,000 non-combatants and incurred 106,594 human casualties (and lost 1,750,000 animals). Indian Government war expenditure was £24,700,000 and other cash from India, including from the wealthy and generous rulers of the princely states, amounted to £2,524,000.[7] Given this, Indian political leaders had urged the British Government to share power with the Indian people and grant India a seat at Imperial Conferences. Edwin Montagu, secretary of state for India (1917–22), was one of the British leaders who understood the vital importance of making a generous gesture to India.[8] In August 1917, the British Government set India upon a new path, announcing 'the progressive realisation of responsible government in India as an integral part of the British Empire'.[9] India was not given dominion status equivalent to the white dominions like Canada and Australia, but was given representation at the Imperial War Cabinet and the Imperial War Conferences of 1917 and 1918. Typically this representation included a British official, a representative of the Indian princely states and a moderate Indian politician.

The particular aspect of foreign policy these Indian representatives, in particular the moderate Indian politicians, directed their energies towards was improving the position of Indians living around the empire. The viceroy and Indian Government were quite supportive of this direction. Indian nationalists were concerned to advocate the rights of Indians to

---

5   Marilyn Lake, 'The Chinese Empire Encounters the British Empire and Its "Colonial Dependencies": Melbourne, 1887', in *Chinese Australians: Politics, Engagement and Resistance*, ed. Sophie Couchman and Kate Bagnall (Leiden: Brill, 2015), 98, doi.org/10.1163/9789004288553_005.
6   Thakur, 'Liberal, Liminal and Lost', 2.
7   Ibid., 4.
8   Hugh Tinker, *Separate and Unequal India and the Indians in the British Commonwealth 1920–1950* (London: Hurst, 1976), 31.
9   Ibid.

participate in political life within India and, ultimately, to some form of self-government. But they were also committed to pursuing the rights of Indians domiciled around the empire and to seeing the promise of equality under British law fully realised. The restrictive policies of South Africa were the chief focus of the nationalists' ire. However, the other white dominions also failed to accord the legal rights of British subjects to Indian subjects of the Crown. Thus, Australia, with the *Immigration Restriction Act 1901*, had instituted the White Australia policy, which prevented new immigrants from the subcontinent travelling to Australia. In Canada in 1914, hundreds of Indians on the *Komagata Maru* were refused entry and the vessel was forced to return to Kolkata.

Indian representatives at the Imperial War Cabinet wanted both recognition of their right to free movement around the empire as well as social and political equality for Indians domiciled in various locations across the empire. The white dominions, however, were determined to control immigration to their shores. In 1917–18, the Liberal Lord Sinha represented India at these conferences along with the Maharaja of Bikaner and a British official. At the 1917 conference, Lord Sinha moved a motion 'calling for reciprocity between India and the dominions with regard to the question of immigration'.[10] This meant that the white dominions and India could regulate their immigration policies. The motion was passed unanimously. This saw India 'waiving her claim to free entry into the Dominions … [while she] hoped to secure a fair treatment for Indians who were already domiciled there'.[11] Sinha appended a list of grievances of the Indian diaspora, but it had little force. By the time of the 1918 conference, Sinha sought to be more forceful and specific, given that the white dominions had done little to address the grievances listed and, indeed, South Africa had added to them. However, the conference resolved 'that each dominion had the right to determine the composition of its population through immigration restrictions'.[12] This meant that Australia, for example, could continue to deny entry to Indians who were British subjects.[13] Having been forced to leave immigration restrictions off the table, Indian representatives now pursued equal civil and political rights for those Indians resident in the dominions.

---

10   Thakur, 'Liberal, Liminal and Lost', 8.
11   Indian Government report, quoted in Maclean, *British India, White Australia*, 144.
12   Thakur, 'Liberal, Liminal and Lost', 9.
13   Peter Prince, 'Aliens in Their Own Land. "Alien" and the Rule of Law in Colonial and Post-Federation Australia' (PhD thesis, The Australian National University, 2015), 121, openresearch-repository.anu.edu.au/handle/1885/101778.

By the time of the next Imperial Conference in 1921, there had been little advance of this resolution. Australia, in line with the 1918 resolution, had developed a scheme to allow resident Indians to apply to bring a wife and minor children to reside with them in Australia, and had agreed to legislate to allow Indian residents access to old age and invalid pensions.[14] However, this had not been legislated, and, in any case, any advances were usually delayed by 'administrative obfuscation'.[15] Sastri was one of the Indian representatives at the conference, along with the Maharao of Cutch and Edwin Montagu, the secretary of state for India. Sastri pointed out that while Indian representatives had conceded in 1918 'that each Dominion should be free to regulate the composition of its population by suitable immigration laws',[16] the 'full rights of citizenship'[17] should be accorded to Indians legally settled in the dominions. Sastri moved a resolution along these lines (a 'Resolution on Equality of Citizenship in the British Dominions') 'to remove the disabilities of Indians properly domiciled in these dominions as soon as possible'. There was a great deal of canvassing by Sastri and Montagu on one side, and on the other by Smuts, the prime minister of South Africa, who sought 'white solidarity'[18] from the other white dominions. As Rao puts it: 'The crux of the question was Empire solidarity versus white solidarity in the Empire.'[19] The putting of the resolution was delayed a number of times until Sastri threatened to resign from the conference if it were not put to the vote. It was passed, with Smuts adding the reservation that South Africa could not accept it 'in view of the exceptional circumstances of the greater part of the Union'.[20] However, while reserving South Africa, Smuts had agreed to the general principle of equality in the empire. Sastri had isolated him in the conference, adding his own reservation to the resolution regretting the South African position and hoping 'that by negotiation between the Governments of India and South Africa, some way can be found, as soon as may, to reach a more satisfactory position'.

---

14   National Archives of Australia (hereafter NAA): 918 INDI 16, Part 1 'India – Equal Rights to Indians in Australia and Territories' 1917–1923; A. T. Yarwood, *Asian Migration to Australia: The Background to Exclusion 1896–1923* (Melbourne: Melbourne University Press, 1964), 133.
15   Maclean, *British India, White Australia*, 136.
16   Pandurang Kodanda Rao, *The Right Honourable V. S. Srinivasa Sastri: A Political Biography* (London: Asia Publishing House, 1963), 99.
17   Ibid., 100. See also Tinker, 46–51.
18   Rao, *The Right Honourable V. S. Srinivasa Sastri*, 100.
19   Ibid., 101.
20   Ibid., 102.

The Sastri resolution on equal citizenship was 'the first time that the rule of unanimity of Imperial Conference resolutions was broken in favour of a majority vote'.[21] It was India, 'a subordinate branch of the British Government', that had isolated Smuts, breaching the white racial bonhomie within the empire.[22] Further, Sastri got on the record his suggestion that India and South Africa should negotiate directly, a tacit recognition of India as an independent actor, rather than merely a colonial subsidiary.

With the passing of the Sastri resolution at the 1921 Imperial Conference, the leaders of Australia, New Zealand, and Canada – at Sastri's suggestion – invited him to make a tour of their countries 'to plead the cause of the Indian therein and to create public opinion favourable to the resolution'.[23] It was a curious invitation, given that the premiers should themselves have taken on this task. Sastri was charged with persuading the general public of the dominions to recognise Indians' rights to 'full citizenship' and implicitly to their full humanity.

Who Was V. S. Srinivasa Sastri PC?

Sastri's life and career were remarkable.[24] The son of a poor Brahman priest, he was born in 1869 and attended the Native High School in his hometown in the Madras Presidency where he excelled, qualifying for a free university education. Although he grew up in an orthodox household, he was nevertheless drawn to reform Hinduism and the Brahmo Samaj. He graduated with a Bachelor of Arts, gaining high honours in both Sanskrit and English. Financial restraints prevented him from continuing his education and studying law.[25] Instead, he taught at high schools before becoming principal of Hindu High School in Triplicane, Madras. There his interest in social questions grew and he took a leading role in the cooperative movement and was a sponsor of the liberal nationalist publication, *Indian Review*.[26]

---

21 Ibid., 103.
22 Thakur, 'Liberal, Liminal and Lost', 15.
23 Rao, *The Right Honourable V. S. Srinivasa Sastri*, 121.
24 See Thakur, *India's First Diplomat*.
25 N. Raghunathan, 'Introduction', in *Speeches and Writings of The Right Honourable V. S. Srinivasa Sastri* (Madras: Right Honourable V. S. Srinivasa Sastri Birth Centenary Committee, 1969), vol. 1, iv.
26 Rao, *The Right Honourable V. S. Srinivasa Sastri*, 5.

Attracted to working for the betterment of Indian society, Sastri gave up his high school position and joined the Servants of India Society in 1907. This select society, founded by the moderate nationalist reformer Gopal Gokhale in 1905, aimed to train 'national missionaries for the service of India in the secular field'.[27] Impelled by patriotism and notions of self-sacrifice for a greater good, Sastri took the membership vows, which involved the renunciation of personal fame and financial career goals. He gained wide experience in Indian politics, first attending the Indian National Congress in 1906 and assisting Gokhale in his roles as secretary of the Congress and as a member of the Indian Legislative Council. Upon Gokhale's death in 1915, Sastri was elected to succeed him as leader of the society. Committed to the gradual inclusion of Indians in the Government of India, in 1913 Sastri accepted the governor's nomination to a position in the Madras Legislative Council. Non-official members like Sastri were very much in a minority and their powers tightly circumscribed but he took the opportunity to 'ask questions, move recommendations to Government and speak on the budget' – or, as Raghunathan writes, 'ventilating grievances, securing minor remedies and educating public opinion'.[28] Sastri advocated the Indianisation of the public service and universal, compulsory and free education. He also promoted the scheme, advanced in 1916 by both the Indian National Congress and the Muslim League, to pressure the British Government to accord more political power to India, so 'she should no longer occupy a position of subordination but one of comradeship'.[29] His publication *Self-Government for India under the British Flag* made the case for self-government 'on a par with the Dominions'.[30]

Sastri was a great enthusiast for the ideal of the British Empire but could also be a severe critic of British administration. He exposed the Indian Government's 'dis-ingenuous attempt to justify reservation of certain services for Europeans and Eurasians on the ground of their superior intelligence'.[31] And he made an 'excoriating denunciation of irresponsible and arbitrary government ... [in] his great speech on the Rowlatt Bill',[32] which ultimately passed as the *Anarchical and Revolutionary Crimes Act 1919*, extending war time emergency policies of imprisonment without trial and preventative indefinite detention.

---

27   Ibid., 6.
28   Ibid., 19; Raghunathan, 'Introduction', vol. 1, xi.
29   Rao, *The Right Honourable V. S. Srinivasa Sastri*, 24.
30   Ibid., 25.
31   Raghunathan, 'Introduction', vol. 1, xiii.
32   Ibid., vol. 1, xii.

Sastri's long political career and the extensive diplomatic experience he had recently gained well fitted him for the task of touring the dominions in 1922. At the Imperial Conference in 1921, Sastri was mixing in the highest level of British politics. He had worked closely with Montagu, the secretary of state for India, and with other leading figures, including Prime Minister Lloyd George. The Sastri resolution on equal citizenship had driven a wedge into the white majority at the conference. While in London, he was made a Privy Councillor and honoured with the Freedom of the City of London. In accepting the latter honour, he reiterated his ideal of racial equality, relating it, cleverly, as always, to the ideals of the British Empire and equating it with an Indian example:

> On the highest authority the British Empire has been declared to be without distinction of any kind. Neither race, nor colour nor religion is to divide man from man as long as they are subjects of this Empire. As in the great temple of Jagannath in my country, where the Brahmin and outcaste, the priest and pariah, alike join in a common devotion and worship.[33]

He urged the British to share their 'great heritage of freedom, representative institutions, Parliamentary government and every form of human equality' and, in due time, to admit Indians 'to be full and equal partners in the glory of Empire and service of humanity'.[34]

Although not an independent nation, India was an original member of the League of Nations and Sastri was part of its delegation in Geneva in September 1921. He then proceeded as leader of the Indian delegation to the Limitation of Armaments Conference in Washington in November 1921. For the Government of India, Sastri appeared a safe choice as a 'native diplomat': with his moderate politics and perfect spoken English, he was 'a living tribute to the success of the civilizing mission'.[35] However, as Thakur argues, Sastri exercised some agency, navigating the arena open to him, namely India's anomalous status as a 'dominion-like colony' with 'dexterity, nuance and purpose'.[36]

It was reported in the Australian press that Sastri came as a result of an invitation by Prime Minister Hughes; however, as has been seen, this invitation arose out of the circumstances of the Imperial Conference. Sastri

---

33   Rao, *The Right Honourable V. S. Srinivasa Sastri*, 106.
34   Ibid., 107.
35   Thakur, 'Colonial Subjects', 79.
36   Thakur, *India's First Diplomat*, 12.

could not count upon Billy Hughes as an ally in his endeavours. Some accounts credit Hughes as being a supporter of the Indians at the 1921 Conference. Thus Cotton writes:

> As a known and vocal champion of White Australia, Hughes nevertheless showed some sympathy with the position of the Indian spokesmen at the conference, even proposing in a draft resolution subsequently accepted by the conference that the Empire had a clear duty to recognise the rights of Indians to citizenship.[37]

However, correspondence between Sastri and his secretary Bajpai,[38] who accompanied him on the tour and at the Imperial Conference, shows Hughes's vacillation during the conference. Indeed, Hughes was caught between the notion of imperial solidarity and the need to maintain the White Australia policy, especially given the impending federal election.[39] It was reported that Hughes was eager for the resolution to be put so that Australia could support it. However, when it became clear that all save South Africa would support it, as Sastri reported, Hughes 'rutted', and it was only with some revisions and the impassioned plea of Lloyd George that Hughes gave Australia's support.[40] Bajpai described the situation:

> At the last moment Hughes defected. He said he could not isolate South Africa particularly as it might involve him in difficulties in Australia. He pleaded that he was afraid of the Chinese and Japanese. The Prime Minister [Lloyd George] however brought him round again. His was a most touching appeal – couched in language of seriousness, simplicity and true pathos. Idealism, even political idealism gains by moving expression. He raised the whole debate to a higher plane.[41]

Sastri and Bajpai soon formed a shrewd assessment of Hughes's ability to deliver any changes to the status of Indians he might promise. Bajpai noted:

> He [Hughes] has only a majority of one in the House of Representatives. He has incurred the everlasting hostility of his former party, Labour. He has made many personal enemies, both

37 James Cotton, 'William Morris Hughes, Empire and Nationalism: The Legacy of the First World War', Australian Historical Studies 46, no. 11 (2015): 109, doi.org/10.1080/1031461x.2014.995114.
38 G. S. Bajpai was, after independence, appointed as first secretary general of the Indian Ministry of External Affairs.
39 Maclean, British India, White Australia, 142.
40 V. S. S. Sastri to Vamana Rao, 4 August 1921, letter no. 360, V. S. Srinivasa Sastri Papers, Correspondence Group IA, Indian National Archives (henceforth INA).
41 G. S. Bajpai to Dr Sapru [undated], enclosed in letter no. 360, V. S. S. Sastri to Vamana Rao, 4 August 1921, V. S. Srinivasa Sastri Papers, Correspondence Group IA, INA.

inside his party and outside. His autocratic ways have rendered him unpopular with a large section of the public … Of course Mr Hughes has promised that if he comes back to power … he would do what we want without consulting anybody.[42]

Indians Resident in Australia

By the 1920s, there were only a relatively small number of Indians living in Australia: Yarwood estimates 3,150 in 1921.[43] These men had come as free immigrants to Australia during the late nineteenth century, generally to work as hawkers, labourers and canecutters. Many had adopted a sojourning practice, alternating long years spent in Australia with visits to homeland and family. These men valued their right as British subjects to free movement within the British Empire and protested strongly as Australian colonial governments introduced immigration restrictions during the 1890s and as the national government passed the Immigration Restriction Act in 1901.[44] Although their numbers declined with the restriction of ongoing immigration, they continued to protest against other restrictions upon their lives in Australia. Along with petitions to state governments, to the British Government and to the viceroy, Indians resident in Australia took action against the new range of discriminations in employment introduced by state governments. Thus, in 1904, Indians in South Australia joined with Chinese and Syrians in the United Asiatic League in protesting the Licensed Hawkers' Bill 1904, which aimed to deny hawkers' licences to those of Indian, Syrian, Chinese and Afghan backgrounds. Bhagat Singh, a merchant and spokesperson for the Indians, argued that it was discriminatory to make 'two laws for the subjects of one Power, applying especially to Indians, who are British subjects just the same as Australians'.[45]

In 1905, Indians in Western Australia joined in petition with local Chinese, Afghans and Japanese protesting against the recently passed *Factory Act*, which imposed harsh and discriminatory conditions upon workplaces where even a single 'Asiatic' was employed. The effect would be to diminish the hours such a business could operate and thus reduce its competitiveness.

---

42   Quoted by L. F. Fitzhardinge, *The Little Digger 1915–1952* (Sydney: Angus and Robertson, 1979), 507.
43   Yarwood, *Asian Migration to Australia*, 163.
44   Margaret Allen, '"I Am a British Subject": Indians in Australia Claiming Their Rights, 1880–1940', *History Australia* 15, no. 3 (2018): 505ff, doi.org/10.1080/14490854.2018.1485505.
45   'The Licensed Hawkers' Bill', *Advertiser*, 7 November 1904, 8.

As British subjects, these Indians argued that they were 'entitled to the privileges accorded their forefathers by the treaties under which the empire was founded' and contested the competence of the colonial legislature to 'interfere with those treaty rights'.[46]

In Queensland, between 1912 and 1919, Indians waged a campaign against the *Sugar Cultivation Act 1913*. This act involved a dictation test, similar to that required under the Commonwealth Immigration Restriction Act. Indians legally domiciled in Australia could be denied work in the sugar industry. It was one of 18 acts passed by the Queensland Parliament between 1910 and 1938 restricting employment in a number of industries unless a person had a certificate showing that they could 'read and write from dictation not less than fifty words in any language determined by the relevant Minister or head of the particular organisation'.[47] The test was aimed at 'Asiatics'. Although exemptions were allowed for Indians and for Japanese already working in the industry, as the numbers of exemptions grew, white workers became more restive, exerting pressure on the state Labor government. When the government limited these exemptions, Indians in Queensland protested to the state government and state governor – and across the empire to the colonial secretary and India Office in London.[48] Pooran Dabee Singh, an Australian-born businessman, emphasised the injustice of Indians as comrades in the Allies' wartime struggles being so treated. In 1915, he noted that many Indians were currently 'serving the Empire' in the war, and that India was giving 'of her wealth and her people'.[49] While Germans, despite their homeland being Great Britain's bitter enemy, could work on the cane fields without restriction, Indians who were British subjects and due 'all the rights and privileges of citizenship' were debarred from such work, 'on account of their colour'.[50] When, in 1919, the government stopped issuing exemptions, the Indians took a test case, that of Addar Khan, who had been found working on a cane field without an exemption certificate, to the local Police Magistrate Court, then the Queensland Supreme Court and finally appealed (unsuccessfully) to the Privy Council.[51]

---

46 Petition from Western Australian traders, enclosure in no. 172, Correspondence 1897–1908 relating to the treatment of Asiatics in the Dominions, Colonial Office (hereafter CO) 886/1/3, National Archives of the United Kingdom (hereafter NAUK).
47 Prince, 'Aliens in Their Own Land', 218.
48 'Indians in Queensland', L/E/7/1246, File 2754/1921, India Office Records (hereafter IOR), British Library (hereafter BL).
49 'Indians Barred', *Brisbane Courier,* 30 August 1915, 4.
50 Ibid.
51 Treatment of Asiatics, CO 886/9/74, NAUK. Also 'Hindoos in the Canefields', *Queenslander,* 13 December 1919, 38.

Upon Sastri's arrival in Perth, members of the Indian community presented a list of grievances that had clearly come from some national consultation. They asked why Indians could not hold government positions; why they were not eligible for the old age pension when they paid rates and taxes; why they, as British subjects, could not hold a miner's right; and why they were not eligible to vote. Referring to the situation in Queensland, they asked why Indians could not work in the cane fields 'whilst Japanese, Chinese, Greeks, Germans and other aliens are allowed to do so?'[52]

In fact, the discriminations suffered by Indian residents varied across the country.[53] Although Indians in Perth raised the issue of the franchise in their appeal to Sastri, some Indians already enjoyed both the state and federal franchise. Indeed, Potts suggests that some 336 Indians were on the federal electoral roll in 1922.[54] Generally, these would be people who had the vote in their state at Federation and, thus, were eligible to be put on the federal roll. Indians were denied all voting rights in Western Australia and Queensland, and others who might have come onto a state roll in Victoria, New South Wales, South Australia and Tasmania after Federation could not get onto the federal roll due to the particular interpretation of section 41 of Australia's Constitution.[55]

Where Sastri Went

During his tour, Sastri met representatives of the Indian communities, state government premiers and Cabinet ministers, and was accorded civic receptions by lord mayors in Sydney, Adelaide and other state capitals. He consulted with leaders of the labour movement and political parties, and addressed numerous public meetings convened by groups such as the YMCA, Women's Non-Party Political Association, Royal Colonial Institute, Rotary Club, Student Representative Council of the University of Melbourne, Australian League of Nations Union, British Empire Union,

---

52   'Grievances', *West Australian*, 2 June 1922, 7.
53   See the list the Australian Government compiled of the 'Disabilities of Aliens and Coloured Persons within the Commonwealth and its Territories', NAA: A981 INDI 16, Part 1.
54   Annette Potts, '"I Am a British Subject, and I Can Go Wherever the British Flag Flies": Indians on the Northern Rivers of New South Wales during the Federation Years', *Journal of the Royal Australian Historical Society* 83 (1997): 109. Being enfranchised in Australia was important to resident Indians and some kept their elector's right among important identity documents when they travelled back to India. See 'Gulab Singh application for permission to return to the Commonwealth', NAA: A1 1911/17264.
55   Pat Stretton and Christine Finnimore, 'Black Fellow Citizens: Aborigines and the Commonwealth Franchise', *Australian Historical Studies* 25, no. 101 (1993): 521–35, doi.org/10.1080/10314619308595934.

Australian Student Christian Movement and Public Questions Society of the University of Sydney. He spoke at the Trades Hall in Melbourne, to the Millions Club in Sydney, was a guest of the Commonwealth Club in Adelaide and the Australian Club in Melbourne, and spoke to students at Melbourne's Scotch College. He met with Indian residents and consulted leading public servants, addressed the Australian Parliament in Melbourne, and conferred with Prime Minister Hughes and his Cabinet. A Commonwealth parliamentary dinner was held in his honour. Sastri followed up particular issues raised by Indian residents – thus Bajpai interviewed the secretary of the Commonwealth Department of Home and Territories about anomalies with the administration of regulations relating to the admission on passports of Indian merchant, student and tourist travellers.[56]

Sastri's Message

In his speeches, Sastri constructed a commonality based upon what he saw as the esteemed values of the British Empire, the English language and shared wartime experiences. He was a renowned speaker, dubbed 'the Silver-tongued orator'. The following description of the British Empire gives some idea of his rhetorical style:

> Imperfect as it was, pressing as it did on the people, in many ways, deaf, as it seemed to be at times to the cries of the people: still on the whole, judged in its good and in its bad aspects, the British Empire stood as the custodians of human liberty, individual and communal: it stood for the ideal of even-handed justice, for the ideal of universal law and jurisprudence, gloriously neglectful of personalities; it stood for the principles of progress, political, commercial and economic, and for every form of equality between man and man, and above all, more than any other known political organization, it had attempted the task of reconciling different races to one another, and – he would not say it had quite succeeded – had made an earnest attempt to weld together the East and West.[57]

Referring to the old age pension and the franchise, Sastri noted:

> My request for equity applies only to those Indians who, for long years, have been resident in the country ... I suggest it would be invidious to treat us as an inferior people.[58]

---

56 'Dr. Sastri Visit to Australia', NAA: A1, 1923/7187.
57 *Adelaide Observer*, 10 June 1922, 30.
58 'India's Claims', *Daily Telegraph*, 15 June 1922, 4.

He appealed to his audiences' better instincts:

> Knowing the great enthusiasm, which Australian people felt for peace, equality and brotherhood and knowing the broad-based and justice-loving democracy upon which Australia was founded, it would be unfair if he entertained any other anticipations than those of brotherly and honourable treatment.[59]

The Imperial Conference of 1918 had agreed 'that each dominion had right to determine the composition of its population through immigration restrictions',[60] and Sastri was careful not to place the issue of immigration restrictions on the agenda, although, when pressed, he shared his own view that the White Australia policy was 'somewhat inconsistent with the integrity of the British Empire'.[61]

He was often asked about Gandhi and his growing movement, and while he had been a colleague of Gandhi in the Indian National Congress for some years and both were devoted to the memory of Gokhale, as a Liberal he disagreed with the methods of the non-cooperation movement and distanced himself from it. He claimed, 'Careful observers are of the opinion that the Gandhi movement is not likely to raise its head again'.[62] He was praised as moderate and restrained, rather than as a dangerous firebrand like Gandhi.

How Successful Was Sastri's Visit?

Sastri's speeches and his visit were widely reported in the Australian press. Most of this was positive, with headlines such as 'A Striking Personality',[63] 'Distinguished Delegate',[64] 'Stirring Speeches' and a 'Remarkable Address'.[65] It was reported that he gave: 'A speech Miltonic in dignity of phrasing and charged with rare eloquence'.[66] Some of his speeches were reproduced at great length. Sastri felt he was lionised in Australia, writing to his daughter:

---

59 *Advertiser*, 8 June 1922, 10.
60 Thakur, 'Liberal, Liminal and Lost', 9.
61 *West Australian*, 2 June 1922, 7.
62 'Political India: The Gandhi Movement', *Brisbane Courier*, 21 June 1922, 9.
63 'Striking Personality', *Age*, 13 June 1922, 6.
64 'Distinguished Delegate', *Argus*, 10 June 1922, 6.
65 'The New India Grievance Specialists, A Remarkable Address, *West Australian*, 3 June 1922, 9.
66 'The New India', *West Australian*, 3 June 1922, 9.

> They treated me very well in Australia. Everywhere the best hotels.
> Special carriages on the railways ... Ministers to escort and look
> after me; grand banquets and receptions; crowded meetings; giddy
> applause; photographs, interviews, autographs.[67]

When Sastri departed from Sydney in July 1922, Prime Minister Hughes
wrote him a letter indicating that legislation would be introduced to grant
the old age pension to Indian residents. Regarding the franchise, Hughes
indicated that Sastri's visit had 'brought within the range of practical policies
a reform which but for your visit would have been most improbable, if not
impossible of achievement'.[68] In his fulsome letter, Hughes continued:

> You have achieved wonders, and in my opinion removed for all time
> those prejudices, which formerly prevented the admission of your
> countrymen resident in Australia to the enjoyment of the full rights
> of citizenship.[69]

Leaders of the federal Country Party and the ALP gave Sastri 'assurances
of sympathy and support', and some state premiers suggested they would
abolish disabilities affecting Indian residents.[70]

Accordingly, Sastri felt his tour was a success. He admired Australian
egalitarianism, its democratic spirit and its prosperity. He reported: 'The
Indians say they already feel several inches taller, while the whites declare
their eyes have been opened.'[71] He felt the Indians he met fared quite well
in Australia:

> Nearly all look prosperous and even when economic prejudice
> operates to their detriment, the remuneration for manual labour for
> each man is seldom less than 12 shillings per day. Of social prejudice
> I saw little trace. A good many Indians have married Australian wives
> from whom they have children and live in friendship and harmony
> with their neighbours. I visited a few families and was assured by the
> wives that they suffered from no social disabilities.[72]

67 Sastri to his daughter Rukmini, 8 July 1922, in *Letters of the Rt Honourable V. S. Srinivasa Sastri*, ed. T. N. Jagadisan, 2nd ed. (London: Asian Publishing House, 1963), 95.
68 *Report by the Right Honourable V. S. Srinivasa Sastri, P.C., Regarding His Deputation to the Dominions of Australia, New Zealand and Canada* (Simla: Government Central Press, 1923), NAA: A1 1923/7187 (Dr Sastri visit to Australia).
69 Ibid.
70 Maclean, *British India, White Australia*, 152.
71 Sastri to his daughter Rukmini, 8 July 1922, *Letters of the Rt Honourable V. S. Srinivasa Sastri*, 95.
72 *Report by the Right Honourable V. S. Srinivasa Sastri*.

Sastri had 'no doubt that my visit will lead to my countrymen being admitted, at an early date, to full citizenship rights'.[73]

But the labour movement and press were suspicious of Sastri, if not openly hostile. Although Sastri often stated that 'no infringement ... is contemplated to the White Australia Policy'[74] and that 'the government of India stood by the reciprocity resolution of 1918', his motives were constantly under suspicion; his 'mission was to the end criticised in certain circles as an insidious attempt to seek a revision of the policy'.[75] *Smith's Weekly* published articles with the headlines: 'What's Sastri's Game?', 'Indian Tiger on the Prowl', 'In Australia with Sheathed Claws', 'An Enemy Invited by W. M. Hughes',[76] and 'Sastri's Poison – A Fatal Dose for White Australia. Will Hughes Administer It?'[77]

A Queensland Labor senator, J. V. McDonald, was very outspoken, declaring: 'Labour with its immovable White Australia ideal, has its hawkeye on the Sastri tour.' He saw Sastri as dangerous:

> [not standing] for the workers or democracy of his own country, he is one of the Indian ruling class who would be very ready to help the Barwells to get cheap and servile coloured labour for Northern Australia.[78]

McDonald was not deceived by Sastri's apparent enthusiasm 'for the removal of the minor political or industrial disabilities of a few hundred or thousands of Indians living in other countries' while ignoring the 'wrongs of workers in India'. Rehearsing familiar claims made by the upholders of White Australia, he denounced the spectre of 'coolie labour', which he predicted would see Australian wages plummet. Then there was the danger of Australia becoming a 'second America', as increased migration from Asia 'would speedily bring to Australia the bitter racial conflicts, lynchings and outrages of South-Eastern United States'.[79]

---

73   *Evening News*, 5 July 1922, 8.
74   'India's Claims', *Daily Telegraph*, 15 June 1922, 4.
75   *Report by the Right Honourable V. S. Srinivasa Sastri*.
76   *Smith's Weekly*, 7 June 1922.
77   Ibid., 15 July 1922.
78   'Snivelling Sastri, Labour Not Deceived by "Nigger Democrat"', *Smith's Weekly*, 29 July 1922, 25. Sir Henry Barwell, premier of South Australia, had been advocating for 'coloured labour' for the Northern Territory.
79   Ibid.

In September 1922, Hughes's letter to Sastri was published in the Australian press and many in the labour movement seized upon this as a sign of Hughes's betrayal of the White Australia policy. Labor was implacably opposed to Hughes, who had defected from the ALP. He was despised as a 'Labor rat'. James Scullin, referring to 'this very extraordinary letter', asked if the concessions were a forerunner of 'the policy of admitting these people freely into Australia'.[80]

Hughes lost office and was succeeded by Stanley Bruce in February 1923. Later that year, Sastri's report was published in India, but nothing was done about the assurances given to him. A group of elderly Indians sought to maintain pressure on the Australian Government about the old age pension; their advocate, James Kavanagh, met with the Cabinet secretary in mid-1924, but to little avail.[81]

The impasse was somewhat broken when a hawker, Mitta Bullosh, a long-term resident in Victoria, challenged his ineligibility for the federal franchise. According to Kama Maclean, Sastri's visit 'helped to reinvigorate a sense of entitlement of citizenship in the Indian community'.[82] Maclean sees the interventions of F. E. Bateman, Bullosh's solicitor, as being crucial in terms of converting the promises made to Sastri into legislative amendments.[83] However, while Bateman may have been influential, it is important to remember that, like a number of Indians in Australia, Bullosh had a history of actively seeking rights in Australia. At Federation he had instructed his solicitor in Chiltern to seek his naturalisation, only to be told this was not necessary as he was a British subject.[84] After a number of years, Bullosh sought to be entered on the Victorian state electoral roll, but when asked whether he was 'naturalized or a natural-born subject', he withdrew his request.[85]

In August 1924, possibly with Bateman's encouragement, Bullosh enrolled to vote in Victorian state elections, but his application to have his name added to the federal roll was rejected. The appeal was heard at the Melbourne Court of Petty Sessions in September 1924 before Police Magistrate Cohen, Bateman arguing against a barrister instructed by the

80   'Mr Hughes Letter to Mr Sastri', *Daily Herald*, 22 September 1922, 4.
81   NAA: A981/INDI 16, Part 2, Rights and Disabilities of Indians in Australia, 1921–1935.
82   Maclean, *British India, White Australia*, 154.
83   Ibid., 156.
84   NAA: A712/1, 1901/N848, Mutta [*sic*] Bullosh, naturalization 1901.
85   NAA: A406 E1925/373, Enrolment of Asiatics, Mitta Bullosh case.

Crown solicitor. Cohen upheld Bullosh's appeal, declaring that his decision was influenced by a statement Justice Higgins had made in the case of Jiro Muramats, a Japanese pearler resident in Western Australia who had also sought the federal franchise.[86] It is possible that Bateman and Cohen were among those whites whose eyes had been opened by Sastri's arguments.

The Australian Government considered appealing Cohen's ruling, but Sir John Latham MHR QC advised Prime Minister Stanley Bruce to reflect upon 'the political aspects of this matter in view of the public statements made by Mr Hughes to Sastri and by yourself'. Latham, a 'supporter of imperial links', cautioned that to continue with the appeal was 'a grave political error, from both an Australian and an Imperial point of view'.[87] The government decided not to appeal the magistrate's decision and paid Bullosh's costs of £70.[88] This meant that Mitta Bullosh and other Indians who sought to be enrolled on the federal roll, like William Fazldad, Nabob Khan and Charles Babakhan in New South Wales, and Charles Sanassee in South Australia, were then able to do so.[89]

This legal decision had the potential to allow other British subjects, such as Indigenous Australians and Chinese residents in Australia, to be added to the federal roll. Perhaps to forestall this, the Australian Government amended the *Commonwealth Electoral Act* in 1925, allowing 'natives of British India' who met certain residency requirements and some naturalised 'Asiatic' Australians, but not other non-Europeans, to be on the federal roll.[90] The following year, another amendment allowed Indians access to the old age

---

86   D. C. S. Sissions, 'Muramats, Jiro (1878–1943)', *Australian Dictionary of Biography*, National Centre of Biography, 1986, adb.anu.edu.au/biography/muramats-jiro-7689.

87   NAA: A981/INDI 16, Part 2.

88   Ibid.

89   NAA: A460 E1925/373, Enrolment of Asiatics, Mitta Bullosh case.

90   Jennifer Norberry and George Williams, 'Voters and the Franchise: The Federal Story', Research Paper 17 (Australia: Department of the Parliamentary Library. Information and Research Services, 2001–2). As the authors note on p. 20, after the 1925 amendment, section 39(5) of the *Commonwealth Electoral Act 1918* read:

No aboriginal native of Australia, Asia, Africa, or the Islands of the Pacific (except New Zealand) shall be entitled to have his name placed on or retained on any roll or to vote at any Senate election or House of Representatives election unless:

a.   he is so entitled under section forty-one of the *Constitution*;

b.   he is a native of British India;

c.   he is a person to whom a certificate of naturalization has been issued under a law of the Commonwealth or of a State and that certificate is still in force, or is a person who obtained British nationality by virtue of the issue of any such certificate.

pension and the invalid pension. Both were passed with Labor support, curiously attracting little controversy in parliament and were justified with references to the undertakings given to Sastri.

The electoral changes did not assist those Indians living in Queensland or Western Australia, which continued to deny them the state franchise. Despite Indians like Shar Mahomed of Silverspur, Queensland, writing to the prime minister to protest his exclusion,[91] and even though there were only around 300 Indians living in Queensland and Western Australia, neither state government would alter its position.

The matter was raised by various figures on a number of occasions, including by Leo Amery, secretary of state for dominion affairs; by Indian representatives who visited Australia with the Empire Parliamentary Delegation in 1926; at the opening of the Australian Parliament in Canberra in 1927; and at a meeting in London in 1930. Queensland finally amended its legislation in 1930 and Western Australia in 1934.

While Indians might have stood taller as a result of Sastri's visit, any actual improvement of their conditions was slow and hard fought. Peter Prince notes that amended regulations allowing Indians to work in the banana industry were conditional on the men being 'continuously … domiciled' in Queensland, which could exclude any who spent some time visiting family in India. Moreover, 'even this type of limited exemption was not provided for British subjects of Indian origin for the purpose of the sugar industry, Queensland's most profitable agricultural undertaking'.[92] Other legal disabilities also lingered. Thus, in 1926, a Western Australian man complained to Gandhi's weekly paper *Young India* that he could not own land or get a miner's right: 'When Mr Sastri came to Australia he was only shown the show part got up for the occasion. They never told him the hardships we had to put up with.'[93] As late as 1940, Sher Ali in Western Australia still could not get a miner's licence.[94] In 1948 there were 10 regulations that prevented Indians working in a number of industries in Western Australia.[95]

---

91   NAA: A981/INDI 16, Part 2.
92   Prince, 'Aliens in Their Own Land', 243–44.
93   *Young India*, 20 May 1926.
94   'Indians in Australia 1928–1947', Collection 108 2A, L/P&J/8/189, IOR, BL; 'The Case of Sher Ali', *Sunday Times*, 17 December 1939, 4.
95   MacLean, *British India, White Australia*, 159.

Conclusion

Sastri's tour of Australia was the first by an Indian representing the Indian Government. That Sastri, a colonial subject of the British Government in India, would come to Australia seeking the rights of full citizenship for Indians resident in Australia speaks to the awkward and in-between position India, as a 'dominion-like colony', occupied during the interwar period. The tour originated at the 1921 Imperial Conference, at which Sastri, an Indian representative, secured majority support for a Resolution on Equality of Citizenship in the British Dominions. His mission saw him informing political leaders and the public in Australia, as well as in New Zealand and Canada, about the justice of granting full citizenship rights to Indian residents. He appealed to his audiences' notions of fair play and always referred to the ideals of the British Empire as a touchstone.

Due to the restrictive White Australia policy, the Australian public had little knowledge of educated Indians and were amazed and enthralled to hear Sastri's eloquent addresses based on his deep understanding of British history and current events. It is difficult to assess how many among his audiences were persuaded to overcome deeply embedded racial ideas. For many, possibly most, the experience of listening to an erudite address delivered by a man with 'brown skin and a turban', while diverting, did not alter their support of the White Australia policy. Indeed, the White Australia policy continued to receive wide support across the nation and remained central to Australia's national identity until late in the twentieth century.

Although Sastri studiously avoided discussing the restrictive immigration policy, his visit was constantly criticised by the labour press and some Labor leaders as being a precursor to the opening up of the country to Indian immigrants. Sastri's discussions with political leaders at state and federal levels led to a number of assurances and even to fulsome praise. However, once he departed Australia's shores, such promises soon receded down the list of political priorities. Prime Minister Hughes lost office shortly after Sastri's visit and any moral imperative he may have felt to honour such promises disappeared with him. In any case, many of the changes needed were under state jurisdiction and, thus, were subject to the whims of local political leaders with little commitment to more generous interpretations of imperial citizenship and fraternity.

A number of studies point to changes to the federal franchise and to the granting of the old age pension to Indian residents; however, it is important to note that such changes came about as a consequence of continued pressure and activism on the part of Indian residents and their supporters, not (just) Sastri's visit. Further, while some of the changes Sastri sought were eventually made, they were achieved slowly and rather grudgingly. Indeed, some were not made until after World War II. Maclean suggests that Sastri's visit reinvigorated 'a sense of entitlement in the Indian community'. It took Mitta Bullosh's legal action in 1924 (successfully appealing the registrar's rejection of his application for federal enfranchisement) to prompt the Australian Government to deal with the issue of Indian British subjects who were on some state rolls but excluded from the federal franchise. The enfranchisement of Indians in Queensland and Western Australia took much longer, finally being achieved some 12 years after Sastri departed Australian shores. Employment restrictions also lingered, especially in Queensland and Western Australia.

Indian access to pensions had been promised at the Imperial Conference in 1918 and again by Hughes in 1922. During this period, numerous elderly Indian men, some in their late eighties, had somehow to make their living without the aid of kin. These men had come to Australia before 1901 and some had been paying Australian taxes for up to 33 years.[96] Finally being entitled to the old age pension in 1926 would have been of great assistance to such men, but other disabilities endured. Thus, Kodanda Rao, who visited Australia in 1936, found that Indians still suffered disabilities in relation to other benefits such as the widow's pension and family endowment in New South Wales.[97] These remaining disabilities, Rao reported, were a 'humiliating insult to India, wholly gratuitous in the present situation'.[98]

96 NAA: A981/INDI 16, Part 2.
97 'Notes on the Status of British Indians in Australia' by P. Kodanda Rao (c. 1936) Sastri papers Group III (b), Private no. 51 INA.
98 Ibid.

5

'Australian Is an Alien': The Position of Australian Women Married to 'Aliens', 1920–49

Emma Bellino

If I wanted to go from my home in Nedlands on a Sunday to visit members of my family in Claremont, I wasn't allowed to go without a travelling permit.[1]

Introduction

Phyllis Eve Pick was born in Australia and she married a Hungarian man, Alexander Pick, on 5 May 1942. In March 1945, Perth's *Daily News* used her story to highlight the absurd nature of marital denaturalisation – a law whereby women who married 'aliens' lost their original nationality and were deemed to acquire that of their husbands. As Phyllis's husband was an 'enemy alien', she was legally regarded the same way: she was required to register as an alien, she had to obtain a travel permit to visit her family who lived in a different suburb and she was prohibited from owning a camera. Prior to marrying, she had served as a voluntary driver in the Red Cross and had been a member of a field unit. She lost her position a week before she

---

1   'Australian Is an Alien', *Daily News*, 17 March 1945, 15.

married. She recalled that when she went to register as an alien: 'The only photograph I had to take with me … was in [my] Army uniform, and the official I had to give it to laughed.'[2]

Alexander Pick had renounced his Hungarian nationality and applied for an Australian naturalisation certificate in February 1945.[3] Women whose husbands were naturalised during the course of their marriage were required to seek naturalisation to regain their British nationality. This was in keeping with the policy that women whose husbands lost their British nationality after they were married were not automatically 'maritally denaturalised' but could make a declaration of alienage if they chose to. Phyllis's story highlights this aspect of dependent nationality and shows the interesting, inconvenient and, at times, tragic position that women married to aliens could find themselves in during wartime. Importantly, until 1949, 'Australian citizenship' was not legally defined. Instead, people born or naturalised in Australia had the legal status of 'British subject'.

To underline Phyllis's predicament, the *Daily News* stated that she was:

> an Australian-born girl, daughter of Australian parents, wife of an Australian [as Alexander had recently been naturalised], and mother of an Australian child, [she] has never been out of Australia – but she is a Hungarian.[4]

In many ways, Australian women married to aliens were still considered to be Australian. However, as Phyllis's story demonstrates, the experience of wartime alien registration exacerbated the difficulties associated with marital denaturalisation and made women social 'others' as well as legal 'others'. Phyllis's story was published on page 26 of the newspaper beside an article on Australian efforts in World War II (WWII). The tone suggested that her situation was peculiar, as not only was Phyllis Australian-born but also her Hungarian husband had satisfied the domicile requirements and had been granted naturalisation. Yet, despite her place of birth, she was still required to apply for naturalisation to once again become a British subject.

2   Ibid.
3   National Archives of Australia (hereafter NAA): A714, 24/10571.
4   'Australian Is an Alien', *Daily News*, 17 March 1945, 15.

Gender and 'Citizenship' in Australia

In the late nineteenth and early twentieth centuries, gender and marital status were essential factors in determining an individual's position under nationality laws. For women, marriage with an 'alien' caused them to be stripped of their own nationality and be deemed to have obtained their husband's nationality. This policy was practised in many nations around the world, including Australia and throughout the British Empire. Historian Joan Beaumont argues that, during this period, notions of allegiance and military service were central to ideas of nationality and citizenship.[5] These were highly gendered notions and likely informed marital denaturalisation laws.

Under the ancient rules of British common law that applied in Australia, a person's place of birth created indelible allegiance to the sovereign of the land. 'Natural-born' British subjects could not revoke their allegiance and take up another nationality of their own accord.[6] But, as Helen Irving notes, this was overridden by the United Kingdom's *Naturalization Act 1870*, including for women who married foreigners or 'aliens'. Allegiance to the British sovereign became less important than allegiance (or subservience) to the husband. As Irving says:

> The *Naturalization Act 1870* had already reversed the common law principle that a British national could not lose or change nationality by any voluntary action, and had applied legislation to British nationality. The act of marriage, while voluntary, was deemed also to include the voluntary transfer of allegiance (even if the latter was, in reality, a legal fiction) … A man owed allegiance to, and therefore belonged to his own country; a woman owed allegiance to her husband, therefore belonged to her husband's country. A woman lost her citizenship upon foreign marriage, and (in principle at least) gained her husband's citizenship.[7]

---

5   Joan Beaumont, 'Australian Citizenship and the Two World Wars', *Australian Journal of Politics and History* 53, no. 2 (2007): 172, doi.org/10.1111/j.1467-8497.2007.00452.x.

6   J. W. Salmond, 'Citizenship and Allegiance' (1902) 18 LQR 49, 52, cited in Peter Prince, 'Aliens in Their Own Land. "Alien" and the Rule of Law in Colonial and Post-Federation Australia' (PhD thesis, The Australian National University, 2015), 17, openresearch-repository.anu.edu.au/handle/1885/101778.

7   Helen Irving, *Citizenship, Alienage and the Modern Constitutional State: A Gendered History* (New York: Cambridge University Press, 2016), 73–4, doi.org/10.1017/CBO9781107588011.

This British marital denaturalisation law was adopted by Australian colonies. For example, section 7 of the *Act to Amend the Law Relating to Aliens 1875* (NSW) declared that 'every married woman shall in this Colony be deemed to be a subject of the State of which her husband is for the time being a subject'. Other colonies had similar laws that carried over after Federation. Marital denaturalisation was reinforced in the *British Nationality and Status of Aliens Act 1914* and adopted at a national level in Australia in section 18 of the *Nationality Act 1920* (Cth), which declared that 'the wife of a British subject shall be deemed to be a British subject, and the wife of an alien shall be deemed to be an alien'.

Beaumont discusses the complex nature of Australian 'citizenship' during World War I (WWI) and WWII, and argues that, 'since the birth of the modern democratic state, military service has been the quintessential demand that the state makes of the citizen'. She suggests that this is a key reason 'why citizenship has been gendered, with the rights of men who serve as combat soldiers being considered superior to the rights of women'.[8] Similarly, Helen Irving argues that, 'historically, what distinguished a citizen (in a constitutional sense) from an alien, was allegiance', which was 'demonstrated principally in military terms'.[9] Since women were barred from demonstrating allegiance through military combat, their claim to nationality was less secure than that of men.[10]

Marital denaturalisation caused emotional and physical hardship for women. Australian-born women married to aliens were ineligible to vote in federal elections, were unable to purchase land, faced difficulty obtaining a passport, lost any teachers' superannuation they had accrued, were barred from working in certain professions, including the public service, were required to register as aliens during wartime, and could even be considered 'enemy aliens' (depending on their husband's nationality). This was the case for all Australian women regardless of their racial background. For non-white Australian women married to aliens, racial restrictions compounded their experience of marital denaturalisation. For example, Hilda Maclean notes that, in Queensland during WWI, Aboriginal women who married

---

8   Beaumont, 'Australian Citizenship', 172.
9   Irving, *A Gendered History*, 41.
10   Ibid.

Chinese husbands became 'aliens in their own land' and were subject to federal alien restriction regulations in addition to prohibitions imposed by the state's Aboriginal 'protection' laws.[11]

Wartime and Denaturalisation

The consequences of marital denaturalisation were harsher during wartime. This chapter examines wartime experiences to highlight the complexities and emotional toll on maritally denaturalised women in Australia. As noted by barrister Elizabeth Trout in an article for the *Daily Telegraph* in 1939, nationality was 'the factor [that determined] the flag under which a person [was] entitled to seek protection in wartime'.[12] During wartime, the loss of nationality meant the loss of political protection, assistance, allegiance and the right to freedom of movement and association, all of which were less problematic during peacetime. Aliens were not entitled to government assistance and protection; under the law, they did not owe their allegiance to the nation, and, conversely, the nation did not owe protection to them. Neither were they guaranteed the rights and freedoms that (white) subjects took for granted.

Alien registration rules and restrictions were essential components of Australian maritally denaturalised women's experiences during the early twentieth century. Australia practised alien registration between 1916 and 1926 and 1939 and 1971. During this time, aliens were required to register at their local police station to assist the government in monitoring the whereabouts of those seen as potential security threats. Restrictions were placed on their freedom of movement and right to associate with others, and they were prohibited from owning cameras, radios or land. Prior to 1946, Australian-born women married to aliens who had not been naturalised or made a declaration of their intention to retain their nationality rights under section 18A of the Nationality Act were also required to register as aliens.

Restrictions and regulations were more severe for those classed as 'enemy aliens'. These were legal aliens whose country of nationality was at war with Australia. Women married to enemy aliens were also considered to have this

---

11   Hilda Maclean, 'Chinese-Aboriginal Families of Northwest Queensland – A Focus on Archival Resources', Lecture 7, 2 December 2021, Institute for Australian and Chinese Arts and Culture, Western Sydney University.
12   'Women without a Country: Often the Price of Marriage to an Alien Is to Be an Outcast', *Daily Telegraph*, 25 September 1939, 4.

legal status because they had acquired, or had been deemed to acquire, the nationality of their husband. As well as restrictions on their right to freedom of movement and association, enemy alien regulations provided that they could be interned or detained. They were also required to regularly report to the police.[13] Enemy aliens were restricted from possessing firearms or other weapons, cameras and surveying apparatus, motor vehicles, cipher or coding tools, telephones, broadcasting transmitters, and naval or airforce maps and handbooks.[14]

War precautions affected both 'friendly' and 'enemy' aliens. Historian Daniel Leach discusses instances of internment of 'friendly aliens' in Australia during WWII. He argues that local authorities were unsure whose authority it was to enforce the *National Security Act 1939* (Cth), and that xenophobia and distrust of those who were non-British influenced Australian security policies.[15] Leach suggests that, in contrast with the processes governing the internment of enemy aliens, authorities were careful to 'establish solid cases' before interning friendly aliens.[16]

Iyko Day and D. C. S. Sissons examine the internment of Japanese aliens in Australia during WWII. Day looks at the internment of Japanese 'enemy aliens', noting that because Australia's 'wartime internment policy' was already in place, it was possible to 'round up nearly all Japanese individuals from Australia and surrounding nations within twenty-four hours of the bombing of Pearl Harbor'.[17] Sissons discusses Japanese migrants in Australia between 1871 and 1971. He argues that in 1941 'all Japanese residents and with very few exceptions their Australian-born children – a total of 958 – were interned'. Sissons notes that, at war's end, 'the Australian-born were permitted to remain but all but 75 of the Japanese-born were compulsorily returned to Japan'.[18]

---

13 Defence (National Security – Aliens Control) Regulations 1939 (Cth), regs 19, 20, 24.

14 Ibid., regs 14, 22.

15 Daniel Leach, '"This Way of Treating Friendly Aliens Seems Strange to Me": Australian Security Services, Allied Governments-in-Exile, and the Surveillance and Internment of "Friendly Aliens" from Occupied Europe, 1939–45', *International History Review* 37, no. 4 (2015): 842, doi.org/10.1080/070 75332.2014.980298.

16 Ibid., 858.

17 Iyko Day, 'Alien Intimacies: The Coloniality of Japanese Internment in Australia, Canada, and the U.S', *Amerasia Journal* 36, no. 2 (2010): 107, doi.org/10.17953/amer.36.2.v2780054171w0666.

18 D. C. S. Sissons, 'Immigration in Australian–Japanese relations, 1871–1971', in *Bridging Australia and Japan: Volume 1*, ed. Arthur Stockwin and Keiko Tamura (Canberra: ANU Press, 2016), 202.

Despite having no legal claim to British nationality, Australian-born, maritally denaturalised women – at least those with an ethnically British background – were still considered members of the Australian community by virtue of their birth and upbringing in Australia, and their presumed commitment to Australian values and ideals. Oftentimes, public opinion, politicians and the women themselves considered maritally denaturalised women to still be Australian, despite their legal status. Legal histories highlight the changing legal–political position of maritally denaturalised women in Australia.[19] In her pivotal work *Citizenship, Alienage, and the Modern Constitutional State: A Gendered History*, Helen Irving considers the legal position of maritally denaturalised women during war and outlines the gendered nature of allegiance and citizenship in the first half of the twentieth century. This chapter builds on Irving's work to examine the emotional toll of marital denaturalisation. It also builds on histories of interracial families in Australia.[20] Notably, it highlights the disconnect between maritally denaturalised women's legal position and their own, often deeply held, identities as British Australian women.

19   See Irving, *A Gendered History*; Helen Irving, 'When Women Were Aliens: The Neglected History of Derivative Marital Citizenship', *Sydney Law School Research Paper* 12, no. 47 (2012): 1–10; Kim Rubenstein, *Australian Citizenship Law in Context* (Sydney: Lawbook Co, 2002); Harriet J. Mercer, 'Citizens of Empire and Nation: Australian Women's Quest for Independent Nationality Rights, 1910s–1930s', *History Australia* 13 (2016): 213–27, doi.org/10.1080/14490854.2016.1185998; Victoria Rigney, 'For Richer or Poorer, I Give Up My Citizenship: Citizenship, Alienation and Marriage', in *Exploring the British World: Identity, Cultural Production, Institutions*, ed. Stuart Mcintyre (Melbourne: RMIT Publishing, 2004).
20   See Ann Curthoys, 'Race and Ethnicity: A Study of the Response of British Colonists to Aborigines, Chinese and Non-British Europeans in New South Wales, 1856–1881' (PhD thesis, Macquarie University, 1973); Kathy Cronin, *Colonial Casualties, Chinese in Early Victoria* (Melbourne: Melbourne University Press, 1982), 78–79, 128–30; Andrew Markus, *Fear and Hatred: Purifying Australia and California 1850–1901* (Sydney: Hale & Ironmonger, 1979), 18, 258–59; Kate Bagnall, 'Anglo-Chinese and the Politics of Overseas Travel from New South Wales, 1898 to 1925', in *Chinese Australians: Politics, Engagement and Resistance*, ed. Sophie Couchman and Kate Bagnall (Leiden: Brill, 2015), 203–39, doi.org/10.1163/9789004288553_009; Victoria Haskins and John Maynard, 'Sex, Race and Power', *Australian Historical Studies* 37, no. 126 (2005): 191–216, doi.org/10.1080/10314610508682920; Ann McGrath, *Illicit Love: Interracial Sex and Marriage in the United States and Australia* (Lincoln: University of Nebraska Press, 2015), doi.org/10.2307/j.ctt1d98bzf; Katherine Ellinghaus, *Taking Assimilation to Heart: Marriages of White Women and Indigenous Men in the United States and Australia, 1887–1937* (Lincoln: University of Nebraska, 2006), doi.org/10.2307/j.ctt1djmhvp; Angela Wanhalla, *Matters of the Heart: A History of Marriage in New Zealand* (Auckland: Auckland University Press, 2013).

Race and Nationality

Race was an essential component of Australian women's experiences of marital denaturalisation. Although non-Anglo women might still identify as British or Australian, their place in the Australian community was not as sure as that of Anglo women married to aliens. Tellingly, articles and political discussions dealing with married women's nationality rarely mentioned race. Although not explicitly articulated, politicians and the popular press likely assumed that the maritally denaturalised women they considered to be 'Australian' were Australian-born white women. The assumed racial distinction between white 'Australian girls' and their alien husbands is evident in a number of political discussions and articles in the press. For example, in an article discussing the deportation of Malayan and Chinese men who had arrived as wartime refugees, the president of the Australian Natives' Association declared: 'Some of these persons have married women of their own race; others have married Australian girls. In both cases they are multiplying.'[21] This distinction between 'Australian girls' and 'women of their own race' demonstrates that Australian women were presumed to be Anglo rather than ethnically Chinese or Malay, even though such women were also Australian by birth and upbringing.

Social Citizens, Legal Aliens

To explore the contrast between maritally denaturalised women's position as both 'social citizens' and legal aliens, the remainder of this chapter examines their depiction in three arenas: political debates, the popular press and women's applications to government. The effect of the two world wars, which strengthened women's existential ties to their original nationality, runs through each section to emphasise that these women were legal aliens and were subject to laws limiting their rights, while – in the case of white women – they remained socially and emotionally Australian/British and were largely seen that way by the communities around them.

---

21   See, for example, 'Girls May Lose Their Chinese Husbands: Deportation of Seaman Will Upset Wartime Marriages', *Sun* (Sydney), 9 November 1947, 3; 'Malays to Be Deported: Australian Wives', *Adelaide Chronicle*, 4 December 1947, 6.

Parliamentary debates across the first half of the twentieth century reveal that Australian politicians were generally favourable towards women married to aliens. Debates surrounding certain rights or privileges, such as those around the maternity allowance introduced in 1912, combined with debates on nationality legislation, show how politicians attempted to assist women married to aliens while negotiating the commitment of successive federal governments to maintain unity in nationality law throughout the British Empire.[22] Newspapers and women's magazines assumed a similar posture in asserting that Australian-born women deserved their independent nationality and in advocating for the restoration of their rights.

Women's applications to government provide a rich history of women's agency and their love for Australia/Britain. Many applications were made by women who seemed unlikely to engage in politics or political advocacy. However, the realisation that they had lost their dearly held original nationality and the practical difficulties this brought, especially in wartime, led them to engage with government on this issue. In these records, women highlight their connections to Australia and Britain and argue that, although they had forfeited their birth nationality through marriage, they had not lost their love for Australia/Britain.

Australian Political Debates on Married Women's Nationality

Discussions and debates in Australian parliaments during the early twentieth century demonstrate that, in general, Australian politicians were in favour of women's independent nationality and viewed maritally denaturalised (white) women as still being Australian/British despite their altered legal status. There were a number of reasons why Australian governments legislated in favour of marital denaturalisation in the first half of the twentieth century, the most pervasive of which was to maintain uniform nationality laws throughout the British Empire, as agreed at the 1911 Imperial Conference.

Marital denaturalisation legislation in Australia remained relatively unchanged from 1920, when it was established in federal law, to 1936, when the Nationality Act was amended to include a new section, 18(2), which declared that Australian women who married aliens would only lose their British nationality if they received their husband's nationality through

---

22   See Emma Bellino, 'Married Women's Nationality and the White Australia Policy, 1920–1948', *Law & History* 7, no. 1 (2020): 175–78.

marriage. This major amendment to prevent women becoming stateless through marriage was in direct response to an international convention held at The Hague in 1930 that discussed married women's nationality and the resulting international complications. The second pivotal amendment in 1936 was the introduction into the Nationality Act of section 18A, which allowed Australian-born women married to aliens to declare their intention to retain their nationality rights and obligations.

The enactment of section 18A demonstrates how Australian politicians negotiated the conflicting goals of restoring women's independent nationality and maintaining the common code of nationality legislation throughout the British Empire. Significantly, section 18A had no extraterritorial power. Hence, rights retained under the provision were applicable only while the recipient was in Australia and its territories. The Act declared that:

> Any woman to whom this section [18A] applies, whether her marriage is still continuing or not, may … make a declaration in the prescribed form and manner that she desires to retain *while in Australia or any Territory* the rights of a British subject, and thereupon she shall, *within Australia or any Territory*, be entitled to all political and other rights, powers, and privileges, and be subject to all obligations, duties and liabilities, to which a natural-born British subject is entitled or subject.[23]

Section 18A demonstrates that politicians looked favourably upon the possibility of granting women independent nationality. Further, it suggests that Australian lawmakers still considered maritally denaturalised women to be important members of the Australian community. Although they were legal 'others', they were not necessarily social or cultural 'others'. Their Australian birth and upbringing meant that, despite their new legal status, Australian-born women married to aliens were still 'Australian' in the eyes of politicians.

Women's organisations played a pivotal role in demanding political change in the early twentieth century.[24] Developments in marital denaturalisation laws in Australia were influenced by campaigns, conferences and deputations by women's organisations, both within Australia and around the wider Commonwealth, arguing in favour of women's independent nationality

---

23 *Nationality Act 1920* (Cth), section 18A, inserted by section 7 of the *Nationality Act 1936* (Cth). Emphasis added.
24 See Marilyn Lake, *Getting Equal: The History of Australian Feminism* (Sydney: Allen & Unwin, 1999), 75.

rights. Both state-based and national organisations lobbied members of parliament on the issue of marital nationality, sending deputations and letters to ministers urging them to bring marital denaturalisation before parliament and enact legislative changes. For example, the National Council of Women Australia (NCWA) and the Australian Federation of Women Voters (AFWV) both appealed to Prime Minister Joseph Lyons for support in 1933.

Capitalising on international affiliations was an essential aspect of women's organisations' strategic approach to advancing women's rights, including their fight to end dependent nationality.[25] Women's organisations staunchly rejected the 1930 League of Nations *Convention on Certain Questions Relating to the Conflict of Nationality Law* (The Hague Convention) because it effectively wrote the principle of women's inferiority to men into international law. The AFWV called it 'an insult to women'.[26] Recognising that the issue required agreement around the British Empire, organisations united to urge governments around the world to reject the recommendations of The Hague Convention. At an NCWA executive meeting in Melbourne in January 1934, May Moss, the NCWA's first president, noted that she had attended a 'private interview' with Prime Minister Lyons that 'did not give [her] much hope', describing the issue as 'a sort of see-saw between the Dominions and the British Empire'.[27]

The parliamentary discussions that led to the development of section 18A reveal politicians' support for the rights of Australian-born maritally denaturalised women. On 14 March 1935, during the second reading of the Nationality Bill in the House of Representatives – that is, before section 18A had been developed – Sir Donald Cameron, United Australia member for Lilley in Queensland, asserted that the proposed Bill's 'provisions fall very far short of what we would desire'. Cameron alluded to the tireless campaigning of women's organisations, stating that 'countless thousands of women in every country have made it very clear that their objective is

---

25   For more on the international affiliations of Australian women's organisations, see Judith Smart and Marian Quartly, 'Mainstream Women's Organisations in Australia: The Challenges of National and International Co-operation after the Great War', *Women's History Review*, 21, no 1 (2012): 63–64, doi.org/10.1080/09612025.2012.645673.

26   Records of the Australian Federation of Women Voters, 1920–1983 [manuscript], National Library of Australia (hereafter NLA): MS 2818/33/24.

27   Very early minutes and notices, 1924-1936, Guide to the Records of the National Council of Women of Australia, 1924–1990, NLA: MS 75833/11/unnumbered.

absolute equality of nationality for married women'.[28] He proposed that Australia include a provision similar to one New Zealand had adopted in its *British Nationality and Status of Aliens (in New Zealand) Amendment Act 1934*, which allowed women to retain their rights as British subjects, if not their actual British nationality. The wording of section 18A closely followed New Zealand's 1934 amending legislation.

On 13 November 1936, the Nationalist member for Perth, Walter Nairn, having urged the government to repeal dependent nationality on several occasions, noted Cameron's absence and proposed the inclusion of what would become section 18A. Nairn emphasised that its purpose was to 'remove disadvantages that are suffered by many of our womenfolk'.[29] Thomas Paterson, Country Party member for Gippsland in Victoria, who supported the amendment, observed that, 'strictly speaking, in law she would still be regarded as an alien outside of Australia', but concluded that the new provision 'would go a long way towards meeting, in Australia at all events, the wish of our womenfolk to be treated on an equality basis'.[30] No arguments against the clause were presented, and, when put to a vote, section 18A was passed.

Apart from the inclusion of section 18A in 1936, debates in both houses of federal parliament across the first half of the twentieth century show that many Australian politicians supported improved rights for maritally denaturalised women, expressing a belief they should not lose their British nationality upon marrying an alien. For example, on 27 October 1920, during the second reading of the Nationality Bill, Frank Brennan, Labor member for Batman in Victoria, declared that 'a great deal of dissatisfaction and indignation [had] been engendered among the people of this country' on the topic of marital denaturalisation. Echoing Senate debates from 1903, he asserted that, despite Australia's advances in giving women rights and 'privileges equal to those possessed by the mere man ... in connexion with naturalization we are still pursuing the antiquated policy of bracketing her with lunatics and idiots'[31] (as the Nationality Act 1920 did in its definition of 'disability').[32] He deemed this state of affairs both unjust and illogical.

---

28   Commonwealth of Australia, *Parliamentary Debates*, House of Representatives, 14 March 1935, 85–6.

29   Ibid., 13 November 1936, 1865–66.

30   Ibid., 13 November 1936, 1866.

31   Ibid., 27 October 1920, 6025.

32   Section 5 defined 'disability' as 'the status of being a married woman, or a minor, lunatic or idiot'.

Bert Lazzarini, Labor member for Werriwa, agreed, arguing on 3 November 1920 that marital denaturalisation was 'absurd'. He asserted: 'I think that men and women should have equal treatment in matters of this kind.'[33] Labor member for Melbourne Ports, James Mathews, also considered marital denaturalisation 'preposterous' and disagreed with inadvertently 'limit[ing] the field of matrimony to any Australian-born woman'.[34] He declared:

> in Australia we should take the stand that women should have the same privileges as men … Nobody has a right to deprive any native-born Australian woman of her birthright.[35]

Sentiments such as these were racialised as well as gendered; Australian-born women who were not white had different levels of access to their 'birthright' than white women. For example, it was not until 1962 that all Aboriginal and Torres Strait Islander women (and men) were able to vote at federal elections, whereas white women over 21 years of age were granted this right in 1902.[36]

On 4 February 1926, in the House of Representatives, Nationalist member for Boothby John Grant Duncan-Hughes suggested that 'the loss of her nationality, of the franchise, and, in certain circumstances, of her property, is a severe penalty for marrying an alien'. He further remarked:

> It would be idle to pretend that there are no objections [to repealing marital denaturalisation], but the reasons in favour of a change seem to me to far outweigh those for the retention of the present system.[37]

Duncan-Hughes proposed:

> That, in the opinion of this House, a British woman should not lose, or be deemed to lose, her nationality by the mere act of marriage with an alien, but that it should be open to her to make a declaration of alienage.[38]

---

33   Commonwealth of Australia, *Parliamentary Debates*, House of Representatives, 3 November 1920, 6140.
34   Ibid., 6137.
35   Ibid.
36   Anna Hough, 'The 120th Anniversary of Women's Suffrage in Australia', Parliament of Australia, 15 June 2022, www.aph.gov.au/About_Parliament/Parliamentary_Departments/Parliamentary_Library/FlagPost/2022/June/Womens_suffrage.
37   Commonwealth of Australia, *Parliamentary Debates*, House of Representatives, 4 February 1926, 679.
38   Ibid., 677.

In response, Prime Minister Stanley Bruce, who, like Duncan-Hughes, was a member of the Nationalist Party, declared:

> The right of women who marry to retain their nationality is of the very greatest importance, and we all must sympathize with a great number of women in this and other countries who, through marriage, have forfeited their original nationality.[39]

Further, Bruce argued that:

> a woman naturally attaches the same importance to nationality as does a man and has at least as much patriotic feeling for her native country. For that reason women are entitled to demand that there shall be no avoidable differentiation in nationality rights between citizens of different sexes.[40]

In the early twentieth century, numerous Australian politicians – many more than represented here – made speeches and engaged in debates asserting the right of Australian women to independent British nationality. Such women were not seen as 'others', but as Australian women who, having married 'aliens', had had the misfortune of forfeiting their dearly held nationality.

Further amendments to the Nationality Act in 1946 allowed Australian maritally denaturalised women, with few exceptions, to retain their British nationality rights automatically and without the need for a declaration under section 18A. Finally, in 1949, following a great deal of campaigning by women's organisations, individuals, newspapers, magazines, lawyers and politicians, Australia repealed dependent nationality for women.

Married Women's Nationality and the Popular Press

Newspapers and women's magazines also addressed marital denaturalisation sympathetically, elaborating on the difficulties it caused and presenting women's nationality as being 'very dear to them', regardless of the nationality of their spouses.[41] Such articles indicate that, in the popular press, maritally denaturalised women were still largely considered 'Australian'. In relation to marital denaturalisation, newspapers and women's magazines discussed the changing legal situation, presented (limited) political updates, commented on women's organisations and activism, described the work of key feminists, advertised meetings and events, and discussed various

39   Ibid., 25 February 1926, 1138.
40   Ibid.
41   'Gossip from Sydney', *Telegraph*, 19 April 1947, 12.

national and international conferences. Therefore, for historians, Australian newspapers and women's magazines are essential sources of information about married women's nationality, offering valuable insights into how marital denaturalisation was presented to the Australian public.

Occasionally, stories of individual women's experiences and hardships, like Phyllis Pick's, were discussed in newspaper and magazine articles. Such articles relayed the experiences of both high-profile and lesser-known 'everyday' women who had married aliens, and often accompanied articles about political debates and/or female activism on marital denaturalisation. The content and tone of these articles highlighted the absurd position such women faced as a consequence of getting married, indicating a level of public understanding that marital denaturalisation left women in a strange situation, to say the least.

Yet, considering the number of women affected, marital denaturalisation was often underreported during the early twentieth century. Although newspapers and women's magazines discussed it to varying degrees, these discussions were not numerous. There was no increase in the number of articles following the introduction of statutory marital denaturalisation in Australia in 1920. In contrast, in the lead up to and following The Hague Convention, there was a noticeable increase in the number of articles attempting to educate women on their rights and advocating for the repeal of dependent nationality laws.

Focusing on Australian newspapers that have been digitised and are available on Trove, a free online library database, between 1900 and 1949, married women's nationality was discussed or mentioned just over 3,400 times. During the period when marital denaturalisation was federally legislated (1920–48), there were 2,571 articles on married women's nationality: 636 in the 1920s, 1,485 in the 1930s and 450 in the 1940s. Across the country, the number of articles on married women's nationality varied.[42] Between 1900 and 1949, newspapers in New South Wales reported on married women's nationality 868 times, Queensland 723 times, Victoria 717 times, Western Australia 412 times, South Australia 401 times, Tasmania 259 times, the Australian Capital Territory 22 times and the Northern Territory nine times.

While some newspapers contained columns or pages specifically designed to appeal to women, they were often written with a broader audience in mind. In contrast, women's magazines featured literature, humour and

---

42   These data are dependent on the number of newspapers printed and digitised in each state.

articles aimed at a female readership.[43] These magazines often contained columns on mothercraft and homemaking, gossip about popular celebrities and, when relevant, articles on political issues deemed of interest to women, including the state of dependent nationality. By discussing marital denaturalisation, women's magazines presented the issue for a wider female readership, indicating that it was an issue of concern to more than just politicians, women's political organisations and followers of political developments via newsprint. Importantly, marital denaturalisation was seen as a women's interest story and something that women should be educated about. Women's magazines both informed and reflected women's interest in, and rejection of, dependent nationality laws.

The language and phrasing of articles in the popular press demonstrate widespread support for better conditions and rights for maritally denaturalised women and a general feeling that they were still Australian despite the formal loss of their nationality. In November 1936, an editorial in the Hobart *Mercury* declared:

> Now comes the recognition of the fact that because a woman is married she does not therefore pawn her privileges as a citizen and merge her birthright of nationality in that of another person.[44]

In reality, the amendment to the Nationality Act that year did not untangle a woman's birthright from that of her husband. Instead, it allowed for the restoration of the nationality rights of a British subject upon making a declaration. It did not alter the legal status of Australian women so affected. Unless they would otherwise become stateless by marriage, such women were technically still aliens. Regardless, the sentiment that the law was finally catching up to the 'fact' that women had their own 'birthright of nationality' is significant. This demonstrates support for married women's independent nationality and that (white) women married to aliens were still largely seen as Australian.

In an article in the *Australian Women's Weekly* in November 1933 entitled 'Australian Girl Became an Alien', Lorna Maneschi, the daughter of a senior Victorian Government official who had married an Italian man, Edigio Maneschi, in London in 1928, commented 'it is a strange experience to

43   For analysis of women's periodicals and their uses for historians, see Sean Latham, 'The Mess and Muddle of Modernism: The Modernist Journals Project and Modern Periodical Studies', *Tulsa Studies in Women's Literature* 30, no. 2 (2011): 407–28; Barbara Green, 'Around 1910: Periodical Culture, Women's Writing, and Modernity', *Tulsa Studies in Women's Literature* 30, no. 2 (2011): 429–39.
44   'Day by Day: Women's Nationality-Deprivation by Marriage', *Mercury*, 16 November 1936, 8.

return to my home as an alien'.[45] The year 1933 was the midpoint between The Hague Convention (1930), which led to substantial changes in marital denaturalisation law, and the *Nationality Act 1936* (Cth), which amended Australia's nationality legislation in line with The Hague Convention, providing for women to declare their desire to retain their nationality rights after marriage with an alien. Across this period, ongoing political discussion and female advocacy calling for changes to married women's nationality influenced articles on the topic.

In its article on Lorna Maneschi, the *Australian Women's Weekly* attempted to engender sympathy for women who found themselves in a similar 'ridiculous situation'. The article began by asking: 'How would you feel if you found yourself treated as a foreigner in your own country, subjected to all sorts of humiliations and red tape?'[46] It presented facts and figures, and claimed that one well-known Sydney divorce barrister, Stanley Vere Toose, knew of 50 deserted women who, owing to laws that viewed a wife's legal domicile as being that of her husband, had 'no legal standing in any divorce court'. Borrowing the words of Melbourne solicitor Joan Rosanove, the article stressed that: 'Women's organisations have no juster or stronger claim to any reform than they have in their campaign to permit married women to retain their nationality.'[47] Emphasising its view of marital denaturalisation as humiliating and unjust, the article concluded that: 'It is a sharp reminder that any Australian woman who marries a foreigner is admitted to her native county only on sufferance.'[48]

Articles that relayed the stories of well-known and lesser-known Australian women who had married aliens attempted to make women who had not married aliens familiar with their situation to help them see it as a problem that could affect all Australian women. In 1935, the *Sydney Morning Herald* printed the words of Linda P. Littlejohn, a prominent feminist and founder of the League of Women Voters in Australia:

> Suppose your daughter falls in love with and marries a good-looking Swede, then her country is finished with her. She cannot keep the nationality of her land, which is just as dear to her as to you or your husband.[49]

---

45   'Australian Girl Became an Alien', *Australian Women's Weekly*, 25 November 1933, 4.
46   Ibid.
47   Ibid.
48   Ibid.
49   'Feminist Cause: What It Fights For. Mrs. Littlejohn's Address', *Sydney Morning Herald*, 15 February 1935, 4.

This was a problem that every Australian woman needed to care about. In choosing a 'good-looking Swede' as the hypothetical match, Littlejohn was making it clear that even women who married white, 'friendly' aliens would lose their nationality: marital denaturalisation was not just an issue for women who married 'undesirable' or 'coloured' aliens – it was an issue for *all* women who married aliens.

In media portrayals of the issue, white Australian women who married aliens were still called 'Australian' or 'British'. Most articles argued for the repeal of marital denaturalisation and the restoration of women's independent nationality. The language used in newspaper reports addressing married women's nationality status stressed the importance of the issue for women and lamented that dominion governments were not taking reasonable steps to repeal the offending legislation. In 1930, quoting the words of Dr Ethel Dentham to the United Kingdom's House of Commons, the Adelaide *Advertiser* noted that there was 'a growing revolt' against the 'doctrine of sex subordination'. Dentham had argued that:

> The grievance is not merely sentimental; the legal principle objected to may inflict injury of a practical kind. A woman married to a foreigner may stand in need of all the protection her country's laws and diplomacy can give her, quite as much as her spinster sister, perhaps more so.[50]

According to Dentham, nationality afforded practical and physical protection for women married to aliens. The suggestion that such women were in greater need of protection than their 'spinster sisters' may have alluded to newspaper reports – often highly sensationalised – about women who had followed their alien husbands overseas and experienced certain hardships.[51] The idea that such women might require the protection of 'her country' reinforced the perception that British women married to aliens were still British despite their formal legal status.

---

50   'Nationality of Married Women', *Advertiser*, 2 December 1930, 8.
51   See Kate Bagnall, 'A Journey of Love: Agnes Breuer's Sojourn in 1930s China', in *Transnational Ties*, ed. Desley Deacon, Penny Russell and Angela Woollacott (Canberra: ANU E Press, 2008), 115–34, doi.org/10.22459/tt.12.2008.07; Kate Bagnall, 'Golden Shadows on a White Land: An Exploration of the Lives of White Women Who Partnered Chinese Men and Their Children in Southern Australia, 1855–1915' (PhD thesis, University of Sydney, 2007).

Women's Agency and Engagement with Government

Women's correspondence with government officials, as well as their declarations under section 18A, reveal that Australian women married to aliens valued their former British nationality and rights and continued to view themselves as Australian/British. The declarations indicate that, despite their changed legal position, these women still held emotive and existential ties to their British nationality. Historian Rachel Bright argues that enemy alien women in Australia (some of whom were likely maritally denaturalised) attempted to prove their desirability as Australian citizens in their naturalisation applications during WWI.[52] In much the same way, maritally denaturalised women emphasised their Australian birth and Australian or British parentage (where relevant), as well as their abiding affection towards Britain/Australia, to highlight their desire to be Australian and their desirability as citizens/subjects. Further, as many section 18A declarations and alien registration applications demonstrate, some maritally denaturalised women were unaware they had lost their British nationality, indicating that, in all likelihood, they considered themselves to be Australian/British.

The exact number of declarations made under section 18A of the Nationality Act is unknown. However, records indicate that between 1936 and 1948 at least 2,100 maritally denaturalised women made declarations under section 18A. To make a declaration, women requested the relevant forms from the Department of the Interior (from July 1945, such requests went to the Department of Immigration). Some women wrote directly to the secretary of the department, others contracted lawyers to oversee the process on their behalf and, occasionally, some wrote to their local member of parliament. The department then forwarded the relevant forms for the women to complete and return. During WWII, security checks were introduced. These had to be completed before further forms, identical to those already supplied, were sent with instructions to complete both copies and to send birth and marriage certificates, if these had not already been sent. A £10 administration fee also applied.

---

52   See Rachel Bright, 'Rethinking Gender, Citizenship, and War: Female Enemy Aliens in Australia during World War I', *Immigrants and Minorities* (2021): 8–9, 15, doi.org/10.1080/02619288.2021.1977126.

Once satisfactorily completed, the declaration was lodged with the department and the applicant or their representative was informed. Section 18A declarations were time restricted and required the applicant to submit a declaration within 12 months following her marriage. Women who applied outside this timeframe had to furnish the department with an explanation as to why their application was late. Common reasons included ignorance of the law (either not knowing about marital denaturalisation or, more commonly, not knowing about section 18A) and ignorance of the need to make a declaration: some women thought that section 18A applied automatically. Security checks were completed after a reason for the late application was provided. I only came across one rejected late application in my research: it presented a perceived security risk and will be discussed below.[53] This willingness to approve applications made outside of the specified time frame indicates a level of goodwill on the part of government officials and ministers, reflecting a desire to restore married women's nationality.

On rare occasions, perceived security risks could lead to a declaration being rejected. One woman whose section 18A declaration was refused was Mavis Leonie Kai Tze Loh, née Chinn. A later application was accepted. Mavis Loh was born in Australia to Chinese parents. She was an accomplished violinist and Melbourne schoolteacher. She married Frank Kai Tze Loh, a Chinese Government official, in Melbourne in 1938 before leaving for China with her new husband. Mavis and her family were well known in Melbourne and, after her marriage, she spoke publicly of her support for China and the Chinese people, especially in relation to their struggle against the invading Japanese. In May 1941, the *Age* reported that Mavis had 'told of the courage of the women in Chungking in the terrible air raids which came at very frequent intervals', that 'her own home [had been] bombed' and that she had been a member of a committee:

> to assist the women of China during the war period, and [i]t was her work to organise the women of the Department of Overseas Affairs [China] in their efforts for refugees and war orphans.[54]

---

53   'LOH Mavis Leonie – Declaration under Section 18A of the Nationality Act – born 7 January 1914 – Chinese by Marriage', NAA: A435, 1946/4/5946.
54   'Woman's Life in Chungking', *Age*, 2 May 1941, 3.

It was also reported that Mavis edited a magazine for the Chinese Department of Overseas Affairs that was 'written in English for the department to send to the Chinese abroad in other countries'.[55]

Mavis initially applied to make a declaration under section 18A in June 1939. Two years later, in August 1941, interdepartmental correspondence outlined her situation, noting:

> shortly after her marriage she left Australia for China with her husband. Before her departure, Mavis asked to be supplied with the necessary form to enable her to make a declaration under the Nationality Act. In September 1939, she completed the declaration in China before a British Consul.[56]

Mavis's sister, Eunice Chinn, communicated with Australian authorities on her sister's behalf and expressed a strong desire for her sister to retain her British nationality rights. However, her application was rejected. Eunice and Mavis were told this was because she had signed the required statutory declaration in front of the British Consul in China and not in front of a designated Australian official. However, further departmental discussions around Mavis's application indicate that, although this was a technical reason for section 18A declarations to be rejected, her strong connections with Chinese Government officials, and the perceived security risk this carried, was the real reason her application was refused.

In March 1940, Mavis and her husband Frank, who, at the time, was the special commissioner for Chinese Overseas Affairs, visited Sydney. The 1941 interdepartmental memo noted that, while her second attempt to declare was 'in order', Mavis intended to 'leave Australia with her husband'.[57] Thus, her application was once again denied, as it was 'not the practice to permit Declarations under section 18A to be made by women who intend to leave Australia'.[58] This was not always true. Other women had been permitted to make declarations under section 18A after expressing their intention to leave Australia indefinitely and their desire to have their nationality in order before departing.[59] In Mavis's case, the memo stated that as her 'husband is practically a Chinese official it is suggested that it would be undesirable to grant her a concession which would enable her to

---

55 Ibid.
56 NAA: A435, 1946/4/5946.
57 Ibid.
58 Ibid.
59 See 'Mrs. J. Shashoua – Retention of British Nationality', NAA: A1, 1938/18342.

travel on a British passport'.[60] Although Mavis had planned to travel with her husband, political unrest in China meant that she ended up staying in Australia. In June 1942, following another application under section 18A, the Attorney-General's Department advised that Mavis would be remaining in Australia 'indefinitely' and was teaching at Melbourne Girls Grammar. Her new application was accepted with 'no military objection'.[61]

Mavis's original application was rejected because it was seen as a potential security risk to have an Australian-born, British national so closely connected with Chinese Government officials retain her British nationality rights. As well as being ethnically Chinese, her strong ties with the Chinese Government and obvious respect for, and friendship with, the Chinese people resulted in Mavis being regarded as an 'other' and denied access to Australian rights through section 18A. However, when Mavis was unable to return to China, her application was accepted. It was not until she was permanently settled in Australia, and her affiliation with the Chinese Government weakened, that she was treated as British/Australian again and allowed to retain her rights. This suggests that, once the security objections were resolved, she was no longer regarded as an 'other' against whom Australia needed protective measures, but as a member of the Australian community. That Australia and China were now fighting a common enemy, Japan, also helped her cause, even overcoming perceptions of her 'otherness' due to her ethnicity or race. The rarity of this situation suggests that the government usually regarded Australian women married to aliens as Australian/British and did not consider them to be a credible threat, despite alien registration restrictions. This also explains the government's willingness to allow women to declare under section 18A specifically to circumvent alien registration restrictions.

Women's correspondence with government departments, specifically the Departments of the Interior and Immigration, reveal that some women were not aware that they had lost their nationality until it became incumbent on them to register as aliens. Elizabeth Agnes Coon, née Jeanes, was born in Camperdown, New South Wales, on 17 December 1885. On 12 January 1910 in Sydney, she married James Coon, a Chinese man from Canton. On 24 October 1939, Elizabeth wrote to the Department of the Interior, stating:

---

60   NAA: A435, 1946/4/5946.
61   Ibid.

I was advised to apply to you, as I wish, would be very pleased to resume my former status as A British Subject. I have never been out of N.S. Wales I don't ever intend to, I have always been a good Citizen.[62]

Elizabeth supplied details regarding her parents and her marriage and noted that her husband had been 'resident in N.S. Wales over 50 years never at any time went out of N.S.W'. On 27 October 1939, three days after writing to the department, Elizabeth registered as an alien. In November 1939, when asked why her application under section 18A was made outside the specified 12-month period, she declared:

I did not think there was any occasion to make a Declaration, as I was born in N.S. Wales and not having any intentions to leave Australia. It was owing to the war, when all Aliens were asked to Register, I found out I had to apply to the Minister. During the time when Section 18A came into force I was in very bad health and also had financial worries. If I had known, I would have most decidedly applied before. I am very sorry I was ignorant of the matter.[63]

Elizabeth's reply suggests that re-naturalisation became important to individuals when they needed to access rights or did not want to be burdened by a lack of them. Her letter demonstrates a strong affinity for her Australian/British nationality. Her section 18A declaration was registered on 25 January 1940.[64]

During the war, many women took advantage of section 18A to avoid alien registration requirements. The number of women who made declarations under section 18A after registering as aliens suggests that many women were informed of the provision's existence by police officers when attempting to register. Mary Mon Ping, who married Chou Mon Ping in September 1920 in Canton, applied for a section 18A declaration form in October 1939. She stated:

I was not aware I could have my British nationality returned to me until it was necessary for aliens to register, when I was advised that before doing so, to make an application for the consideration of my case, and if granted, I would then not have to register as an alien.[65]

---

62 'Coon, Elizabeth Agnes – Retention of British Nationality', NAA: B659, 1939/1/14820; 'Elizabeth Agnes COON – Nationality: Chinese – [Australian Born] [Box 36]', NAA: SP11/5.
63 NAA: B659, 1939/1/14820.
64 'Elizabeth Agnes COON – Nationality: Chinese – [Australian Born] [Box 36]', NAA: SP11/5.
65 'Ping, Mary Mon – Retention of British Nationality', NAA: A659, 1939/1/14061.

Mary's application was approved in January 1940. That officials had provided advice on section 18A was frequently mentioned in women's applications, further demonstrating official support for their right to retain their nationality after marriage and the perception that they were still Australian/British, despite their formal legal status.[66]

Not all women mentioned how they became aware of section 18A. Some made a declaration soon after registering as an alien, the short interval suggesting that they became aware of the existence of section 18A when registering. Marjorie Lowe, née Wong, was born in Strathfield, Sydney, on 12 March 1918. She married Wellington (Wing) Hong Lowe in Sydney on 22 August 1942.[67] On 23 September 1942, Marjorie registered as an alien. The following month she declared under section 18A. Her declaration was registered on 9 December 1942. Another woman, Rita Betsy Ping, wrote to the secretary of the Department of Immigration requesting the 'necessary papers to regain [her] British Nationality' on the same day she registered as an alien.[68] Her declaration was registered on 16 May 1946; by 31 May, she had produced her declaration to the local police station to have her alien registration cancelled.

For women married to 'enemy aliens', the effects of marital denaturalisation during wartime could be severe. Some women married to enemy aliens were interned. The *Commonwealth War Book* directed that: 'As a general rule women of whatever nationality will not be interned. When the interests of public safety so demand, they will be kept in custody.'[69] A report for the secretary of the Department of Defence Co-ordination on 8 August 1940 asserted that: 'It is not anticipated that large numbers will be affected [detained], as women are not generally so involved in organising activities inimical to the Empire as men of enemy nationality.'[70] Although internment was relatively uncommon, women married to enemy aliens still faced more restrictions than women married to 'friendly aliens'.

66 See 'Wong Young Tai, D – Retention of British Nationality', NAA: A659, 1939/1/13646.
67 'Marjorie LOWE – Nationality: Chinese – [Australian Born] [Box 115]', NAA: SP11/5; 'Lowe, Marjorie [Chinese by marriage – born in Australia] [Box 595]', NAA: C123, 20900.
68 'Rita Betsy PING – Nationality: Chinese – [Australian Born] [Box 150]', NAA: SP11/5; 'PING Rita Betsy – Declaration under Section 18A of the Nationality Act 1920–1936 – born 9 December 1924 – British', NAA: A435, 1945/4/5899.
69 NAA: A816, 54/301/3; Irving, *A Gendered History*, 124.
70 Ibid.

Ada Shibuya's file in the National Archives of Australia provides insight into what life was like for some maritally denaturalised women married to enemy aliens. Ada was born on 15 July 1896 in Cobram, Victoria. In 1919, she travelled to Japan where she married Haruka Shibuya. The couple had two children, Joseph and Hannah, before Haruka's death in 1922. Following her husband's death, Ada returned to Victoria. In 1926, she moved to Sydney where she married Sakuhei Suzuki, a Japanese man who was a long-term resident in Australia, and together they had three more children. After her second marriage, her two eldest children also went by the name Suzuki.[71]

On 8 December 1941, the day after Pearl Harbor was attacked, Sakuhei Suzuki, who had been resident in Australia for 42 years, was interned at Liverpool Internment Camp, New South Wales. Ada had registered as an alien on 16 September 1939 when the war with Germany began. With Japan's entry into the conflict, she became the wife of an 'enemy alien' and was treated with suspicion by officials. Despite this, she regarded herself as a loyal Australian woman. Sakuhei was transferred to No. 6 (Hay) Internment Camp, New South Wales, on 19 December 1941. He was moved to several other internment camps before being released on 10 September 1946. Ada's children by her first marriage, Joseph and Hannah, having been born in Japan, were legally Japanese, and were also interned as 'enemy aliens' at No. 6 Internment Camp. Hannah was released on 22 May 1942. In early 1942, Ada applied to regain her British nationality under section 18(6) of the Nationality Act, which allowed wives of enemy aliens to apply to resume their British nationality. Following security checks, Ada's application was accepted on 3 October 1942. She was granted a certificate of naturalisation, making her once again a British subject under the law.[72] The existence of section 18(6) indicates that Australian politicians viewed Australian-born women married to enemy aliens as 'Australian'. Section 18(6) enabled such women to regain their nationality, thereby avoiding the most severe effects of being an enemy alien.

However, even after Ada was naturalised, her request for a wireless licence was viewed with suspicion. On her alien registration questionnaire in 1939, she noted that she had given her wireless to a friend. However, when her husband was interned in December 1941, a wireless set was listed among his possessions. A letter from Sakuhei to Ada in March 1942 made reference to Ada attempting to sell a motorcycle, wireless and telephone. In October

---

71   'Shibuya, Ada May – aka Suzuki, Ada May; Quinn, Ada May', NAA: A11797, WP8670.
72   Ibid.

1942, Ada applied for a Broadcast Listener's Licence. In December that year, the deputy director of security for New South Wales wrote to the director-general of security in Canberra arguing that:

> Even though Ada May Shibuya is a British Subject, in view of her background, and the possible effect it would have on local residents, it is considered desirable to ensure that wireless receiver could not be used on the premises occupied by her and her children.[73]

Although there was no record of Ada having participated in subversive activity, her application was deemed undesirable. It was claimed that her husband still lived with her and that he was a 'dominating force'. However, as Sakuhei was then interned, the director-general of security rejected these claims, declaring that 'it would be unnecessarily harsh to prohibit [Ada] from having a wireless of any sort'. He suggested restricting her wireless access to medium band reception with checks conducted 'from time to time' to ensure her compliance.[74]

Ada was advised accordingly. The deputy director of security's reluctance to provide Ada with a wireless licence demonstrates that some level of suspicion of Australian-born wives of enemy aliens continued even after they had regained their nationality. In this case, the concern was that Ada's enemy alien husband would gain control of the wireless and/or persuade Ada to act in a disloyal manner. However, this suspicion was mitigated by Ada's British status and upbringing – and Sakuhei's absence in an internment camp – and she was allowed a wireless with some restrictions.

In her letters to the government and her family, Ada displayed anti-Japanese sentiments that officials considered 'somewhat unusual from the wife of a Japanese man'. She considered herself Australian and showed no affinity for Japanese people. She expressed frustration that her children had been interned when 'full-blooded Japanese' people had not been. In a letter addressed to her son Joseph on 8 May 1942, she stated:

> Hannah was telling me that old Japanese woman Mrs Yeghel had been discharged 9 days ago, and as she went into camp the day after Hannah it is only natural Hannah would feel hurt. I don't know who gave the camp permission to discharge Mrs Yeghel. What I can't understand is Mrs. Yeghel's son, he is a full blooded Japanese born

---

73   Ibid.
74   Ibid.

in Australia, and [he] escapes the Military call up, and goes about at liberty, while the Australian born Japanese with Australian Mothers, are all interned.[75]

Evidently, Ada considered herself to be Australian and not Japanese.

During the war, at a time of heightened patriotic feelings, women's applications were explicit in their love for Australia and Britain. Dorothy Wong Yong Tai (discussed later) declared: 'I have been deprived of all the rights of British citizenship since my marriage'.[76] She 'sincerely beg[ged]' for the retention of her nationality, which was clearly important to her. Lilian Hock Hing, née Gray, was born on 23 May 1892 in Pyrmont, Sydney. On 7 February 1916, she married Louie Hock Hing, a Chinese man, in Sydney.[77] On 16 September 1939, Lilian reported to a Sydney police station to register as an alien and, while there, heard about section 18A. Three days later, she applied to make a declaration under the section, writing directly to Prime Minister Robert Menzies. Noting her Australian birth and that both her parents were British subjects, her father having been born in England and her mother in New South Wales, she stated:

> I only married my husband for my children. I was one of those women who had to get a name for my children. I am not happy and have not spoken to my husband for three years.

Lilian declared her love for Australia:

> My three sons are willing and will fight for Australia and so will I if that time comes. I do not suppose I would do anything to my country – I love Australia.[78]

In Lilian's mind, her connection to Australia had never been forfeited. Even though she had been denied her nationality, she, and many others like her, still felt Australian.

During WWII, alien registration made some women feel they were being treated like criminals for the mere act of marrying a foreigner. Lilian's application to Prime Minister Menzies demonstrates how humiliating, upsetting and difficult alien registration could be for Australian-born,

75 Ibid.
76 NAA: A659, 1939/1/13646.
77 'Hock King [nee Gray], Lilian (Chinese [by marriage – born in Australia]) [Box 451]', NAA: C123, 14749.
78 Ibid.

maritally denaturalised women. In desperation, Lilian asked the prime minister: 'Do you think you could do something to help me out of this so I can get back my nationality. I have been trying for a long time with the wrong people.' She continued:

> I am counted as an Alien. I do not mind that so much but when it comes to those fingerprints and photos I nearly broke my heart. I have never been in a Police Court for that in my life. Now I am made a criminal, my photo in a Police Station.[79]

Clearly, alien registration could be very distressing for Australian-born women. It could also be humiliating, as Rose Inagaki explained in a letter to the Department of Defence:

> If necessary of course I will fill in the papers, but both my husband and myself feel keenly loyal to the Allied Cause, feel keenly the humiliation of having to furnish a description of ourselves, in the same manner demanded of enemy residents and criminals.[80]

Lilian's and Rose's letters suggest that alien registration was upsetting and offensive to maritally denaturalised women because it treated them like criminals, rather than as Australian women who had married foreigners.

In relation to Lilian's case, a letter from Inspector D. R. B. Mitchell to Victoria Barracks on 10 October 1939 asserted that:

> the requiring of photos and the taking of prints under clause 8 of Statutory Rule No. 88 of 1939 is discretionary, and perhaps discretion could have been exercised in regard to people who were born British and lost nationality through marriage. I have had a few bitter complaints of the nature of that made by Mrs. Hing.[81]

Mitchell's suggestion that discretion be used in the taking of photographs and prints shows that Australian officials did not want to unduly distress maritally denaturalised women by insisting that they complete registrations in the same manner as other legal aliens. It demonstrates that the government and officials regarded these women differently to other aliens and criminals. Indeed, they were rarely viewed as a threat. There is no record

79 Ibid.
80 'Rose C. Inagaki', NAA: MP16/1, 1916/1378; 'INAGAKI Rose: Nationality – Australian [Japanese]: Date of Birth – 27 April 1881: Date of Arrival – Born in Victoria: First Registered at Caulfield – Victoria', NAA: MT269/1.
81 NAA: C123, 14749.

of further correspondence between Lilian and the Prime Minister's Office. However, it appears she made a declaration under section 18A following her initial presentation at the police station. On 28 November 1939, Lilian's declaration was approved.

Alien registration sometimes served as the means by which Australian maritally denaturalised women discovered they had lost their nationality. This ignorance of their legal status speaks to the nature of nationality at the time and suggests that, while some Australian women married to aliens utilised the rights of their British nationality, or at least attempted to do so before becoming aware of their altered nationality status, others lacked either the means or the desire to access such rights. Further, their apparent ignorance of their changed status indicates that, even though women married to aliens legally lost their nationality, they still considered themselves – and were considered by most others – as very much Australian.

Conclusion

Marital denaturalisation, as federally legislated from 1920 to 1949, could have significant negative consequences for Australian women married to aliens. The correspondence of such women with government officials suggests that, even though they had become legal aliens, they still considered themselves to be Australian. The emotion that such women expressed in response to the loss of their nationality and the requirement to register as aliens shows that this was keenly felt. The fact that many Australian women married to aliens did not realise they had lost their nationality demonstrates that they felt themselves to be British/Australian. The need to register as aliens during WWII, a period of heightened patriotism when the loss of nationality deprived women of tangible rights and privileges, made the loss of nationality more obvious, problematic and emotionally distressing for women.

Australian politicians' support for repealing dependent nationality, and for other legislative changes where practicable, demonstrates that women married to aliens (especially white women) were not regarded as 'others'. The existence of sections 18(2), 18A and 18B of the Nationality Act, and the willingness to give women the tools to avoid alien registration, can also been seen as evidence that Australian politicians were in favour of restoring women's independent nationality and did not regard (white) women married to aliens as undeserving of their British nationality. The discussion of married women's nationality in the popular press demonstrates that there was widespread support for maritally denaturalised women and suggests that many Australians, even those unaffected by marital denaturalisation, considered such women to be Australian, despite their altered legal position. Although they were legally 'other', in politics, society and their own minds, by virtue of their Australian birth and assumed shared values and culture, maritally denaturalised women were still regarded as Australian/British.

6

'Our Natives Have No Constitutional Right to Equal Privileges with White People' Western Australia's *Natives (Citizenship Rights) Act 1944*

Peter Prince

Note of warning

This chapter references deceased Aboriginal people, their words, names and images. Although all such words and images are already in the public domain, individuals and communities should be warned that they may read or see things in this chapter that could cause distress. In addition, some statements by white officials, politicians and newspapers that are recognised as racially offensive today are quoted to illustrate the thinking at the time. These quotations include derogatory terms such as 'native', 'full-blood' and 'half-caste', which were part of the colonial language of subjugation. As Bruce Buchan observes, 'the ongoing struggle of Indigenous peoples … has been one fought *as much against the language* as against the institutions of colonization'.[1]

---

1   Bruce Buchan, *Empire of Political Thought: Indigenous Australians and the Language of Colonial Government* (London: Pickering and Chatto, 2008), 2–3. Original emphasis.

Figure 6.1: Sally Morgan, *Citizenship*, 1988.

Source: © Sally Morgan/Copyright Agency, 2022/Copyright Agency, 2023. Powerhouse collection. Purchased 1989. Photograph: Marinco Kojdanovski.

Introduction

Sally Morgan's painting (Figure 6.1) mocks Western Australia's *Natives (Citizenship Rights) Act 1944*, showing that Aboriginal Australians derided their 'certificate of citizenship' as a derogatory 'dog licence'. In 2002, Wongutha man Leo Thomas told the Federal Court:

> When I was about 21 years old … [the] football team would go drinking, but if I was caught getting a beer at a hotel my mate would be fined … The President of the football club asked for me one day they said that we have to go to court … so they ended up giving me the citizenship rights … a little black book … *the dog collar, I used to call it* … Getting citizenship rights meant that you were no longer dealt with as an Aborigine under the Act.[2]

As Western Australia's solicitor-general told the commissioner of native affairs in 1951, unlike the United States, 'our natives have no constitutional right to equal privileges with white people'.[3] This included the 'privilege' of legal belonging and Australian citizenship itself.[4] Until 1971, Western Australia forced Aboriginal Australians to 'dissolve tribal and native associations' and display 'the manner and habits of civilised life' for two years before they could apply for the 'privilege of citizenship' to escape apartheid-type restrictions under state law.

This chapter uses personal stories to argue that the history of the Natives (Citizenship Rights) Act was largely one of disrespect for the rule of law. Those administering the Act showed little regard for the proper legal status of Aboriginal people or for the actual requirements of the legislation itself. Disdain for the law was accompanied by humiliation of First Nations peoples. Applicants suffered intrusive medical examinations, personal inspection of their homes, had to separate from traditional clan groups and were treated like accused criminals by magistrates hearing their applications. Worst of all, if successful, they were deemed 'no longer a native or aborigine' for the purpose of state law.

---

2   *Harrington-Smith v. Western Australia* (No. 9) [2007] FCA 31, Annexure F [5966]. Emphasis added.
3   State Records Office of Western Australia (hereafter SRWA): S2030 Cons1733, 1263/45, folio 48.
4   At least until the High Court's decision in *Love & Thoms* (2020) 397 ALR 597, 94 ALJR 198, which held that First Nations peoples could not be 'aliens' or treated as not 'belonging' under the Australian Constitution.

There has been passing reference to the Natives (Citizenship Rights) Act in other works.[5] In 1973, Peter Biskup wrote that the 1944 Act 'was one of the strangest enactments ... lifted almost verbatim from U.S. legislation promulgated in 1886 relating to American Indians ... and repealed by Congress a decade earlier'.[6] Tamara Hunter, in 2001, noted that, under the Commonwealth *Nationality and Citizenship Act 1948*, Aboriginal people in Western Australia 'were declared subjects of Her Majesty and considered to be Australian citizens'. However, 'being citizens of the Commonwealth did not mean that they were full citizens in their own state'.[7] Both Biskup and Hunter relied heavily on evidence to the 1961 federal parliamentary inquiry into 'Voting Rights of Aborigines'.[8] This chapter adds more detailed analysis, using files from the State Records Office of Western Australia, including correspondence between ministers and senior bureaucrats, as well as publicly available court records about individual 'citizenship' applications.

The 'Citizenship' Lie

There is a reason why most references to 'citizenship' in this chapter are in quotation marks. An obvious point, but one ignored in Western Australia, is that, from the time of Federation in 1901, nationality and 'Australian citizenship' were matters of federal not state law.

---

5   Richard Broome, *Aboriginal Australians*, 5th ed. (Crows Nest, NSW: Allen & Unwin, 2019), 209–10; Brian Galligan and John Chesterman, 'Citizenship and Its Denial in Our Federal State', in *Citizenship in Australia: Democracy, Law and Society*, ed. S. Rufus Davis (Carlton, Vic: Constitutional Centenary Foundation, 1996), 171, 183–86; John Chesterman and Brian Galligan, *Citizens without Rights: Aborigines and Australian Citizenship* (Cambridge: Cambridge University Press, 1997), 132–33, 165–69, doi.org/10.1017/CBO9780511518249; John Chesterman and Brian Galligan, eds, *Defining Australian Citizenship – Selected Documents* (Carlton, Vic: Melbourne University Press, 1999), 32–33; J. C. McCorquodale, *Aborigines and the Law: A Digest* (Canberra: Aboriginal Studies Press, 1987), 98–101; Garth Nettheim and Larissa Behrendt, 'Aborigines and Torres Strait Islanders, Constitutional Status, Citizenship and Electoral Rights', as at 1 January 2010, *Laws of Australia*, online resource (Pyrmont, NSW: Lawbook Co); Kim Rubenstein, *Australian Citizenship Law*, 2nd ed. (Pyrmont, NSW: Thomson Reuters, 2017), 64; Christine Choo, 'A Challenge to Human Rights: Aboriginal Women in the West Kimberley', *Studies in Western Australian History* 19 (1999): 48, 55.
6   Peter Biskup, *Not Slaves Not Citizens. The Aboriginal Problem in Western Australia* (St. Lucia, Qld: University of Queensland Press, 1973), 207–8.
7   Tamara Hunter, 'The Myth of Equality: The Denial of Citizenship Rights for Aboriginal People in Western Australia', *Studies in Western Australian History* 22 (2001): 69. See also Tamara Hunter and Tony Ozies, 'Just an Ordinary Thing': Tony Ozies' Application for an Aboriginal Citizenship Certificate', *Studies in Western Australian History* 22 (2001): 63.
8   Commonwealth of Australia, *Report of Select Committee on Voting Rights of Aborigines* (Canberra: Parliament House, 1961).

In 1961, World War II (WWII) soldier and long-term Aboriginal activist George Abdullah[9] wrote to the *West Australian* demanding that Aboriginal people be given the 'rights of citizenship' to which their legal citizenship status entitled them. Abdullah had a better understanding of nationality and citizenship law in Australia than state government ministers and officials. He wrote:

> *The Australian aboriginal is a natural-born citizen* … The aboriginal people will not be satisfied with any half-hearted measure. We are demanding freedom from restrictive legislation, with equal rights and opportunities as our white brothers and sisters, and then we can join them in developing a greater Australia.[10]

The following year, Abdullah called for a 'more militant native approach to citizenship problems', observing that:

> Every native child born in Australia was hamstrung from birth because he was not free. *Full Australian citizenship was the natives' birthright*, but even the most degraded white Australian had more rights than the native. To deprive a person of civil rights was to destroy his self-esteem and his incentive to become a responsible citizen.[11]

Under the law imposed from 1788 with European settlement, First Nations peoples always had full legal membership status, first as 'British subjects', then, from 1949, also as 'Australian citizens'. As the High Court of Australia noted in 2020:

> two distinct rules of the common law operated in temporal sequence to confer the status of a British subject on the indigenous inhabitants of Australia. The first, applicable at the time of acquisition of sovereignty over territory, was that by which *every inhabitant of that territory alive at that time immediately became a British subject*. The second … was that by which *every person born within that territory became a British subject from birth* simply by reason of their place of birth … *neither drew any distinction based on race or indigeneity*.[12]

---

9   Yasmin Jill Abdullah, 'Abdullah, George Cyril (1919–1984)', *Australian Dictionary of Biography*, National Dictionary of Biography, 2007, adb.anu.edu.au/biography/abdullah-george-cyril-12117.

10   *West Australian*, 13 September 1961, SRWA: S2030 Cons 993 1961-0854, folio 117. Emphasis added.

11   *West Australian*, 17 September 1962, SRWA: S2030 Cons 993 1961-0854, folio 117, item 77. Emphasis added.

12   *Love & Thoms* (2020) 94 ALJR 198 [104] (Justice Gageler). Emphasis added.

The Commonwealth *Nationality Act 1920* confirmed the principle of 'birthright nationality' under which Aboriginal and Torres Strait Islander people became 'natural-born' British subjects from the moment of birth. Under the Nationality and Citizenship Act 1948, all British subjects in Australia, including all Indigenous people, received the new status of 'Australian citizen', while retaining their subject status.

Dating back to early colonial times, however, Anglo-Celtic institutions in Australia repeatedly denied First Nations people equal membership status under the law.[13] In Western Australia, this extended into the 1970s. Government ministers and bureaucrats peddled the lie that Aboriginal people had to apply under the Natives (Citizenship Rights) Act to become 'Australian citizens'. In doing so, they were responsible for promoting the wilful confusion between 'citizenship' as a 'bundle of rights' and 'citizenship' as formal legal membership status. As the minister for the north-west, A. M. Coverley, stated in September 1944 when introducing the Natives (Citizenship Rights) Bill to parliament:

> This Bill while being quite a small one, is in my opinion, very important. It consists mainly of one principle, contained in one clause ... The main principle underlying the Bill is to provide an opportunity for adult natives to apply for *full citizenship as Australians.*[14]

Mr Graham from East Perth supported the legislation but said successful applicants should not be in danger of having their 'Australian citizenship' suspended or stripped:

> when natives have made application to a magistrate and been accepted, they should be *Australian citizens* in fact ... [There] should be no discrimination against those who, though previously natives, have been *accepted as Australian citizens* ... Either a person is or is not a *citizen of this country*; that is how I view the position.[15]

State government files show wilful confusion on the part of government officials between the 'rights of citizenship' and citizenship as legal status. Reviewing the operation of the Natives (Citizenship Rights) Act in 1950,

---

13   Peter Prince, 'Aliens in Their Own Land. "Alien" and the Rule of Law in Colonial and Post-Federation Australia' (PhD thesis, The Australian National University, 2015), ch. 1, openresearch-repository.anu.edu.au/handle/1885/101778.

14   Western Australia, *Parliamentary Debates*, Legislative Assembly, 28 September 1944, 825. Emphasis added.

15   Ibid., 5 October 1944, 970. Emphasis added.

District Officer Anderson from the Department of Native Affairs admitted his ignorance of Australia's nationality law. He had heard of the federal Nationality and Citizenship Act but was unfamiliar with its contents, fearing it meant 'citizenship' given to Aboriginal people in Western Australia could not be taken away:

> About a year ago some legislation was passed by the Commonwealth Government declaring all residents within the Commonwealth to be citizens of Australia. *I am not versed with this bit of legislation* but I fear that it means that if a native becomes a citizen he cannot lose those rights.[16]

Applicants themselves (at least according to records made by court clerks) appeared to believe they would be getting formal citizenship. Court files list their applications for 'citizenship' or 'native citizenship'.[17] In 1948, Eva Bickley, aged 47, told Magistrate Taylor in Derby: 'I require citizenship as I live a civilised life and I think I am entitled to the privileges of the Act.'[18] In 1949, Agnes Molloy, aged 21, a worker at the Derby Hospital, said: 'I require my citizenship in order that I may live and have the privileges of white person.'[19] In 1955, Jack Shandley, head stockman at Gogo Station near Fitzroy Crossing, travelled 300 kilometres to the Derby court declaring he wanted 'to be Australian and be free to travel'. His application was refused, with no reason given.[20] Some magistrates hearing these matters called themselves 'Courts of Citizenship',[21] recording the outcome as 'Citizenship granted'.[22]

As Chapter 1 discussed, the word 'citizenship', like other terms of identity and belonging, has more than one meaning. In a non-legal sense, it means, essentially, freedom to participate in the political and social community. After Federation, regulation of the lives of First Nations peoples in Australia and control of their 'citizenship' in this non-legal sense remained with the

---

16   SRWA: S2030 Cons993 1944/0463, folio 52. Emphasis added.
17   SRWA: S1629 Cons1404, folios 78, 85, 88, 97, 105–8, 110 ff.
18   SRWA: S1103 Cons 4706 1, folio 33.
19   Ibid., folios 36–37.
20   Ibid., folios 60–61. Mr Shandley was forced to re-apply a year later. Along with his wife Rita and three children he was then granted a certificate of citizenship with the support of a local Citizenship Board member, Mr Rowell. Ibid., folio 69. Western Australia, *Gazette*, 11 January 1957, 29.
21   SRWA: S1103 Cons 4706 1, folios 88 (Margaret Albert), 89 (Gladys Edgar).
22   SRWA: S1629 Cons1404, folios 70–72 (Sylvia Newman, Millicent Daisy Bell Smythe, Josephine Pandi, Millie Long, William Albert Cooper).

states.[23] In 1962, Shirley Andrews, campaign organiser for the Federal Council for Aboriginal Advancement, summarised the legal restrictions on First Nations peoples across Australia. All mainland states, including Western Australia, expressly restricted the political and social freedom of Aboriginal Australians.[24] But Western Australia was the only state to add 'citizenship' legislation on top of this.

In 1942, future federal minister for territories and later governor-general, Paul Hasluck – born in Western Australia and with a strong interest in Aboriginal affairs in his home state – detailed the extensive control over people categorised as 'natives' under Western Australia's *Native Administration Act 1936*,[25] including those described by the derogatory term 'half-caste':

> By the 1936 Act no native parent or other relative living has the guardianship of an aboriginal or half-caste child … no native … can move from one place to another without the permission of a protector and the giving of sureties … Natives may be ordered into reserves or institutions and confined there … the property of any native may be taken over by consent or if it is considered necessary to do so to provide for its due preservation … Natives may be ordered out of town or from prohibited areas … Subject to the right of appeal, the Commissioner of Native Affairs may object to the marriage of any native.[26]

As Hasluck pointed out, in the period before the introduction of the Natives (Citizenship Rights) Act:

> The native's only escape … is through a certificate of exemption from the [Native Administration] Act granted by the Commissioner and experience does not indicate that the procedure is as satisfactory as it might be.[27]

---

23 Until section 51(xxvi) of the Australian Constitution (the notorious 'races power') was amended in 1967 to allow federal parliament to legislate for Aboriginal Australians.
24 Shirley Andrews, 'The Australian Aborigines: A Summary of Their Situation in All States in 1962', accessed 11 August 2022, www.nma.gov.au/__data/assets/pdf_file/0005/697091/australian-aborigines. pdf. Hard copy reference: State Library of Victoria, Council for Aboriginal Rights (Vic.) Papers, MS 12913, Box 3/4.
25 The *Native Administration Act* became the *Native Welfare Act* in 1954.
26 Paul Hasluck, *Black Australians: A Survey of Native Policy in Western Australia, 1829–1897* (Melbourne: Melbourne University Press, 1942), 160–61.
27 Ibid., 161.

The Department of Native Affairs admitted that 'natives ... have been refused exemptions on the flimsiest of grounds'.[28] Moreover, an exemption under the Native Administration Act offered only partial escape from draconian state control. As Chief Secretary Kitson explained in the Legislative Council:

> An exemption certificate does not relieve them of disabilities and disqualifications imposed on native persons by various Acts, such as the Land Act, the Mining Act, the Electoral Act, the Licensing Act and others. They are still *natives in blood* and this disqualifies them from enjoying any of the rights which a white man has under the Acts I have mentioned.[29]

In contrast, under the *Natives (Citizenship Rights) Act 1944*, which commenced operation in early 1946, a successful applicant was deemed to be no longer 'a native or aborigine' and, therefore (in theory), beyond the reach of state laws controlling Aboriginal people. So it is not surprising that many Aboriginal applicants under this Act used the term 'citizenship' as a synonym for freedom from state control. But they were encouraged by the government to believe the 1944 Act conferred something more – namely, formal 'Australian citizenship', even though they already possessed full membership status under federal law. As the inscription on Sally Morgan's painting (Figure 6.1) states: 'In 1944 Aborigines were allowed to become Australian citizens.' This misrepresentation by state authorities exasperated Aboriginal activists who (like George Abdullah) understood nationality law in Australia better than their white counterparts.

In 1954, Noongar man George Howard, a 33-year-old Department of Native Affairs welfare officer who described himself as 'a Native and ... proud of that fact', addressed a Rotary luncheon at the Savoy Hotel, Perth. His very presence at the event contravened a prohibition on 'natives' entering licensed premises.[30] As Perth's *Daily News* reported, Mr Howard's exemption certificate under the Native Administration Act 'did not bar him from restrictions' under the *Licensing Act* and other legislation. The newspaper pointed out that 'he could get full legal rights by getting a certificate of citizenship'. But, as Mr Howard remarked:

---

28   W. A. Gordon to acting commissioner of native affairs, 11 September 1947, SRWA: S2030 Cons 993 1944/0463, folio 79.
29   Western Australia, *Debates*, Legislative Council, 18 October 1944, 1174. Emphasis added.
30   His entry into the Savoy Hotel, Perth, to speak on Aboriginal rights is listed by the Australian Broadcasting Commission as one of the significant events of the 1950s. See '1950s', ABC Archives and Library Services, [entry 30 April 1954], accessed 21 August 2022, www.abc.net.au/archives/timeline/1950s.htm.

to get this certificate, I must pay fees and undergo personal investigation by a board, *with the end result of being told I am what I am – a natural-born Australian*.[31]

Moreover, he continued:

neither of these two certificates secures me from personal interrogation or investigation. I have to produce them on demand, like a tram ticket, presumably to show that I have paid my way.[32]

In the parliamentary debate on the Natives (Citizenship Rights) Bill in October 1944, Mr Needham from Perth observed that:

The tenor of the debate so far suggests that all members will vote for this measure. All contend that the natives should be granted the status of full citizenship … I am of the opinion that before a measure of this nature was submitted to Parliament some attention should have been given to the education of natives as to what is meant by citizenship.[33]

Given their lack of knowledge about nationality law, it might have been better if members of parliament and state officials had been educated about 'citizenship' in Australia.

What the Legislation said

In force until 1971, the Natives (Citizenship Rights) Act purported to grant 'rights of citizenship' to Indigenous applicants who 'adopted the manner and habits of civilised life'. A successful applicant received 'all the rights, privileges and immunities … of a natural-born or naturalised subject of His Majesty'. The person was given a 'certificate of citizenship' signed by a magistrate that had 'affixed thereto a photographic likeness of the applicant in the manner of a passport'.[34] The certificate granted in 1950 to James Brennan, one of Australia's 'Rats of Tobruk' in WWII,[35] is shown in Figure 6.2.

31 'Native Breaks Law to Talk on Law', *Daily News*, 30 April 1954, SRWA: S76 Cons1910 1964–1910, folios 20–21. Emphasis added.
32 Ibid.
33 Western Australia, *Parliamentary Debates*, Legislative Assembly, 5 October 1944, 971.
34 Section 5(4).
35 Nathan Morris, 'Meet James Brennan, an Aboriginal Stockman Turned Guerrilla Fighter', *ABC News*, 17 October 2016, www.abc.net.au/news/2016-10-17/aboriginal-stockman-turned-guerrilla-fighter/7934792.

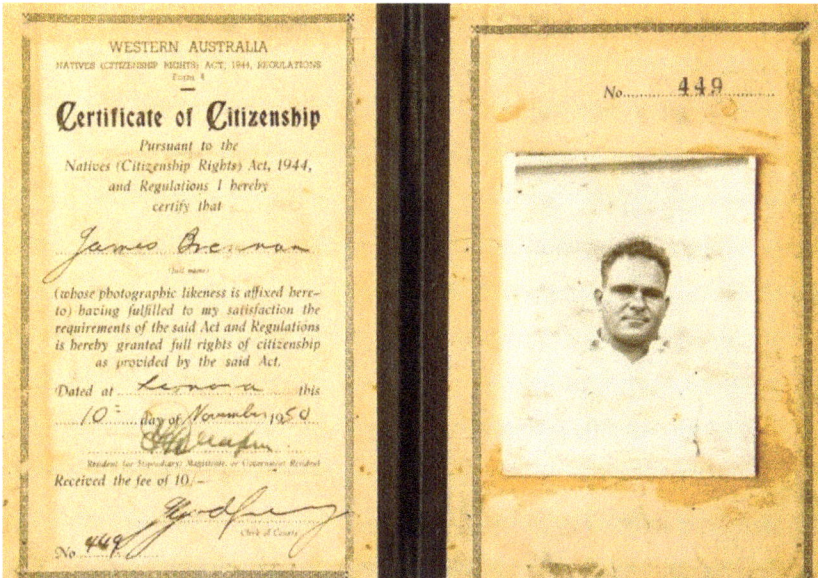

Figure 6.2: Certificate of citizenship issued to James Brennan, 10 November 1950.

Source: Nathan Morris, 'Meet James Brennan, an Aboriginal Stockman Turned Guerrilla Fighter', *ABC News*, 17 October 2016.[36]

Any adult who was 'a native within the meaning of the Native Administration Act'[37] could apply for a citizenship certificate. Written references were required from two 'reputable citizens', together with a signed statutory declaration saying that the applicant had 'dissolved tribal and native association' for the past two years 'except with respect to lineal descendants or native relations of the first degree'. A magistrate had to be satisfied that the person had adopted a 'civilised life', was 'of good behaviour and reputation', 'reasonably capable of managing his own affairs', and that the 'full rights of citizenship' were 'desirable for and likely to be conducive to' his or her welfare.[38] In addition, the applicant had to be 'able to speak and understand the English language' and could not be suffering from 'active

---

36   Ibid.
37   Under the Native Administration Act 1936, a 'native' was defined as 'any person of the full blood' or 'less than full blood' 'descended from the original inhabitants of Australia' not including 'quadroons' (unless a Magistrate decided otherwise) or 'a person of less than quadroon blood'. The 'blood test' remained in use in Western Australia until 1972. John McCorquodale, 'The Legal Classification of Race in Australia', *Aboriginal History* 10 (1986): 7, 13, doi.org/10.22459/AH.10.2011.02.
38   Sections 4 and 5.

leprosy, syphilis, granuloma[39] or yaws'.[40] It was Minister Coverley himself who insisted that these diseases should disqualify Aboriginal people from 'citizenship'.[41]

The grant of a certificate of citizenship was conditional only. A magistrate could suspend or cancel a certificate upon complaint *from any person* if the holder contracted one of the specified diseases, committed even a minor offence or was not adopting a 'civilised' life.[42]

Copying America's 'Black Laws'

In the breakthrough 'Aboriginal belonging' case *Love & Thoms* (2020), the High Court of Australia stated that, after European settlement, First Nations peoples were always regarded as British subjects and part of the Australian political community.[43] Indeed, as Justice Gageler remarked, in Australia it had:

> never been thought necessary to enact legislation along the lines of the *Indian Citizenship Act 1924* (US), specifically conferring the status of subjects or citizens on members of indigenous societies.[44]

Chapter 7 discusses the High Court's idealised version of the history of Indigenous belonging in Australia after 1788 in more detail. For the purpose of this chapter, it must be concluded that, in *Love & Thoms*, the High Court overlooked Western Australia's Natives (Citizenship Rights) Act – even though it remained in operation until the early 1970s, forcing First Nations peoples to apply for 'certificates of citizenship' on their own land. Justice Gageler's remark that it was never thought necessary to copy United States' legislation because Aboriginal Australians were already accepted as subjects or citizens could not have been more misleading. In fact, Western Australia did look to the United States. However, rather than replicate the 1924 federal legislation conferring citizen status on Indian tribes,[45] it adopted nationality laws from an earlier (racist) generation.

---

39 A cluster of inflammation, often in the lungs, as in tuberculosis.
40 A skin disease with swelling and ulcers.
41 Commissioner of native affairs to state crown solicitor, 11 September 1944, SRWA: S2030 Cons993 1944/0463, folio 109.
42 Section 7.
43 *Love & Thoms* (2020) 94 ALJR 198, see e.g. 261 [314] (Justice Gordon); 287 [449] (Justice Edelman).
44 Ibid., 223 [103].
45 Under US law, Indian tribes were treated as independent political powers and until 1924 were not automatically citizens.

In 1943, at the suggestion of State Solicitor-General James Walker,[46] Commissioner of Native Affairs Francis Bray asked the American consul in Perth 'whether the Red Indians [*sic*] of the United States enjoy the ordinary rights of citizenship', explaining that he was considering a proposal for 'certificates of citizenship' to be issued in Western Australia 'to some of our *better types of Australian natives*'.[47] The US consul replied in terms of 'citizenship status', stating that American Indians were recognised as birthright citizens under the *Nationality Act 1940* (US),[48] which confirmed America's 1924 federal legislation. But Commissioner Bray refused to recommend similar recognition for First Nations peoples in Western Australia, despite the birthright nationality and 'citizenship' they were already entitled to under Australian law.

In July 1944, Solicitor-General Walker alerted Minister Coverley to the forthcoming federal '14 powers referendum', which, among other measures, proposed giving the Commonwealth power to make laws about 'aboriginals or natives'. The solicitor-general recommended postponing the Natives (Citizenship Rights) Bill 'until the result of the referendum is known in August', warning the minister about the potential inconsistencies with federal law should the referendum succeed:

> if the Commonwealth Parliament should make laws *with respect to aboriginals*, such laws will automatically supersede State laws relating to aboriginals insofar as the latter are in any respect inconsistent with such Commonwealth laws.[49]

As Charlie Fox notes: 'The referendum failed and so did the Aboriginal clause … [meaning] that power over Aboriginal people remained with the States for a further 23 years.'[50] The solicitor-general did not warn the minister or Commissioner Bray about inconsistencies with the existing Commonwealth nationality law. Despite the Natives (Citizenship Rights) Bill deeming the holder of a certificate of citizenship to have 'all the rights, privileges and immunities … of a natural-born or naturalised subject of His Majesty', the solicitor-general made no mention of federal legislation expressly excluding state law in these areas (see below).

---

46   SRWA: S2030 Cons993 1944/0463, folio 121.
47   Ibid., folio 132. Emphasis added.
48   Ibid., folio 129.
49   Ibid., folio 121. Emphasis added.
50   Charlie Fox, 'The Fourteen Powers Referendum of 1944 and the Federalisation of Aboriginal Affairs', *Aboriginal History* 32 (2008): 27, doi.org/10.22459/ah.32.2011.02.

Instead of adopting the current US legislation recognising the birthright nationality of First Nations peoples, Commissioner Bray copied racially discriminatory provisions on citizenship from the outdated 1918 United States Federal Code (also supplied by the US consul) into Western Australia's 1944 legislation.[51] As Biskup observed, these were 'lifted almost verbatim'.[52] So, at the same time as the United States was going through a fundamental change in relation to who should properly be regarded as legal members of society as part of its leading role in promoting a new world after WWII, it bequeathed a regressive, deeply racist legislative legacy on citizenship to Australia, with strong echoes of the notorious 'Black Laws' from the American South in the 1820s and 1830s.[53]

'Some of Our Better Types of Australian Natives'

In October 1944, Chief Secretary Kitson told the Western Australian Parliament who the 'better types of Australian natives' intended to benefit from the new measure were:

> It is an inspirational measure for *those natives who live under white standards*, and it opens up more clearly the transitional path from native circumstances to white standards for detribalised natives, *particularly the half-caste* who is justly deserving of consideration *since he is no more black than white*.[54]

Forwarding the draft Natives (Citizenship Rights) Bill for Minister Coverley's approval, Commissioner Bray noted:

> an enlightened policy is desirable in respect of those natives who by reason of character, standards of intelligence, and development, are deserving of consideration in connection with the acquisition of citizenship rights, and in my opinion this worthy progressive amelioration of their conditions might be achieved by the issue of certificates of citizenship.[55]

---

51 SRWA: S2030 Cons993 1944/0463, folios 127–29.
52 Biskup, *Not Slaves Not Citizens*.
53 See Martha S. Jones, *Birthright Citizens: A History of Race and Rights in Antebellum America* (Cambridge: Cambridge University Press, 2018).
54 Western Australia, *Debates*, Legislative Council, 18 October 1944, 1176. Emphasis added.
55 Commissioner of native affairs to minister for north-west, 23 May 1944, SRWA: S2030 Cons993 1944/0463, folio 122.

According to political scientist Colin Tatz, A. O. Neville, the notorious chief protector of Aborigines in Western Australia from 1915 to 1940, believed that the government:

> could do nothing for Aborigines, who were dying out, but ... *could absorb the 'half-castes'* ... These were the sort of people who should be elevated 'to our own plane'. In this way, it would be possible to 'eventually forget that there were ever any Aborigines in Australia'.[56]

Tatz argued that 'Neville's legacy – his mishmash of nineteenth-century race theory, twentieth-century eugenics, his own brand of assimilationism, and illogic – [was] to be found in the quite astonishing' Natives (Citizenship Rights) Act.[57] As Kitson stated, 'citizenship' in Western Australia was intended to reward 'detribalised natives', especially 'the half-caste who is ... no more black than white'.

The First Approvals

In January 1946, the first 'certificate of citizenship' was granted in the Geraldton Court of Petty Sessions to Patrick Farrell – a labourer who did tomato gardening work – despite objections from the Department of Native Affairs. The magistrate ruled that evidence that Farrell was an industrious worker with a clean house living 'according to a white man's standard' outweighed his sole conviction for drunkenness.[58]

The next month, Commissioner Bray appeared in person at the Perth Police Court to support the state's second application, this time by 66-year-old Samuel Isaacs. Later, the *Mail* announced: 'For the second time in history, a half-caste aboriginal has been admitted to rights of full citizenship of Australia.'[59] Samuel's father had received the Bronze Medal of the Royal Humane Society for his role in a famous sea rescue in 1876.[60] In addition, four of Samuel's sons had served with the Australian military, including two

---

56   Colin Tatz, *Genocide in Australia*, AIATSIS Research Discussion Papers, no. 8 (Canberra: Aboriginal Studies Press, 1999), 25, aiatsis.gov.au/publication/35772.
57   Ibid.
58   'Citizenship Rights Case in Geraldton. Successful Application', *Geraldton Guardian and Express*, 9 January 1946, 4.
59   'Full Citizen Status to Half-Caste', *Mail*, 23 February 1946, 3.
60   *West Australian*, 23 February 1946, 6.

overseas with the AIF in World War I.[61] Newspaper reports found it 'most fitting' that 'citizenship' had been granted to a member of a family that had served the white establishment so well.

Disregarding Their Own Law

In April 1946 the *Northern Times* announced the first approvals in the north of Western Australia under the Natives (Citizenship Rights) Act:

> *Three new Australian citizens were created* in the Broome Police Court on Monday by Mr M. Harwood, R.M. They were Robert Hunter (28), Mary Bernardine Puertollano and Monica Dolby (25). All were natives within the meaning of the Native Citizenship Rights Act of 1944 … the trio hold certificates of citizenship number four, five and six.[62]

The *Daily News*, in the state capital Perth, reported that the three new certificates of citizenship would 'permit these natives to proceed south of the line' – referring to the 'leper line' that forbade Aboriginal people living above 20 degrees latitude (a little to the north of Port Hedland) travelling south of that boundary.[63] The paper reassured its white readers anxious about 'natives' flooding into the south of the state that 'migration of northern natives to southern areas is not expected. In most instances northern natives have no desire to proceed south of their usual habitat.'[64]

The Broome cases reveal much about the thinking behind the 'citizenship' legislation, the operation of the Act itself and official attitudes to the rule of law. All three applications were opposed by Police Inspector O'Neill on behalf of Commissioner Bray. Bray thought the three Broome applicants were not the 'better type of Australian natives' he intended to reward with

---

61 'Citizen Rights. Award to Half-Caste', *West Australian*, 23 February 1946, 6. Records indicate that a fifth son, Henry Isaacs, enlisted but was discharged on racial grounds, i.e. for 'not being of substantially European origin'. National Archives of Australia (hereafter NAA): B2455, Isaacs Henry. This, in turn, meant his own application in 1946 for a certificate of citizenship was refused because he did not receive an 'honourable discharge' from the military in accordance with section 4(2)(a) of the 1944 Act.

62 'Citizens' Rights Native Applications. Three Granted at Broome', *Northern Times*, 12 April 1946, 15. Emphasis added.

63 Imposed in 1941: see *Native Administration Act Amendment Act 1941* (WA) section 2. For a great account of the leper line and protests against it by Indigenous people, see Anne Scrimgeour, '"Battlin' for Their Rights": Aboriginal Activism and the Leper Line', *Aboriginal History* 36 (2012), 43, doi.org/10.22459/ah.36.2013.03.

64 'Natives Become Citizens', *Daily News*, 10 April 1946, 6.

'citizenship'. He made his 'personal reasons for objection' available to Police Magistrate Harwood before the hearings[65] and was angered when he was ignored. Despite legal advice from the state Crown solicitor supporting Harwood's approvals,[66] Bray complained strongly to Minister Coverley about the decisions.[67]

Inspector O'Neill provided a detailed report on the Broome proceedings. Mary Puertollano's application was heard first.[68] She 'was represented by Bishop Raible and Dr Oldmeadow who were both subject to cross-examination by myself and questioning by the Magistrate, as also was the applicant herself'.[69] Bray complained that Mary had 'not dissolved native association for two years' prior to her application and that 'her misconduct with at least one Asiatic' meant 'the full rights of citizenship were not desirable for and likely to be conducive to the welfare of the applicant'.[70] He claimed that Harwood's approval of Mary's application would cause 'apprehension as to the success of the new law at Broome in view of the sordid reputation of that town as regards association between natives and Asiatics'.[71] However, as Inspector O'Neill reported:

> With regard to association between Asiatics and coloured women, I do not think the Magistrate is impressed by any expression of 'National Policy' unless it is supported by legislation which would enable him to deal with offenders.[72]

In other words, as Magistrate Harwood had noted, there was no provision in the Natives (Citizenship Rights) Act allowing him to take into account prejudice against relationships between Aboriginal women and Asian men in deciding 'citizenship' applications. But Bray waved Harwood's finding

---

65   SRWA: S2030 Cons 1733 1945–1263, folio 96.
66   Ibid., folio 83.
67   Ibid., folio 82.
68   The Puertollanos were a well-established family in the north of Western Australia. Their name appears many times in Broome and Derby 'citizenship' hearings. In 2019, David Puertollano from Broome's Yawuru people attended a ceremony in Germany where remains of more than 40 Indigenous Australians, including seven Yawuru, were handed back to their community. Nick Miller, 'Enslaved, Exported, Then Made into an Artefact, One Young Girl Is Finally Coming Home', *Age*, 16 April 2019, www.theage.com.au/world/europe/enslaved-exported-then-made-into-an-artefact-one-young-girl-is-finally-coming-home-20190416-p51ejh.html.
69   SRWA: S2030 Cons 1733 1945-1263, folio 96.
70   Ibid., folio 86. Emphasis added.
71   Ibid., folio 85. Emphasis added.
72   Ibid., folio 94.

aside, insisting that the Department of Native Affairs interpret the Act's requirement for 'good behaviour and reputation'[73] according to the racial bias of the day:

> the Department will continue to observe the law as it stands and will object on the grounds of ... unfavourable reputations, including association with Asiatics ... If the Magistrate feels that association with coloured persons is not a good reason [for rejecting an application], *even though the Act stipulates that it is* ... then I am unable to do anything about the difficulties in question.[74]

Robert Hunter was also granted a citizenship certificate in Broome that day. His case shows that Bray's refusal to accept the wording of the legislation he helped create was not the only aspect of established law he ignored. Bray objected that Hunter, too, had 'not dissolved native association for two years prior to his application' and was 'not of industrious habits and of good behaviour and reputation'. Two years previously, Hunter had been convicted of 'disorderly conduct' and 'resisting arrest', receiving a caution on both charges.[75] According to O'Neill, Magistrate Harwood 'expressed the opinion that two convictions did not debar a man from Citizenship rights'[76] and that he required actual proof of Hunter's 'bad reputation and behaviour'. Much to the consternation of Commissioner Bray, O'Neill explained that:

> before [Magistrate Harwood] will refuse an application [he] will require definite proof of previous continued misconduct, in this I mean he will be unlikely to accept the opinion of Police Officers or Departmental officers unless the opinions *can be substantiated by actual evidence.*[77]

Bray rejected the need for allegations to be backed by 'actual evidence', declaring:

> it seems to me that Hunter is not a person of good reputation. *This is a question of fact*, and in my opinion it should be accepted in its aspects.[78]

---

73   Section 5(1)(e).
74   SRWA: S2030 Cons 1733 1945–1263, folio 93. Emphasis added.
75   Ibid., folio 86.
76   Ibid., folio 96.
77   Ibid., folio 94. Emphasis added.
78   Ibid., folio 92. Emphasis added.

As this shows, Bray thought it was his prerogative to determine the 'better types of natives' deserving 'citizenship', and he demanded that his view of a person's character and reputation be accepted by magistrates regardless of evidence.

In the case of Monica Dolby, Inspector O'Neill said there was 'no suggestion of any previous misconduct', but Bray opposed her application anyway – again because she had 'not dissolved native association for two years' and the 'full rights of citizenship' were 'not desirable for and likely to be conducive to' her welfare.[79]

As the Broome hearings demonstrate, a failure to 'dissolve tribal and native association' was a major ground for opposing applications for 'citizenship'. Yet this was not consistent with the wording of the Natives (Citizenship Rights) Act. As Bray admitted to Minister Coverley, while applicants had to sign a statutory declaration saying they had dissolved 'native associations', this was not one of the criteria in the Act for granting a certificate of citizenship:

> Section 4 provides that an applicant must have dissolved native associations for two years before applying. In the issue of a Certificate, however, the Magistrate only has to be satisfied as regards the stipulations in section 5. These stipulations *do not mention the question of association with natives.*[80]

As Magistrate Harwood understood, this enabled a commonsense approach. Inspector O'Neill reported that:

> [The Magistrate] holds the view that the average half-caste or coloured person is not accepted by white persons in the North therefore they cannot do other than associate with persons of the same colour as themselves therefore it is impossible that they could avoid association with natives in law.[81]

The Crown solicitor told Bray that Harwood acted within his jurisdiction under the Act by overruling 'evidence of previous association with natives' and 'there is therefore no ground for reviewing his decision … There is no other way of attacking his decision through the court.'[82] But the commissioner ignored this formal advice from Western Australia's highest-ranked government lawyer. As Bray told the minister:

---

79 Ibid., folio 96.
80 Ibid., folio 82. Emphasis added.
81 Ibid., folio 94.
82 Ibid., folios 83, 86.

It was never intended that an associate of natives should be eligible for a Certificate. This is the view held by the Magistrates, except Mr Harwood ... The question of non-eligibility on the ground of association with natives is an important aspect. It is as much an important consideration as the requirement that the applicant must be a native.[83]

Contrary to the Crown solicitor's legal advice, and at Bray's urging, the Department of Native Affairs continued to oppose applications for 'citizenship' on this basis.[84] Moreover, as Bray indicated, other magistrates did not follow Mr Harwood's example:

Mr Ansell, the Magistrate at Geraldton ... refused to grant an application by a man named Harris at Mullewa recently on the grounds that he associated with natives. This decision was of interest, since it was in direct contradiction to the decision of Mr. Harwood in the three cases he dealt with at Broome.[85]

Rewarding Aboriginal people who 'dissolved native associations' (i.e. abandoned their own communities) to live 'according to white standards' was fundamental to the national policy of 'assimilation'. As Hasluck said when federal minister for territories in 1951, 'it is expected that in the course of time all persons of aboriginal blood or mixed blood in Australia will live like White Australians'.[86] In Western Australia, according to Biskup:

The heyday of this policy was the twenties and thirties, but as late as 1944 the Natives (Citizenship Rights) Act required that a candidate for citizenship rights should have dissolved all 'tribal and native' associations ... and even four years later the Bateman Report saw the splitting of generations as the only solution to the aboriginal problem.[87]

---

83 Ibid., folio 82.
84 See e.g. SRWA: S1629 Cons 1404-1, folios 34 (Herbert Binder, 31 July 1946); 41 (Jack Hume October 1946); 49 (Raymond Smith, 19 November 1947); acting commissioner native affairs to Mr T. Ansell, magistrate, Geraldton, 14 January 1948 (re Robert Drayton), SRWA: S2030 Cons 1733 1945–1263, folios 74–5.
85 SRWA: S2030 Cons 1733 1945–1263, folio 85.
86 Commonwealth of Australia, *Native Welfare, Meeting of Commonwealth and State Ministers held at Canberra*, 3–4 September 1951 (Canberra: Commonwealth Government Printer, 1951).
87 Biskup, *Not Slaves Not Citizens*, 264.

The 1946 Broome hearings show the scant respect of Commissioner Bray and his officials for the 'rule of law' even in the 'formal' or 'thin' sense of that concept.[88] Bray and the Department of Native Affairs thumbed their noses at established law, denying the need for evidence to support allegations of bad reputation and insisting that not associating with either 'natives' or 'coloured persons' was a prerequisite for 'citizenship', despite the absence of any such requirement in the Natives (Citizenship Rights) Act itself.

Besides a failure to adhere to the provisions of the legislation or to basic principles of common law, there were also broader questions about the legality of the Natives (Citizenship Rights) Act.

Contrary to the Constitution

In 1951, Bray's replacement as commissioner of native affairs, Stanley Middleton, notified his department of six new 'certificates of citizenship' granted in various towns in Western Australia:

> Accordingly the said Regina Manado, Charles Olocko Councillor, Ivan Williams, Margaret Shiosaki, Gloria Mary Fogarty, and Rosie Gilligan are deemed to be no longer natives or aborigines, and *shall have all the rights, privileges and immunities and shall be subject to the duties and liabilities of natural-born or naturalised subjects of His Majesty* unless and until the certificates are cancelled.[89]

Yet, after Federation, Western Australia had no power to grant either British subject status or legal citizenship. At the time the Natives (Citizenship Rights Act) came into force in 1944, the Commonwealth Nationality Act operated to nullify any conferral of British subject status ('naturalisation') under state law:

> The right to issue certificates of naturalization in the Commonwealth shall be exclusively vested in the Government of the Commonwealth, and no certificate of naturalization or letters of naturalization issued … under any State Act shall be of any effect.[90]

---

88 Denise Meyerson explains the contest between a 'formal' or 'thin' conception of the rule of law, 'which places no constraints on the content of law and is therefore compatible with great iniquity in the law', and, conversely, a 'substantive conception' that also involves 'moral constraints on the exercise of state power'. Denise Meyerson, 'The Rule of Law and the Separation of Powers', *Macquarie Law Journal* 4 (2004): 1, 2.
89 SRWA: Item 1948/1149 AU, WA S268 cons 1003, folios 117–18. Emphasis added.
90 Section 33.

In the same way, from 1949, the federal Nationality and Citizenship Act invalidated any conferral under state legislation of either British subject status or Australian citizenship:

> The provisions of this Act shall apply to the exclusion of any provisions, providing for British nationality or Australian citizenship, of any law of a State, whether the law was passed or made before or after the commencement of this section.[91]

In *Australian Citizenship Law* (2017), Kim Rubenstein argues that the Natives (Citizenship Rights) Act 'was inconsistent with the Commonwealth legislation and, therefore, unconstitutional by virtue of s 109 of the *Constitution*'.[92] Similarly, Garth Nettheim and Larissa Behrendt in *Laws of Australia* (2010) argue that the Western Australian law 'throughout its life was inconsistent with the Commonwealth legislation'[93] and was, therefore, unlawful.

'Freedom ... for the Children's Sake'

Obtaining 'citizenship' in the sense of freedom from government control was the main motivation for applications under the Natives (Citizenship Rights) Act. Applicants were lured by the prospect of freedom from laws controlling where they could live and work, banning them from voting or buying alcohol, and even restricting who they could marry. In 1947, Rita Bargas told Magistrate Harwood in Derby that she wanted a certificate of citizenship 'to enable me to live as a free citizen'.[94] Petronella Puertollano said she sought a certificate 'to get away from control by Native Affairs'.[95] Dorothy Roberts stated: 'I desire certificate in order to improve my position and live as white people and to be out of native control' (i.e. beyond the restrictions over 'natives').[96] In 1948, David Bickley told Acting Magistrate Hogg in Derby: 'I am applying for citizenship rights for the reason that I wish to be free from the Native Affairs Department.'[97] Twenty-seven-year-old Catherine Frazer Rodriguez – married to a Spanish national working as

---

91 Section 52.
92 Rubenstein, *Australian Citizenship Law*, 64, fn 9.
93 Nettheim and Behrendt, 'Aborigines and Torres Strait Islanders'.
94 SRWA: S1103 Cons4706 1, folio 19.
95 Ibid., folio 18.
96 Ibid., folio 27.
97 Ibid., folio 31.

a carpenter across the north – told Magistrate Taylor: 'I require citizenship because my husband does not come within the Act and I desire to move freely wherever he does.'[98]

Apart from their own freedom, applicants also sought 'freedom' for their children. Under section 8 of the Native Administration Act:

> The Commissioner [of Native Affairs] shall be the legal guardian of every *native child* notwithstanding that the child has a parent or other relative living, until such child attains the age of twenty-one years.[99]

A daughter or son included in a certificate of citizenship would be deemed to be no longer a 'native child' under state law and, therefore, supposedly, beyond the power of the commissioner to remove against the parents' wishes. A consolidated list of 'Citizenship holders' at the end of June 1954 sent by Commissioner Middleton to the commissioner of public health contains many entries listing children on the citizenship certificates of their parents.[100]

In March 1954, Robert Hunter's name appeared again, this time in the Derby Magistrates Court. In 1953, his certificate of citizenship had been suspended for 12 months 'for supplying liquor to natives'.[101] This meant he was deemed once more to be 'a native or aborigine' for the purpose of state law.[102] As a consequence, he had also been convicted and fined for 'receiving liquor as a native'.[103] Pleading for the return of his citizenship certificate, Hunter promised that he had 'learned [his] lesson' and had been 'in no trouble since' losing his certificate. Declaring that he 'would like rights back for the children's sake', he asked for his seven children to be added to his certificate. 'All children of age are going to school. There are beds for all the children.' His request was approved.[104]

---

98   Ibid., folios 33–34.
99   Emphasis added.
100 Commissioner of native affairs to commissioner of public health, 25 August 1954, SRWA: S268 cons1003 1948/1149, folio 4.
101 An offence under section 48(1) of the Native Administration Act.
102 Section 7(2) *Natives (Citizenship Rights) Act*.
103 Under section 48(2) of the Native Administration Act, it was an offence for any 'native to knowingly receive any liquor or opium'.
104 SRWA: S1103 Cons 4706 1, folio 45.

However, far from conferring equal rights and 'freedom' from racist laws, gaining 'citizenship' in Western Australia could mean increased racial targeting. After the 1944 Act came into effect, the commissioner of police warned that 'the holder of citizenship rights will have all the privileges and rights of a white person, including the right to purchase intoxicating liquor', which could be illegally supplied to 'natives'.[105] In 1947, Police Constable Brown observed suspicious activity in Wellington Street, Perth:

> I saw the native, Sport Charles Jones, holder of the certificate of citizenship No. 152 walking across the street from the direction of the Imperial Hotel. He was carrying two bottles bearing labels, which appeared to be Emu Bitter Beer Labels.[106]

Constable Brown arrested Jones, who was 'convicted and fined £4 with 4/6 costs' for supplying beer to a 'native'.[107] On another occasion, Brown:

> questioned a native named Samuel Charles Isaacs, holder of Certificate No. 50, concerning his attempting to obtain bottled liquor after having been seen talking to some natives in Royal St, East Perth. I was satisfied that Isaacs intended obtaining the bottles of liquor for these natives. He did not get his Bottles as the Hotel … closed in the meantime.[108]

Samuel Isaacs was the son of the second certificate holder (see above) in Western Australia. He was a decorated WWII soldier, having fought in Africa, New Guinea and the Pacific.[109] But neither his certificate of citizenship nor distinguished war service saved him from humiliation when buying a beer. As 'Rotten Legislation for Coloured Australians', an article 'prepared by natives and written by a native',[110] observed:

> The ex-serviceman who is prepared to sink his pride and apply for the right to carry one of these *dog licences* must, often in the presence of a crowd of white citizens, at the demand of a none-too-polite barman or barmaid, or white-coated waiter present this card as evidence of his right to join his white friend in a social drink. 'A State which dwarfs its men'. Indeed![111]

---

105 Western Australia, *Notice for Gazette*, 9 November 1945, SRWA: 1964–1910, folio 39.
106 SRWA: S2030 Cons993 1944/0463, folio 77.
107 Ibid., folios 75–76.
108 Ibid., folio 76.
109 NAA: B883, WX19177.
110 Similar articles a few weeks before in the same paper were written by Commissioner Middleton. Biskup, *Not Slaves Not Citizens*, 251–52.
111 *West Australian*, 5 November 1952, 3. Emphasis added.

As well as being targeted as potential suppliers of liquor, 'citizenship' holders required a special permit to visit Aboriginal reserves or missions.[112] And, despite 'becoming white' under state law, they were not wanted where white people lived.[113]

Humiliation

There were many humiliations in Western Australia's 'citizenship' process. Aboriginal applicants had to find two well-known white people to certify that they were of 'good character and industrious habits'. Mary Puertollano in Broome had asked the town doctor and Catholic bishop to support her. Further, applicants were required to sign a statutory declaration, punishable by imprisonment for a false statement, in front of the local postmaster, schoolteacher or policeman stating that they kept away from traditional Aboriginal people and were living, in effect, as a white person. They also faced the ignominy of personal inspection of their homes to ensure they were kept to a 'civilised' or 'white' standard. During Robert Hunter's hearing in Broome, 'the Court was adjourned to allow the Magistrate to personally inspect the dwelling house of the applicant and observe his living conditions'.[114] As the *Northern Times* informed its readers, Hunter's 'home on the foreshore was … inspected by the magistrate, who found it of reasonable standard and in a high state of cleanliness'.[115] In 1948, the Derby Magistrates Court granted Catherine Rodriguez 'citizenship', noting: 'House inspected and found to be clean and tidy and applicant herself seems to have adopted and be capable of maintaining civilised standards of living.'[116] Eva Bickley's application was also approved, with the court declaring: 'Applicants living quarters inspected. Everything clean, tidy and well-kept, and in accordance with civilised standards.'[117]

In 1944, the Women's Christian Temperance Union of Western Australia strongly objected to the proposal for 'citizenship' applicants to show they were free from certain diseases, claiming this 'was outside the realm of any government to legislate upon … Since when has health and morals been a bar

---

112 Section 39, Native Administration Act.
113 See e.g. Secretary Katanning Road Board to Mr Nalder MLA, 13 October 1955, SRWA: S2030 Cons 1733, 1945/1263, folio 32.
114 Ibid., folio 96.
115 *Northern Times*, 12 April 1946, 15.
116 SRWA: S1103 Cons 4706 1, folios 33–34.
117 Ibid., folio 33.

to Citizenship anywhere?'[118] But the requirement for a humiliating medical inspection was included in the final legislation. Applicants had to show proof to the court. In 1949, 31-year-old labourer George Ryder told the Derby Magistrates Court: 'I produce a medical certificate … showing that I am free from active syphilis, granuloma, leprosy or yaws.'[119] As social historian Tamara Hunter observes: 'For many Aboriginal people this was a humiliating and degrading process and they resented having to expose their private lives in open court.'[120] No consent was required for these medical examinations. Under the Native Administration Act, an 'authorised person' could use 'such means as may be necessary to compel any native to undergo examination'. Refusing to submit to an examination was a criminal offence.[121]

There was further degrading treatment in the 'citizenship' hearing itself, which was conducted more like a criminal trial. Applicants appeared before a police magistrate[122] with local police attending as key witnesses. In Robert Hunter's case in Broome, Inspector O'Neill 'called Sergt. Campbell to give evidence as to Hunter's general reputation and behaviour'.[123] In their conflicting role as 'protectors of natives',[124] the police acted at the behest of the commissioner of native affairs.[125] In 1945, Western Australia's chief of police told his officers that the native affairs commissioner 'requests that every care be exercised … to see that certificates are not issued to *doubtful types of natives*'.[126] As O'Neill reported in relation to the Broome cases, applicants and their supporting referees were 'subject to cross-examination' by both the magistrate and police.

Some magistrates openly treated 'citizenship' applicants as if they were accused criminals. In 1950, Magistrate Smith in Perth granted a certificate to Alfred James Mippy but warned 'should he appear before him in Court again he would appear as a white man and in view of his past crime record, he would have *no hesitation in sending him to gaol*'.[127] The magistrate dealt with Mippy as if he was on his last warning before being sent to prison.

---

118 SRWA: S2030 Cons993 1944/0463, folio 93.
119 SRWA: S1103 Cons4706 1, folios 34–35.
120 Hunter, 'The Myth of Equality', 78.
121 Section 16.
122 In 1951, the Act was amended so that hearings were held by a board consisting of a magistrate 'and a person nominated by the Minister as a district representative'.
123 SRWA: S2030 Cons993 1944/0463, folio 96.
124 Biskup, *Not Slaves Not Citizens*, 230.
125 Or, as Biskup puts it, the Department of Native Affairs was 'for all practical purposes an appendage of the Police Department'. Biskup, *Not Slaves Not Citizens*, 179.
126 SRWA: Item 1964/1910, folio 39. Emphasis added.
127 SRWA: S2030 Cons993 1944/0463, folio 56. Emphasis added.

In a final humiliation, the original version of the Natives (Citizenship Rights) Act deemed successful applicants for 'citizenship' 'to be no longer a native or aborigine'. In 1951, Commissioner Middleton argued for removal of this provision, saying it 'implies black can be made white by Act of Parliament; at least it tends to destroy a pride of race which should not be the intention of any legislation'.[128] Minister for Native Affairs Victor Doney agreed, declaring:

> No Act of Parliament should have the effect of depriving a person of his race … an aborigine or part-aborigine never can be a European, and there seems to be no sound reason why Parliament should seek to make him other than what he is.[129]

Middleton recognised the humiliation for Aboriginal people, telling all 'Field Officers, Missions and Institutions' that 'this offensive section has been deleted so pride of race can be maintained even under Citizenship'.[130]

The Hollowness of Aboriginal 'Citizenship'

For some time after his appointment as commissioner in 1948, Middleton had little knowledge of the relevant nationality law. In 1951 he had to ask Solicitor-General G. W. Wood: 'does a state of citizenship exist in law?' Middleton was about to attend the inaugural conference of the Australian Council of Native Welfare in Canberra at which 'citizenship status' was the lead item. The solicitor-general's response appears to have been a turning point for Middleton. In a handwritten note, Middleton observed: 'Citizenship is already vested in natives. Their very birth in Australia confers on them automatic citizenship.'[131] He concluded that if Aboriginal people were already 'Australian citizens', only discriminatory state and federal legislation prevented them having 'full citizenship' in the broader sense. He urged the Canberra conference to 'press for the removal of all discriminatory legislation, and insist on the recognition of all aboriginal natives as native citizens of Australia having full citizenship rights'.[132] But federal and state ministers said Australia's First Nations peoples still had to earn the right to

---

128 Ibid., folio 36.
129 Western Australia, *Debates*, Legislative Assembly, 30 October 1951, 317.
130 SRWA: S2030 Cons 993 1944/0463, folio 16.
131 SRWA: S2030 Cons 1733 1945/1263, folios 45–50.
132 Western Australia, *Annual Report of the Commissioner of Native Affairs for the Year Ended 30th June, 1952* (Western Australia: Department of Native Affairs, 1953), 4.

'full Citizenship'.[133] Reporting on the conference, Minister for Territories Hasluck made no mention of equal rights for Aboriginal Australians based on equal citizenship, emphasising instead the Australian Government's objective of 'assimilation'.[134]

In 1959, Mr Sandy McDonald, born in the Northern Territory, wrote to Hasluck stating that he was living with his son 'as an Australian citizen' at Hall's Creek in Western Australia. However, when they went to the 'pub to buy few bottles beer, publican refuse to serve us because we have not got WA Citizenship rights'.[135] McDonald particularly objected to the treatment of his son who had been born in Western Australia:

> how could the State by-laws class a man with his birthright and civic status as ward of the State and you know Mr Hasluck that not right. I am British Subject, citizen of Empire and Australian citizen and therefore I know that I am Australian – law must give me my right to defend my status as Australian. Well Mr Hasluck would appreciate it if you could get this for us.[136]

Hasluck had extensive experience as a federal minister and he also had considerable knowledge of Aboriginal affairs. Yet he had to ask the federal attorney-general, Sir Garfield Barwick QC, 'whether a person who has obtained full and irrevocable Australian citizenship in a Commonwealth territory can lose that citizenship when he crosses the border into a State of the Commonwealth', adding 'I ought to be better informed about the legal questions that may be raised than I am'.[137] Barwick's response reflected the lack of value for Aboriginal people of formal citizenship under federal law:

> Mr McDonald is an Australian citizen wherever he may be in Australia ... but this does not mean that he is necessarily entitled to all the rights enjoyable by a non-Aboriginal citizen throughout Australia.[138]

---

133 Ibid., 3–4.
134 Ibid., 4. In *Black Australians*, Hasluck acknowledged that First Nations peoples had equal membership status as 'British subjects' under the law applying in Australia. However, he asserted that 'it was impracticable for them to have, and in fact they never did have, exactly the same position at law as other British subjects'. See Hasluck, *Black Australians*, 129.
135 NAA: A432 1966/3171, folio 29.
136 Ibid., folio 21.
137 Ibid., folio 20.
138 Ibid., folio 13.

The senior legal officer in Hasluck's department advised that all mainland states had legislation 'relating to the welfare and control of persons wholly or partly descended from aboriginal natives of Australia', and noted that:

> any person who satisfies the definition of 'native'… is, while present in the State in question, subject to the provisions of the legislation in force in that State relating to 'natives' … This is so irrespective of citizenship.[139]

As John Chesterman and Brian Galligan argue: 'Divorcing citizenship status from rights and benefits facilitated exclusion on racial grounds, but it also debased Australian citizenship status as a hollow, even hypocritical, formality.'[140] Barwick discounted assertions that the Natives (Citizenship Rights) Act conferred either Australian or state citizenship, advising that the 'so-called certificate of citizenship … is really no more than a certificate of exemption from the operation of certain statutes of Western Australia'.[141]

While modern-day legal commentators such as Kim Rubenstein, Garth Nettheim and Larissa Behrendt state that Western Australia's Natives (Citizenship Rights) Act was unconstitutional, in his 1959 legal advice to Minister for Territories Hasluck, Barwick (soon to be appointed chief justice of the High Court) made no mention of any potential inconsistency under the Australian Constitution.[142] Similarly, Commonwealth Solicitor-General Kenneth Bailey said nothing about any possible constitutional invalidity in his evidence to a federal parliamentary inquiry in 1961, remarking only that:

> the language [of the Citizenship Rights Act] is not very apt because of course under the law of the Commonwealth an Australian aboriginal is a natural-born subject of Her Majesty, and the terms of the provision rather imply the contrary.[143]

---

139 Ibid., folio 26.
140 Chesterman and Galligan, *Defining Australian Citizenship*, 9–10.
141 NAA: A432 1966/3171, folio 6.
142 Ibid.
143 K. H. Bailey, 'Voting Rights of Aborigines', Commonwealth of Australia, *Report of Select Committee on Voting Rights of Aborigines* (Canberra: Parliament House, 1961), Appendix VIII.

Conclusion

In a 2017 native title hearing, the Federal Court explained the ongoing 'human tragedy' caused by Western Australia's Natives (Citizenship Rights) Act:

> Lindsay Todd said that his father was Kariyarra,[144] his parents were married and had *citizenship cards* … He said that the '*[c]itizenship right* meant that you had to act as white people … and you had no contacts with the, well, I'd hate to say it, full bloods' … his parents could not teach him Aboriginal language and the family could not associate with the Aboriginal population …

> The *human tragedy* is that, although the Todd respondents undoubtedly have indigenous ancestry, they appear to have lost the ability to identify accurately, and connect fully with, their heritage or to enjoy the benefit of inclusion as part of a claim group in a determination of native title … Accordingly, I do not accept … that they have any knowledge that is relevant to establishing their claim to be Yindjibarndi.[145]

The Federal Court found that the constraints of 'citizenship' had been imposed 'inappropriately with the benefit of hindsight',[146] but it did not consider legal opinions regarding the validity of Western Australia's 1944 law or how this would affect the native title claimants.

The story of the Natives (Citizenship Rights) Act involves an overwhelmingly negative reflection on the myth that modern Australia has been built on the 'rule of law'. Government ministers and officials wrongly conflated legal and non-legal types of citizenship in describing the 1944 Act. The minister sponsoring the legislation disregarded the obvious point that nationality was a federal not state responsibility, insisting that the Act conferred 'Australian citizenship' despite no such legal status existing at the time. Solicitor-General Walker failed to advise Commissioner Bray or Minister

---

144 One of the many language groups in the Pilbara, see 'Kariyarr', Wangka Maya Pilbara Aboriginal Language Centre, accessed 16 December 2022, www.wangkamaya.org.au/pilbara-languages/kariyarra.
145 *Warrie (on Behalf of the Yindjibarndi People) v. Western Australia* [2017] FCA 803 (20 July 2017) [438], [450], [453]. Emphasis added. The Yindjibarndi are another language group in the Pilbara. See "Yindjibarndi', Wangka Maya Pilbara Aboriginal Language Centre, accessed 16 December 2022, www. wangkamaya.org.au/pilbara-languages/yindjibarndi. Similar cases include *Daniel v. Western Australia* [2003] FCA 666; *Moses v. Western Australia* [2007] FCAFC 78; *Harrington-Smith on Behalf of the Wongatha People v. Western Australia* (No. 9) [2007] FCA 31.
146 *Warrie* [2017] FCA 803 [452].

Coverley about any inconsistency between the Western Australian Act and federal nationality law. Commissioner Bray wanted to personally determine the 'better types of natives' deserving of 'citizenship', and demanded that his department's prejudiced views on character and reputation be accepted by magistrates regardless of evidence. Bray and the Department of Native Affairs persisted in treating 'tribal and native association' as a disqualifying factor, disregarding explicit advice to the contrary from the state's most senior lawyer. Native title claimants continue to be hamstrung today by this unlawful application of the legislation. While Magistrate Harwood refused to accept prejudiced 'national policy' about associating with 'natives' or 'coloured persons' (instead applying the actual criteria in the legislation), he was, as Bray caustically observed, the exception among the magistrates in Western Australia. The local police failed to act as an impartial arm of the law, actively opposing applications on behalf of the commissioner of native affairs. And, in the actual 'citizenship' hearings, applicants were treated like accused criminals, facing cross-examination along with their supporting witnesses.

As Marxist historian E. P. Thompson says about England and the rule of law, it has to be concluded that, for Western Australia's governing elite, the law about nationality and citizenship was, in relation to First Australians, 'a nuisance, to be manipulated and bent in what ways they could'.[147] Commissioner Middleton eventually realised that white lawmakers and bureaucrats in Western Australia had the 'citizenship' process the wrong way round. They should have used as a starting point the irrevocable legal membership status of First Nations peoples under Australian law. But wilful ignorance of federal nationality law and a racist, Darwinian view that Aboriginal Australians could not be their equals meant that white officials in Western Australia could not accept their equal legal status – let alone that they should have full 'citizenship rights' as a logical consequence of such equal status. Instead, white administrators saw 'citizenship' as a 'privilege' that the 'better types' of Australia's original inhabitants had to earn through the process of 'assimilation'.

Far from gaining 'full citizenship as Australians', as Minister Coverley claimed, successful applicants faced increased racial harassment, not least being targeted as potential suppliers of liquor. As Middleton said, they were 'suspended between two communities, that of the white man on the one

---

147 E. P. Thompson, *Whigs and Hunters: The Origin of the Black Act* (London: Allen Lane, 1975), 266.

side and of the aboriginal native on the other'.[148] Even those who showed the ultimate commitment to their nation by fighting for Australia had to show their citizenship 'dog tag' to get a drink in a hotel.

According to Justice Edelman of the High Court in *Love & Thoms*:

> The Aboriginal inhabitants of Australia had community, societies and ties to the land … that established them as belonging to Australia and therefore to its political community. Whatever the other manners in which they were treated … Aboriginal people were not *'considered as Foreigners in a Kingdom which is their own'*.[149]

The First Nations peoples of Western Australia, forced until 1971 to apply for 'citizenship' to obtain a 'passport' with freedom to travel and enjoy other rights as Australians, might question Justice Edelman's view that they were not treated as foreigners in their own country.

---

148 Western Australia, *Annual Report of the Commissioner of Native Affairs for the Year Ended 30th June, 1952*, 4.
149 *Love & Thoms* (2020) 94 ALJR 198 [392]. Emphasis added.

7

Was Namatjira an Alien? The High Court's Flawed History of Belonging in Australia

Peter Prince[1]

Note of warning

Aboriginal and Torres Strait Islander readers are advised that the following chapter contains names, words and images of people who have died. Such words and images are already in the public domain. In addition, statements by white officials, politicians and newspapers that are recognised as racially offensive today are quoted to illustrate the thinking at the time. Readers are warned that the chapter contains words and descriptions that may be culturally sensitive and would not normally be used in public or community contexts.

Introduction

In 'Why High Court Judges Make Poor Historians', Rob McQueen notes the observation of Italian historian Alessandro Portelli:

> The distinction between legal and historical truth deserves one final comment. Historical truth is hardly ever more than a descriptive hypothesis: legal truth has a performative nature. Whether things

1   The author thanks Dr Eve Lester for her insightful comments on an earlier draft of this chapter.

happened as the court says or not, to all practical purposes they now did: a court's [decision] creates truth … legal truth, in turn has a tendency to become historical truth as well.[2]

As McQueen says, 'once a particular version of history is given the imprimatur of "authenticity" by a superior court, it becomes the definitive account of the particular event'.[3] Statements about Australian history by the nation's High Court have particular significance. This chapter contends that the High Court needs to better confront racialised conceptions of national identity and belonging from the era of White Australia in order to resist the enduring influence of such attitudes and policies – and that failure to do so unavoidably perpetuates them. The laws of any country reflect the values of society and the time period in which they were made. The chapter argues that laws from earlier periods of Australian history in which white privilege was the foundation of the social order cannot be applied to contemporary society in an uncritical manner.

Using three case studies, the chapter examines the fragmented way the High Court has been willing to engage in a postcolonial reckoning with the country's past discrimination. Individuals in each case study faced deportation. Their fate depended on the court's assessment of whether they legally belonged. For each occasion, the judicial approach to the historical context can be questioned. In the first two examples, the High Court failed to acknowledge the pervasive legal discrimination in nineteenth- and twentieth-century Australia against First Nations peoples and other non-European inhabitants. In the last instance, the High Court glossed over the positive discrimination throughout the same period in favour of ethnic Anglo-Celtic and other 'Aryan' residents.

First, in the landmark 'Aboriginal belonging' case, *Love & Thoms* (2020), the High Court claimed that Aboriginal people had never been considered 'aliens' or 'foreigners' in their own country. Yet, as the shameful treatment of world-famous artist Albert Namatjira shows, this does not accurately reflect the experience of First Nations peoples following European colonisation.

---

2   Rob McQueen, 'Why High Court Judges Make Poor Historians: The Corporations Act Case and Early Attempts to Establish a National System of Company Regulation in Australia', *Federal Law Review* 19, no. 3 (1990): 245–6, doi.org/10.1177/0067205x9001900304, citing A. Portelli, 'The Law and the Making of History: The April 7 Murder Trial', *History Workshop* 20 (1985): 31, doi.org/10.1093/hwj/20.1.5.
3   Rob McQueen, 'History, Court's Use of', *The Oxford Companion to the High Court of Australia*, ed. M. Coper, T. Blackshield and G. Williams (South Melbourne, Vic: Oxford University Press, 2001), 326, doi.org/10.1093/acref/9780195540222.001.0001.

Without disputing the outcome of the case – that 'Aboriginal Australians' could not validly be subject to draconian federal powers over 'aliens' – this chapter argues that the High Court presented an idealised view of what the law should have been on Indigenous belonging in nineteenth- and twentieth-century Australia, ignoring the unpalatable reality of what it actually was. An understanding of the deficiencies in Aboriginal 'citizenship' under imposed white law in post-1788 Australia would add strength to calls in the *Uluru Statement from the Heart* for constitutional enshrinement of an Indigenous 'Voice' to the Commonwealth Parliament.

Second, in 2021, Mr Troyrone Zen Lee, born as an Australian citizen in the former territory of Papua, won a long battle in the Federal Court to regain his Australian passport (and, hence, his career and access to his wife and family overseas). The Department of Home Affairs had revoked his passport five years earlier based on the High Court's decision in *Ame's Case* (2005). The High Court said Papuans born before independence in 1975 were never 'real Australians' because they were denied entry to the mainland and lacked other rights of Australian citizens. However, the court failed to acknowledge that this reasoning was directly linked to the White Australia–era policy of excluding 'dark-skinned' Papuans to protect the aspiration for a white continent. Because the High Court in *Ame's Case* avoided confronting this historic racism, it continues to cause personal hardship well into the twenty-first century. Unable to question the High Court's precedent, the Federal Court had to distinguish Mr Lee's situation before it could order the return of his passport and livelihood.

Third, in *Falzon* (2018)[4] and *Chetcuti* (2021),[5] the High Court ruled that two men who had arrived as small boys from the British colony of Malta in the mid-twentieth century and had lived in Australia ever since did not 'belong' and could be deported to their country of birth. Their right to remain in Australia was cancelled after they were convicted of serious crimes. Mr Falzon had made Australia his home for over 60 years and Mr Chetcuti for more than 70 years! Like other British subjects, they possessed full 'citizenship rights' from the time they arrived and had no need to formally become Australian citizens. Mr Chetcuti was even part of the conscription ballot during the Vietnam War. But they were caught by the High Court's retrospective declaration that any British subjects from the United Kingdom or its former colonies who disembarked, even before

---

4   *Falzon v. Minister for Immigration and Border Protection* [2018] HCA 2.
5   *Chetcuti v. Commonwealth of Australia* [2021] HCA 25.

the creation of Australian citizenship in 1949, could be treated as 'aliens' from the time of their arrival if they had not been naturalised as citizens. The chapter contends that this idealised rewriting of history denies the inherent allegiance and loyalty to the 'home country' of Anglo-Australians from previous generations. It is difficult to imagine an Australian court in the 1950s or 1960s labelling white British subjects in Australia as 'aliens' or 'outsiders' who could be expelled from the country.

Idealising Australia's Indigenous History

The first case study looks at the gap between law and history on a fundamental issue for modern-day Australia – the legal treatment of First Nations peoples. The 2020 High Court case *Love & Thoms v. Commonwealth*[6] involved two men of Australian Indigenous background, Daniel Love and Brendan Thoms, each born outside Australia (Love in Papua New Guinea, Thoms in New Zealand), who had not formally become Australian citizens. Both were issued with a deportation order under the *Migration Act 1958* on character grounds. However, by a bare 4:3 majority, the High Court ruled that the spiritual and cultural connection of Aboriginal people with the land and waters of Australia over tens of thousands of years meant that the men could not be categorised as 'outsiders' or 'aliens' in a legal sense.[7] This decision means that no 'Aboriginal Australian',[8] even if born overseas, can validly be deported by a law such as the Migration Act made under the 'aliens power' in the Australian Constitution.

While the narrow ruling in *Love & Thoms* must be welcomed as a landmark recognition – albeit one made 120 years after Federation – of the constitutional belonging of First Australians, disappointingly the High Court presented what might reasonably be described as a 'whitewashed' view of their legal treatment since 1788. Judgments in the case gave the

---

6   (2020) 94 ALJR 198.

7   Ibid., 271 [373–74] (Justice Gordon); 288 [451] (Justice Edelman). As Justice Gordon said, no Australian court had previously considered whether First Nations peoples could be 'aliens' in their own country. At 258 [294].

8   The High Court stated that 'Aboriginal Australians' were those who met the tripartite test in *Mabo v. Queensland* (No. 2) (1992) 175 CLR 1 at 70, where Justice Brennan said that membership of Australia's Indigenous community depended on 'biological descent from the indigenous people and on mutual recognition of a particular person's membership by that person and by the elders or other persons enjoying traditional authority among those people'. *Love & Thoms* (2020) 94 ALJR 198, 290 [458]. The majority in *Love & Thoms* agreed that Mr Thoms satisfied the *Mabo* test and could not be deported as an 'alien'. But they could not agree whether Mr Love satisfied this test and his matter was referred to the Federal Court to determine.

misleading impression that, since European colonisation, Australia's First Peoples had always been understood as having full legal membership status under imposed British law.

Despite the narrow margin, both the majority and minority judges agreed on the relevant history. Chief Justice Kiefel (minority) stated that, from the time of British settlement, 'the legal status of Aboriginal persons in Australia – as subjects of the Crown – has not been different from other Australians'.[9] Similarly, Justice Gordon (majority) said:

> Aboriginal Australians were regarded as British subjects following settlement ... Status as a British subject extended to all inhabitants ... nothing in the [1890s] Convention Debates purported to treat Aboriginal Australians as aliens or within the reach of the aliens power.[10]

Justice Gageler (minority) observed that 'members of Aboriginal and Torres Strait Islander societies have *never been understood* to fall outside the standard common law or statutory rules' regarding British subject or Australian citizen status.[11] Justice Edelman (majority) stated that Aboriginal people had always been 'belongers' (the opposite of 'aliens') in Australia and that, 'even with racial application, alien was not applied to persons described as members of the Aboriginal race':

> Since settlement, Aboriginal people have been inseparably tied to the land of Australia generally, and thus to the political community of Australia ... [At] Federation, the Aboriginal people in Australia were not regarded as aliens to the political community ... Aboriginal people were a necessary part of the 'people of Australia' and the Australian political community ... Aboriginal people simply did not fall within the application of 'alien', a foreigner to the political community.[12]

These statements by the High Court confuse what the law should have been in relation to the legal status of Aboriginal people with how they were actually treated and regarded legally after European settlement.

It was convenient for the High Court in 2020 to deem First Nations peoples, because of what is now accepted as their unique connection with the land and waters of Australia,[13] to have always 'belonged' under white

---

9   *Love & Thoms* (2020) 94 ALJR 198, 206 [9]. Emphasis added.
10   Ibid., 261 [314], 265 [342]. Emphasis added.
11   Ibid., 223 [103]. Emphasis added.
12   Ibid., 274 [396], 278 [410] including heading, 287 [449]. Emphasis added.
13   Ibid., 271 [373–74] (Justice Gordon).

law; however, the historical legal reality is very different. Until a generation ago, the Australian political community was incomplete, precisely because Aboriginal people were excluded from it. As Bri Lee observes:

> Australia only achieved a true democracy in the 1960s when Aboriginal Australians were finally allowed to vote. Indeed, as white women in Australia saw an opportunity to climb to the next rung in the pyramid at the turn of the century, they threw Indigenous Australian women under the bus in the process.[14]

Far from always being regarded as 'belongers' and not 'aliens', Anglo-Celtic lawmakers in the nineteenth and early twentieth centuries refused to accord First Nations peoples even the detested status of 'alien'. Much impressed by Social Darwinism, most thought Aboriginal Australians were a 'dying or doomed race'[15] not worth counting as 'people'. They openly queried whether the continent's first inhabitants were human. In 1902, prominent federal Australian Labor Party member King O'Malley, later minister for home affairs, told the new Australian Parliament that: 'An aboriginal is not as intelligent as a Māori. There is no scientific evidence that he is a human being at all.'[16] As Richard Broome explains, contrary to the current High Court's portrayal of a benign acceptance at Federation of Indigenous Australians as equal members of the political community:

> By 1900 most settler Australians held derogatory views towards Aboriginal Australians, which were a mixture of ignorance, indifference, fanciful racial theories, a belief in white superiority, and the need to rationalise the continued dispossession of Aboriginal land. In this vein, settler Australians shaped the Constitution, which failed to count Aboriginal people with other Australians.[17]

---

14   Bri Lee, *Who Gets to Be Smart: Privilege, Power and Knowledge* (Crows Nest, NSW: Allen and Unwin 2021), 211.

15   Richard Broome, *Aboriginal Australians: A History since 1788*, 5th ed. (Crows Nest, NSW: Allen and Unwin, 2019), 106. As Sven Lindqvist notes:

> in white historiography, the Aborigines long remained an inferior race doomed to 'fade away' on contact with Western culture. There was no investigation of the violence that precipitated this 'fading'. Historians spoke of violence in general terms, without concrete examples. [This] mental block has by no means disappeared … Those involved in their killing naturally enough were ready to equate them with forms of life less than human.

Sven Lindqvist, *Terra Nullius: A Journey through No One's Land* (London: Granta, 2007), 202, citing C. D. Rowley, *The Destruction of Aboriginal Society* (Canberra: Australian National University Press, 1970).

16   Commonwealth of Australia, *Parliamentary Debates*, House of Representatives, 23 April 1902, 11930.

17   Broome, *Aboriginal Australians*, 108.

Section 127 of the Australian Constitution (repealed in 1967) directed that 'aboriginal natives *shall not be counted* … in reckoning the numbers of people of the Commonwealth or a State'.[18] As John Chesterman and Brian Galligan point out, rather than being included as a 'necessary part of the Australian political community':

> for the first half century of Australian nationhood … it was the *'aboriginal native' who was the key boundary marker to Australian citizenship* … the Australian citizen was thought to be simply a 'natural-born or naturalised' person who was *not an 'aboriginal native'*.[19]

In this extract, Chesterman and Galligan are referring to 'Australian citizenship' as a 'bundle of rights'[20] not as a formal legal status. In this practical sense, the clearest indicator of 'belonging to' or being 'a citizen of' a political community is the right to vote. The *Commonwealth Franchise Act 1902* and *Commonwealth Electoral Act 1918* barred any 'aboriginal native of Australia' from voting unless they could already vote at a state level.[21] Queensland, Western Australia and the Northern Territory denied Aboriginal Australians the right to vote until well after World War II, meaning they were also excluded from the political process at the federal level. It was not until 1962 that the Commonwealth Electoral Act was amended to give Indigenous Australians the right to vote in federal elections regardless of state law.[22] However, Queensland did not grant Aboriginal and Torres Strait Islander people voting rights until 1965.[23]

Commonwealth legislation also denied First Nations peoples other rights enjoyed by Anglo-Celtic members of the Australian political community. The *Invalid and Old-Age Pensions Act 1908* disqualified 'aboriginal natives of Australia' from receiving pensions.[24] The *Emigration Act 1910* prevented 'aboriginal natives' leaving Australia except with a permit.[25]

---

18   Emphasis added.
19   John Chesterman and Brian Galligan, *Citizens without Rights: Aborigines and Australian Citizenship* (Cambridge: Cambridge University Press, 1997), 120, doi.org/10.1017/CBO9780511518249. Original emphasis.
20   As explained in Chapter 1, such rights are those that enable equal participation in the sociopolitical community, including freedom of movement, the right to vote, stand for parliament, serve on a jury, decide where to live, work, choose friends, partners etc.
21   *Commonwealth Franchise Act 1902*, section 4; *Commonwealth Electoral Act 1918*, section 39.
22   'Electoral Milestones for Indigenous Australians', Australian Electoral Commission, accessed 15 December 2021, aec.gov.au/indigenous/milestones.htm.
23   Ibid.
24   Sections 16, 21.
25   Section 3(1).

Under the *Maternity Allowance Act 1912*, women who were 'aboriginal natives of Australia' could not be paid an allowance.[26] In 1947, the *Social Services Consolidation Act* maintained the exclusion of 'aboriginal natives of Australia' from invalid and old age pensions, widow's pensions and maternity allowances.[27]

Discrimination by the Commonwealth against 'aboriginal natives' was accompanied by even greater restrictions under state and territory law.[28] Peter Bayne argues that 'a massive edifice of law' discriminating against Indigenous people was erected in the Australian colonies from the middle of the nineteenth century.[29] As the Australian Institute of Aboriginal and Torres Strait Islander Studies notes, so-called protection laws controlled every aspect of the lives of Aboriginal people:

> from the forced removal of children, where they lived, worked, had wages and entitlements withheld (now known as Stolen Wages), owned land, to their personal relationships and contact with family and community. These laws were in force from the 1840s ... and then, after federation, well into the 1960s and even the 1970s for some states.[30]

In Queensland, for example, the *Protection of Aboriginals and Restriction of the Sale of Opium Amendment Act 1934* specified that:

> The Minister may from time to time cause any aboriginal or half-caste ... to be removed to any reserve, institution, or district and kept there, or to be removed from any reserve, institution, or district to any other reserve institution or district, and kept there.[31]

The extensive range of Commonwealth and state laws preventing participation of Australia's First Nations peoples in the political community had a calamitous effect on their lives. As the next part of this section shows, even global fame was no protection.

---

26   Section 6(2).
27   Sections 19, 62, 86.
28   Peter Prince, 'Aliens in Their Own Land. "Alien" and the Rule of Law in Colonial and Post-Federation Australia' (PhD thesis, The Australian National University, 2015), 167ff, openresearch-repository.anu.edu.au/handle/1885/101778.
29   Peter Bayne, 'Politics, the Law and Aborigines', *The Australian People: An Encyclopedia of the Nation, its People and their Origins*, ed. James Jupp (North Ryde, NSW: Angus & Robertson, 1988), 212, 214–15. Emphasis added.
30   'To Remove and Protect', Australian Institute of Aboriginal and Torres Strait Islander Studies, accessed 24 August 2021, aiatsis.gov.au/collection/featured-collections/remove-and-protect.
31   Section 7.

Case Study 1: Albert Namatjira

> In Alice Springs … Namatjira came under intense small-town scrutiny … only Australian citizens were allowed to be in Alice in the evenings, and Albert's children weren't citizens.[32]

Albert Namatjira's story provides a real-life example of how First Nations peoples were treated as 'aliens' or 'outsiders' in the Australian community, contrary to the High Court's portrayal in *Love & Thoms*. In 1935 at Hermannsburg mission, south-west of Alice Springs, Namatjira, an Arrernte man, learnt to paint watercolours in the European style.[33] By the 1950s, reproductions of his paintings hung in schools and loungerooms across Australia:[34]

> The contemporary settler public … saw Namatjira's painting as empirical evidence of a pathway from the primitive to the civilised … Namatjira, the successful artist, represented the potential of all Aborigines to assimilate and to live 'like us'.[35]

Namatjira was introduced to the Queen in Canberra in 1954 as part of a Northern Territory delegation.[36] But, according to Julie Wells and Michael Christie, 'because he was an Aboriginal person, Namatjira was *not in any real sense a citizen*'.[37] The Commonwealth minister for territories, Paul Hasluck, agreed, declaring:

> *The status of Albert Namatjira is that of an aboriginal* as defined in the Aboriginals Ordinance 1918–1947 … as an aboriginal he is free to move about anywhere in native reserves, and in his own tribal area … he is at present legally barred from being in certain prohibited areas.[38]

---

32 Lindqvist, *Terra Nullius*, 180.
33 Ibid., 177.
34 Julie T. Wells and Michael F. Christie, 'Namatjira and the Burden of Citizenship', *Australian Historical Studies* 31 (2000): 110, doi.org/10.1080/10314610008596118.
35 Ibid., 116.
36 National Archives of Australia (hereafter NAA): F425, C33. The Queen accepted a gift from Namatjira of his painting of Heavitree Gap, Alice Springs, 'which he had specially brought with him to Canberra'. He also had to acknowledge in writing that he received the sum of £1 from the secretary of the Department of Territories during his visit.
37 Wells and Christie, 'Namatjira', 110. Emphasis added.
38 Hasluck to Senator Robertson, 10 October 1952, NAA: A431, 1951/1200. Emphasis added.

Figure 7.1: William Dargie, *Portrait of Albert Namatjira*, 1956.
Source: Collection of Queensland Art Gallery | Gallery of Modern Art, © QAGOMA.
Photograph: QAGOMA.

In the 1950s, as Sven Lindqvist explains:

> the Aborigines of the Alice Springs area could still be interned against their will; they were not allowed into white hotels, hospitals or other 'prohibited areas' and could not travel or leave employment without permission. They were outside the social security system and did not receive old age pensions, maternity allowances or any other social benefits. Marriages were prohibited across racial boundaries, except by special permission from the authorities.[39]

Like other First Nations peoples in the Northern Territory, Namatjira's life was overseen by white officials despite his standing as a world-famous artist. As the head of the federal Department of Territories explained in 1957, departmental officials 'look after a trust account for him and advise him from time to time on the state of his account and suggest ways of spending his money advantageously'.[40]

In 1953, Hasluck instigated replacement of the *Aboriginals Ordinance* in the Northern Territory with the ostensibly non-discriminatory *Welfare Ordinance* 'to facilitate the Commonwealth Government's policy of assimilation which is designed to provide opportunities for aborigines to merge into full membership of the greater community which surrounds them'.[41] Despite its race-neutral wording, the Welfare Ordinance was 'almost confined in its application to aboriginals'.[42] It came into effect in 1957 after a 'Register of Wards' was compiled containing the names of over 15,000 First Nations people.[43] After a national campaign in support of his exemption, Namatjira was one of only six Aboriginal people of full descent in the Northern Territory not listed on the register. As a result, Wells and Christie observe, 'Namatjira was made a citizen'.[44] This meant 'he could vote, be served in restaurants and treated in hospitals reserved for white

39   Lindqvist, *Terra Nullius*, 179.
40   A. S. Brown, secretary Department of Territories, to Mr Lock, Brisbane, 6 February 1957, NAA: A463, 1957/17.
41   NAA: A452, 1958/3670 (folio 77).
42   *Namatjira v. Raabe* (1959) 100 CLR 664, 667, 670.
43   Ibid., 667.
44   Wells and Christie, 'Namatjira', 120. In 2022, Australian Government websites still claimed, incorrectly, that Namatjira and his wife Ilkalita (Rubina) became the first Aboriginal Australian citizens in 1957. See e.g. 'Albert Namatjira: His Life and Art', National Film and Sound Archive of Australia, accessed 14 September 2022, www.nfsa.gov.au/latest/albert-namatjira-his-life-and-art.

people. He was free from all restrictions governing the life of "wards".'[45] As Sydney's *Sun* newspaper declared, 'Namatjira was given full citizenship rights. He was made a "white man"'.[46] The backlash was swift:

> In Alice Springs, many thought this was too great an honour for a 'black ape'. Namatjira came under intense small-town scrutiny. Did he have his children with him after dark? He wasn't allowed to do that, because only Australian citizens were allowed to be in Alice in the evenings, and Albert's children weren't citizens. Had he been drinking with his relations? He wasn't allowed to do that, because offering Aborigines alcohol was prohibited.[47]

In 1958, Namatjira was convicted by an Alice Springs magistrate of supplying alcohol to a 'ward', one of his relatives. As Lindqvist argues, 'innumerable white people broke these rules and went unpunished. They earned good money illicitly supplying alcohol to black people.'[48] Immediately there were calls for Namatjira's 'citizenship' to be taken away. While these were rejected by the administrator of the Northern Territory, his statement below shows white officials' wilful confusion (as highlighted in Chapter 6) in relation to 'citizen rights' for Indigenous Australians and 'citizenship' as legal membership status:

> The question of whether Namatjira will retain his citizenship is essentially one for Namatjira himself ... He could lose his citizenship rights only if he himself requested the loss of those rights by asking to be declared a ward, or, if in terms of the Welfare Ordinance, he became incapable of protecting his own interests.[49]

Namatjira was sentenced to six months hard labour. In the Northern Territory Supreme Court, Justice Kriewaldt halved the sentence, declaring: 'All my life the duty of Christians towards heathens ... has been impressed upon me.'[50] When it considered Namatjira's case, the High Court was troubled by the 'block declaration' of ward status for many thousands of Aboriginal people given no opportunity to argue against their inclusion.[51] But it refused leave to appeal, commending the 'protective nature' of the Welfare Ordinance

---

45 Lindqvist, *Terra Nullius*, 180.
46 23 September 1958, NAA: A452, 1958/3670 (folio 133).
47 Lindqvist, *Terra Nullius*, 180. Emphasis added.
48 Ibid., 181.
49 'No Move to Oust Namatjira', *Centralian Advocate*, 29 August 1958, NAA: A452, 1958/3670 (folio 147). Emphasis added.
50 *Albert Namatjira v. Gordon Edgar Raabe*, NTSC 194/1958 (1958) *NT Judgments* 608, 614.
51 *Namatjira v. Raabe* (1959) 100 CLR 664, 668.

and noting the (entirely theoretical) right of judicial review for an individual declared a ward.[52] Showing a similar level of confusion between 'citizen rights' and legal citizenship, Minister Hasluck observed:

> Mr Namatjira is an Australian citizen and his citizenship cannot be revoked. The only way for him to lose his citizenship is for him to make a request himself to be placed under the provisions of the Welfare Ordinance of the Northern Territory.[53]

Fellow artists, including Arthur Boyd and Clifton Pugh, protested against Namatjira's conviction, telling Hasluck that 'Namatjira's humiliation is our humiliation and will already appear so in the eyes of the world'.[54] The Australian Builders' Labourers Federation also wrote to the minister:

> this inhuman gaoling spotlights the outrageous situation aboriginal people are in and relegates them to second class citizenship in their own land. Further, that it holds the whole of the Australian people up to shame before the world and makes a mockery of our United Nations pledges. We urge that … the restricting laws imposed on the aboriginal people be rescinded, giving them equal status with white people in Australia.[55]

Hasluck was unmoved by these entreaties:

> If anything lies on our conscience it is that at a time when Albert Namatjira was under our protection and *was not a citizen*, we did not resist strongly enough the pressure from various quarters, doubtless acting in good faith, to take him away from his own environment … More harm was done to him outside the Territory than anything he learnt in the Territory.[56]

---

52 Ibid., 668–70. As Namatjira's barrister pointed out, 'the right of appeal … is illusory because the Wards Appeal Tribunal has no power to make an order with retrospective effect … and (its decisions) may be disregarded by the Administrator with impunity'. NAA: A452, 1958/3670 (folio 44).
53 Press release, 13 March 1959, NAA: A452, 1958/3670 (folio 29).
54 N. Counihan to P. Hasluck, 10 October 1958, NAA: A452, 1958/3670 (folio 167).
55 P. Malone to P. Hasluck, 14 October 1958, NAA: A452, 1958/3776.
56 P. Hasluck, Press release, 'The Case of Albert Namatjira', 9 October 1958, NAA: A452, 1958/3670 (folio 102). See also Wells and Christie, 'Namatjira', 128. Emphasis added.

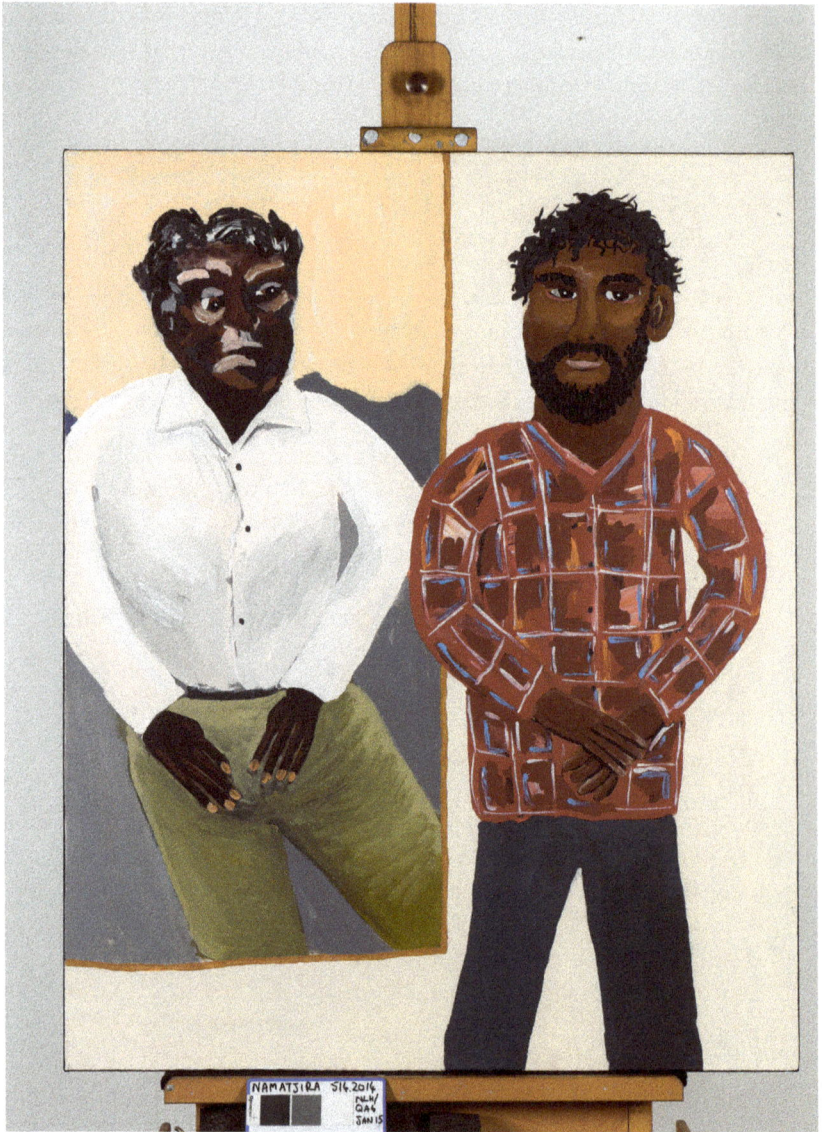

Figure 7.2: Vincent Namatjira, Western Aranda people, *Albert and Vincent*, 2014.

Source: Collection of Queensland Art Gallery | Gallery of Modern Art, © Vincent Namatjira/Copyright Agency. Photograph: Natasha Harth, QAGOMA.

Namatjira served his sentence at an internment camp 200 kilometres north-west of Alice Springs.[57] After his release 'he showed no interest in painting. He seemed to have lost the will to live and died of a heart attack in August 1959.'[58] Wells and Christie reflect that:

> Concerned settler Australians had believed that in *granting Namatjira citizenship* he would be liberated and the last barrier to his full assimilation removed. Surely *when he became a citizen* he would 'live like us'? Namatjira's citizenship, however, was flawed, leaving the nation struggling to come to terms with what had gone wrong.[59]

In *Love & Thoms*, the High Court claimed that First Nations peoples in Australia were never regarded as aliens;[60] yet, as Namatjira's case clearly demonstrates, the standard discourse in Australia about 'citizenship' in the 1950s showed little understanding of, let alone respect for, the automatic and irrevocable equal membership status that Aboriginal people possessed under imposed white law. Under common law rules unchanged since *Calvin's Case* (1608),[61] Aboriginal Australians were automatically 'British subjects' from the time of European settlement; later, they became 'Australian citizens' when that concept was created legally in 1949. But senior Australian Government figures, including Minister Hasluck, claimed that only Namatjira and a handful of other First Nations people in the Northern Territory were sufficiently 'like us' to be 'made citizens' when excluded from the Register of Wards in 1957. In assimilation rhetoric, this meant that these six people, all men, took their place as 'members of the community of the Commonwealth'. In the eyes of Australia's white population, the thousands of other First Nations peoples whose names were on the register were not 'made citizens' but remained 'outsiders' who were not 'one of us' and did not 'belong', even in their own country. As Oodgeroo Noonuccal lamented in a poem presented to the Federal Council for the Advancement of Aborigines in 1962:

> Make us mates, not poor relations,
> Citizens, not serfs on stations.
> Must we native Old Australians
> In our own land rank as aliens?[62]

---

57 Lindqvist, *Terra Nullius*, 181.
58 'Albert Namatjira and Citizenship, 1958–59', National Museum of Australia, accessed 15 December 2021, www.nma.gov.au/explore/features/indigenous-rights/civil-rights/albert-namatjira-citizenship (site discontinued).
59 Wells and Christie, 'Namatjira', 125–26. Emphasis added.
60 (2020) 94 ALJR 198, 287 [449].
61 *Calvin v. Smith* or the *Case of the Postnati* (1608) 7 Coke Report 1a; 77 Eng. Rep. 377.
62 *The Dawn Is at Hand* (Brisbane: Jacaranda Press 1966).

Colonial Legal History and Indigenous Belonging

Australia's colonial legal history was also much more muddled in relation to recognition of the legal belonging of First Nations peoples than statements from the High Court in 2020 might lead us to believe. In cases from the 1820s to the early 1840s, the New South Wales Supreme Court was uncertain about the legal status of Australia's Indigenous people. In *Lowe's Case* (1827), Lieutenant Lowe was acquitted of the murder of an Aboriginal man.[63] His barrister, William Charles Wentworth, claimed that the court had no jurisdiction because Aboriginal inhabitants were neither British subjects nor aliens – indeed, they barely deserved recognition as 'people' at all:

> they are men, no more subject to punishment by our code, than a set of idiots or lunatics … Here are a set of natives one degree just above the beasts of the field – possessing no understanding beyond a confused notion of right and wrong, and that is all.[64]

In a series of cases, the Supreme Court disregarded the law with respect to the subject status of Indigenous inhabitants. *R v. Ballard* (1829),[65] *R v. Murrell* (1836)[66] and *R v. Bonjon* (1841)[67] each concerned the alleged murder of one Indigenous inhabitant by another. Debates about the jurisdiction of colonial courts over Aboriginal 'crimes' formed part of a 'much deeper discourse around the conditions under which indigenous people would be accommodated in settler societies'.[68] According to Lisa Ford:

> the officers of the Crown and the new Supreme Court together *invented jurisdiction* over Aboriginal Australians in New South Wales … The court wrought a revolution in the theory and practice of jurisdiction in New South Wales … a revolution grounded in the logic of territoriality.[69]

---

63 *R v. Lowe* [1827] NSWSupC 32, [1827] NSWKR 4 (18 May 1827).
64 Ibid. Emphasis added.
65 *R v. Ballard* [1829] NSWSupC 26.
66 *R v. Murrell* [1836] NSWSupC 35.
67 *R v. Bonjon* [1841] NSWSupC, Port Phillip District, 16 September 1841, Macquarie University Division of Law, *Decisions of the Superior Courts of New South Wales 1788–1899.*
68 Mark Finnane, 'The Limits of Jurisdiction. Law, Governance, and Indigenous People in Colonized Australia', in *Law and Politics in British Colonial Thought: Transpositions of Empire*, ed. Shaunnagh Dorsett and Ian Hunter (Palgrave Macmillan 2010), 148, 154, doi.org/10.1057/9780230114388_9.
69 Lisa Ford, *Settler Sovereignty, Jurisdiction and Indigenous People in America and Australia, 1788–1836* (Harvard University Press, 2010), 158, doi.org/10.2307/j.ctv1smjszh. Emphasis added.

But the Supreme Court had no need to 'invent jurisdiction' over Indigenous people within the boundaries of New South Wales. Under the law dating back to *Calvin's Case*, any person 'habitually resident' or born in territory annexed by the British in 1788 had the status of a subject under English law and came within the jurisdiction of colonial courts on that basis. Despite having the principles in *Calvin's Case* in front of it,[70] the Supreme Court ignored the established law, focusing instead on levels of 'civilisation' and other non-legal, social factors. The court thought Aborigines incapable of exercising rights and liberties as 'subjects' because of their 'savage', 'barbarous' and 'uncivilised' way of life.[71] Justice Burton, in *Murrell*, stated that Indigenous inhabitants were akin to 'strangers' who had entered the territory of the British sovereign.[72] As Henry Reynolds observed:

> His argument … begged the question of where the Aborigines had come from if they were legally equivalent to foreigners who had entered the society from outside unless, of course, he conceded that unsettled 'Aboriginal' Australia was in effect a foreign country.[73]

In the early decades of European settlement Aboriginal people were seen as a threat and labelled as 'aliens' by prominent colonial figures. According to Peter Bayne:

> Many settlers in violent contact (or, as was often said, at war) with the Aborigines held the view that the Aborigines were not to be regarded as British subjects. Sometimes they were regarded as 'enemy aliens' to justify the use of force against them. Some senior officials, such as the explorer Thomas Mitchell, certainly took this view and acted upon it.[74]

In 1836, Thomas Mitchell, surveyor-general of New South Wales, led an expedition that resulted in large numbers of Aboriginal people being killed. The explorer's report:

> caused consternation at the Colonial Office … due to the fact that Mitchell regarded the Aborigines as 'Aliens with whom war can exist, and against whom HM's Troops may exercise belligerent right'.[75]

---

70 Prince, 'Aliens in Their Own Land', 58, 69–71.
71 Ibid., 60–62.
72 Burton J, 'Arguments and Notes for Judgment in the Case of Jack Congo Murrell', February 1836, *Original Documents on Aborigines and Law 1797–1840*, Document 48 (Centre for Comparative Law History and Governance, Macquarie University and State Records NSW), [251–52].
73 Henry Reynolds, *Aboriginal Sovereignty: Reflections on Race, State and Nation* (St. Leonards, NSW: Allen & Unwin, 1996), 72.
74 Peter Bayne, 'Politics, the Law and Aborigines', 212, 213.
75 Ibid., 214, citing *Historical Records of Australia I*, vol. 19, 48.

For more than a hundred years, there was ongoing warfare with First Nations peoples who resisted invasion of their homelands. Given the ever-present violence on the Queensland frontier in the second half of the nineteenth century:

> few colonists subscribed to the view that hostile Aborigines were rebellious subjects. To most people on the frontier they were enemies who were engaged in a war for control of the territory. The same views, expressed during the 1850s, were common currency forty years later ... It seemed the height of folly to suggest that their enemies were British subjects and should be treated as such.[76]

Contrary to the impression given by Justice Gordon in *Love & Thoms*, there was no discussion of the 'aliens power' at any of the 1890s constitutional conventions,[77] much less any benevolent decision to exclude First Nations peoples from the constitutional concept of 'alien'. There were numerous references at the conventions to 'aliens' in a derogatory racial sense – referring to 'coloured races' even if they were British subjects – especially in the debate on the 'races power'.[78] By this time, 'alien race' was a standard phrase used by Anglo-Celtic lawmakers in Australia to refer to those who were different or 'not one of us' in a non-legal, racial sense.[79] Contrary to Justice Edelman's statement, Aboriginal Australians could also be regarded as an 'alien race' in this general, non-legal sense. Australia's First Nations peoples were excluded from the original version of the 'races power' in section 51(xxvi) of the Australian Constitution not because they were recognised as subjects (and not aliens) under the law, but simply because their regulation was to be left to the states.[80]

---

76   Henry Reynolds, *Forgotten War* (Sydney: New South Publishing, 2013), 76–77, 166–67.

77   As Quick and Garran say, the provision 'was introduced in its present form in 1891, and was adopted in 1897–8 without debate'. John Quick and Robert Garran, *Annotated Constitution of the Australian Commonwealth* (Sydney: Angus & Robertson, 1901), 599.

78   See Prince, 'Aliens in Their Own Land', 136ff.

79   British Indians, Malays, Chinese from Hong Kong, the Straits Settlements and other colonies, as well as 'Kanakas' (Pacific Islanders) from British possessions in the South Pacific were all included, despite their legal status as subjects of the Crown. Prince, 'Aliens in Their Own Land', ch. 3.

80   In its original form, section 51(xxvi) gave the Australian Parliament power to make laws with respect to 'the people of any race, *other than the aboriginal race in any State*, for whom it is deemed necessary to make special laws'. Emphasis added. This provision was amended by the *Constitution Alteration (Aboriginals) Act 1967* (Cth) by exclusion of the phrase 'other than the aboriginal race in any State'.

As Chesterman and Galligan say:

> A comprehensive constitutional treatment of citizenship might be
> considered by some to be preferable, and certainly it would be neater
> and simpler. But that is not the way citizenship has been handled
> in Australia. Those who do not pursue the substantive complexities
> of Australian citizenship remain at the surface, fulminating against
> the supposed ignorance of the founders and the emptiness of
> Australian citizenship.[81]

However, rather than 'fulminate against the ignorance of the founding
fathers', the High Court in *Love & Thoms* provided a false positive impression,
maintaining that Aboriginal Australians had never been seen differently
in terms of legal membership status. As this section has shown, there was
a consistent lack of regard in Australia for Aboriginal legal belonging from
European settlement until at least the 1960s. But the emphasis in academic
writing on 'substantive citizenship' is also misleading. In particular, it fails
to highlight the trashing of the rule of law in colonial and post-Federation
Australia with the repeated failure by Anglo-Celtic lawmakers to treat First
Nations peoples with the equal legal and constitutional membership they were
entitled to. A lack of attention to formal legal membership means historians
have not held past lawmakers to account for their failure to respect the
automatic legal belonging of First Nations peoples under white law and how
that should have flowed through to equal rights of citizenship and protection.

Uluru Statement

The concept of a 'makarrata' or coming together after a struggle called for
in the 2017 *Uluru Statement from the Heart* – facing the facts of wrongs and
living again in peace, involving not only agreement-making but also truth-
telling about Australia's past – would be strengthened by the recognition
that, even under the settler Europeans' own imposed laws, Aboriginal people
were frequently regarded as 'aliens', the 'other' or as 'not belonging'– that
is, as not having the formal citizenship in their own country that they were
legally entitled to. As a group of 40 public law experts from across Australia
said in March 2021:

> Constitutional enshrinement of a First Nations Voice would meet
> the widespread desire among Australians for the Constitution to
> properly reflect Australia's history and values … A constitutionally

---

81 John Chesterman and Brian Galligan, ed. *Defining Australian Citizenship – Selected Documents*
(Carlton, Vic: Melbourne University Press, 1999), 4.

enshrined Voice will develop and sustain a respectful relationship between First Nations peoples and others in Australian society based on respect for equal dignity where, in the past, lack of that respect has contributed to their exclusion and disempowerment.[82]

As Ann Curthoys, Ann Genovese and Alexander Reilly have argued in relation to the 1992 *Mabo* decision,[83] 'the new understandings of history' had become so compelling that 'the High Court was forced to abandon its old legal narrative' of pre-colonial Australia as terra nullius (unoccupied).[84] Three decades later, in *Love & Thoms* there was no comparable appreciation of the history of First Nations peoples in Australia. The majority finding in that case (i.e. that Australia's Indigenous peoples were never 'aliens' or 'outsiders' under imposed settler law) would not have been undermined by recognition that they were, in fact, regarded and treated this way – contrary to the law from the time of European settlement onwards. The danger with this lack of recognition is 'law's assertion of its own sovereignty [or] reliance on its own history', with the consequence that 'the final judgment acts as an authorised version of the past'[85] – however inaccurate that might be – which can only be corrected by the High Court itself if/when a similar case comes before it. The next case study discusses another area in which the High Court has failed, yet again, to confront Australia's racialised history of identity and belonging.

Case Study 2: Excluding Papuan Australians

It is well documented that the 'imperatives' of 'White Australia' were pivotal to the decision to federate the country and the framing of its constitutional powers:[86] political debates on the legislative framework that constituted the White Australia policy are replete with racist rhetoric.[87]

---

82 'Submission: The Imperative of Constitutional Enshrinement', Indigenous Constitutional Law, 18 March 2021, accessed 15 December 2021, www.indigconlaw.org/home/submission-the-imperative-of-constitutional-enshrinement.
83 *Mabo v. Queensland* (No. 2) (1992) 175 CLR 1.
84 Ann Curthoys, Ann Genovese and Alexander Reilly, *Rights and Redemption: History, Law, and Indigenous People* (Sydney: UNSW Press, 2008), 2:2.
85 Ibid., 6:2, referring to Jennifer Clarke, 'Case Note: Cubillo v Commonwealth', *Melbourne University Law Review* 25 (2001): 218–94.
86 See e.g. Eve Lester, *Making Migration Law: The Foreigner, Sovereignty and the Case of Australia* (Cambridge: Cambridge University Press, 2018), 112–58, doi.org/10.1017/9781316779910.
87 Ibid., 122–26.

The absence of a citizenship provision in the Australian Constitution gave the Commonwealth legislature extraordinary latitude to determine who should be regarded as a member of the Australian community and who should not.[88] Therefore, it should come as no surprise that, in late 1901, as Australia's new Commonwealth Parliament called for the transfer from Great Britain of the colony of British New Guinea, Senator Thomas Playford made the avowedly racist and deeply offensive statement that: 'We also wish to know … whether the n*****s will be allowed to cross the narrow strait and find their way into Australia proper.'[89]

The former South Australian premier and his fellow members of parliament supported the expansion of Australia's new Federation into the Pacific as part of its own 'Monroe Doctrine'.[90] However, as Mr Cameron from Tasmania asked in the House of Representatives, 'there are 350,000 natives at present in New Guinea, and if they become part of the Commonwealth, how can we have a White Australia?'[91] In 1905, Australia eagerly passed legislation to accept the transfer of the new territory, renamed Papua.[92] Playford need not have worried. As Adelaide's *Register* explained:

> the new nation does not seek to raise the Papuans to the rank of Australians … on account of their dark pigmented skins they will be regarded as aliens and not be permitted even to visit it.[93]

The racist ideology evident in this statement aligns with some of the most offensive elements of the White Australia policy. Papuans were entitled to Australian birth certificates and passports but they were prohibited from travelling to the mainland for the 70 years that Papua was an Australian territory.[94]

---

88 Kim Rubenstein, *Australian Citizenship Law*, 2nd ed. (Pyrmont, NSW: Thomson Reuters, 2017), 50–52.
89 Commonwealth of Australia, *Debates*, Senate, 20 November 1901, 7480.
90 Michael Wesley, 'The Ties That Bind: The Australia-PNG Relationship', *Devpolicy Blog*, 17 August 2017, devpolicy.org/ties-bind-australia-png-relationship-20170817/?print=print.
91 Commonwealth of Australia, *Debates*, Representatives, 19 November 1901, 7461.
92 *Papua Act 1905* (Cth), section 5.
93 'AUSTRALIAN MONROEISM', *Register* (Adelaide), 2 December 1901, 4.
94 Kim Rubenstein and Jacqueline Field, 'What Is a "Real" Australian Citizen? Insights from Papua New Guinea and Mr. Amos Ame', in *Citizenship in Question: Evidentiary Birthright and Statelessness*, ed. Benjamin N. Lawrance and Jacqueline Stevens (Durham: Duke University Press, 2016), 108, doi.org/10.1215/9780822373483-006.

When Australian citizenship was formally created after WWII, Papuans (like Aboriginal Australians) were given a form of 'pretend' citizenship only. Asked in 1948 if Papuans could travel to mainland Australia and enjoy the right to vote, Immigration Minister Arthur Calwell declared: 'We do not even give them the right to come to Australia … a native of Papua would be an Australian citizen but would not be capable of exercising rights of citizenship.'[95] Even after a major relaxation of the White Australia policy in the mid-1960s,[96] Papuan Australians were not allowed to travel to the Australian mainland (or Tasmania).[97] The exclusion of Papuan Australians continued until they could be kept out as foreigners after Papua New Guinea's independence in 1975. As recently as 2005, Australia's High Court used this history of racial exclusion to justify stripping citizenship rights from Papuans born as Australians before Papua New Guinean independence. It continues to be used today to deprive long-term Australian residents of these rights. This reminds us that, despite abolition of the White Australia policy, attitudes from that time cannot merely be considered a quaint historic relic and consigned to the dustbin of history.

Ame's Case: Avoiding the Racial Issue

The determination throughout the White Australia era to keep dark-skinned people away from the mainland meant Papuans lost their Australian citizenship in 1975.[98] On Papua New Guinea Independence Day, 16 September 1975, regulations made by Australian Governor-General Sir John Kerr removed Australian citizenship from those who became citizens of the new nation.[99] Only a few Papuans already granted permanent residence in Australia did not become citizens of Papua New Guinea and kept their Australian citizenship. When challenged in *Ame's Case* (2005),[100] the High Court stated that Papuans were never 'real Australians'. The Australian Parliament had denied them normal citizenship rights like voting and jury service as well as freedom of movement in and out of the mainland. Further, because it was not considered 'real', their Australian

---

95   Commonwealth of Australia, *Debates*, Representatives, 30 November 1948, 3660.
96   'End of the White Australia Policy', National Museum of Australia, accessed 15 December 2021, www.nma.gov.au/defining-moments/resources/end-of-white-australia-policy.
97   *Minister for Home Affairs v. Lee* [2021] FCAFC 89 [31].
98   Peter Prince, 'Mate! Citizens, Aliens and "Real Australians" – The High Court and the Case of Amos Ame', Commonwealth Parliamentary Library, *Research Brief*, 27 October 2005, no. 4 (2005–6).
99   Commonwealth of Australia, Papua New Guinea Independence (Australian Citizenship) Regulations, 10 September 1975.
100 *Re Minister for Immigration and Multicultural and Indigenous Affairs; Ex Parte Ame* (2005) 222 CLR 439.

citizenship could be unilaterally removed by executive regulation without their consent.[101] The High Court agreed that Mr Ame's birth in Papua in 1967 meant that he had been born in 'Australia' under the *Australian Citizenship Act 1948* (Cth).[102] However, it said the meaning of 'Australia' in 1975 under the *Migration Act 1958* (Cth) was different, excluding Papua and other external territories. Thus, Mr Ame was an Australian citizen but also an 'immigrant' who could be kept out of 'Australia proper'. This meant that he automatically lost Australian citizenship when he became a Papua New Guinea citizen. And, as a non-Australian citizen, he was not legally a member of the Australian community and could be deported from Australia as an 'alien' under the Migration Act.

Only Justice Kirby in the *Ame* decision acknowledged the racism of past Australian lawmakers, saying Calwell's 1948 statement and 'repeated references to ethnicity and race in the parliamentary debates' reflected a concern:

> to preserve to the Commonwealth the power to exclude from entry into the Australian mainland foreign nationals and even British subjects who were 'ethnologically of Asiatic origin' or other 'pigmentation or ethnic origin'.[103]

But, even Justice Kirby was unable to find in favour of Mr Ame. As Kim Rubenstein and Jacqueline Field note, it is striking that the High Court in *Ame* saw no need to engage in a postcolonial reckoning with past discrimination. Instead, the court left the nature and security of Australian citizenship 'floating, adrift on … the tides of prejudice'.[104] In this way, highly racialised policies from early 1900s Australia continue to taint the country's legal system and cause personal hardship into the twenty-first century.

Troyrone Zen Lee: A 'Real Australian'

In 2021, Troyrone Zen Lee, born as an Australian citizen in Port Moresby in 1975, won a long court battle to regain his Australian passport. In 1982, Mr Lee's family moved to Brisbane. His Australian passport was renewed at least four times after first being issued in 1979. In 2016, he was 'dumbfounded' when told by a Department of Home Affairs official during another routine

---

101 *Ame* [34]; Rubenstein and Field, 'What Is a "Real" Australian Citizen?', 111.
102 Replaced by *Australian Citizenship Act 2007*.
103 *Ame* [70].
104 Rubenstein and Field, 'What Is a "Real" Australian Citizen?', 112.

renewal that he was not, in fact, an Australian citizen.[105] Drawing on *Ame's Case*, Home Affairs said he had never been a 'real Australian' and, instead, was a citizen of Papua New Guinea. Senior officials in Papua New Guinea told Mr Lee this was not the case.[106] Deprived of his Australian passport, Mr Lee was unable to pursue his career as an electrical engineer specialising in high-speed rail projects in Asia. He was also separated from his wife and Australian-born son, living in Taiwan.[107] And he was at risk of losing his right to stay in Australia – all because of the Department of Home Affairs' interpretation of the High Court's *Ame* decision, which can be traced directly back to the White Australia–era prohibition against 'dark-skinned' Papuans coming to the Australian mainland.

When Mr Lee challenged the confiscation of his Australian passport, the Federal Court stated that Home Affairs was wrong.[108] However, as a lower court, it could not question the *Ame* precedent set by the High Court. Instead, it found a way around this, noting that when Mr Lee was a child, Australian authorities did not treat him as an 'immigrant'. This meant that he had a pre-existing right of permanent residence on the Australian mainland and therefore did not become a Papua New Guinea citizen at independence. In other words, he had never lost the Australian citizenship he was born with. The Commonwealth appealed to the full Federal Court, which also found in favour of Mr Lee, taking the unusual step of recommending an 'Act of Grace' payment because of the significant 'emotive and economic impact' of the Commonwealth's mistake in depriving him of his Australian passport.[109]

The Commonwealth elected not to appeal the case to the High Court. While this means that Mr Lee will not lose his birthright Australian citizenship, an appeal would have given the High Court the opportunity to reconsider its *Ame* judgment, a decision that has led to such cases. The current legal position, therefore, is that *Ame* continues to be the leading authority on this issue. By deciding not to appeal, the Commonwealth chose not to expose the issue to further scrutiny. Significantly, it also leaves for another day the postcolonial reckoning with past racial discrimination that Rubenstein and Field have called for.

---

105 *Minister for Home Affairs v. Lee* [2021] FCAFC 89, [3].
106 Ibid., [5].
107 Stefan Armbruster, 'Man Born in Pre-Independence PNG Recognised as Australian after Federal Court Battle with Immigration Minister', *SBS News*, 17 April 2020, www.sbs.com.au/news/article/man-born-in-pre-independence-png-recognised-as-australian-after-federal-court-battle-with-immigration-minister/r2z41rekx.
108 *Lee v. Minister for Home Affairs* [2020] FCA 487 (17 April 2020).
109 *Minister for Home Affairs v. Lee* [2021] FCAFC 89, [108].

The first two sections in this chapter have discussed how the High Court did not properly confront historic legal discrimination *against* people of colour in key decisions on Australian identity and belonging. The next section discusses how the High Court has also ignored legal discrimination *in favour* of British subjects who arrived from the United Kingdom and its former colonies. It now deems such people to have always been 'aliens' if they have not taken out citizenship. Two men from the former British colony of Malta who both made Australia their home for more than half a century have been caught up in this rewriting of history, losing High Court appeals against their expulsion.

Cast Study 3: Deporting Maltese 'Belongers'

In July 1948, Frederick Chetcuti, born in Malta and not quite three years old, arrived in Australia with his family. For the next 73 years he lived in Australia. But, in 2021, the High Court had no hesitation in labelling him an 'alien' who had never belonged in the Australian community, upholding his deportation to a country he had left as an infant more than seven decades before.[110] In a similar case in 2018, the High Court ruled that John Falzon, who also arrived from Malta as a small boy – in his case 61 years before – could be deported as an 'alien' because he never belonged in Australia.[111] Neither Mr Chetcuti nor Mr Falzon had formally become Australian citizens. Both committed crimes for which they were punished with lengthy terms of imprisonment. The responsible minister cancelled their 'absorbed persons' visas and right to stay in Australia under section 501 of the Migration Act, satisfied they failed the 'character test' due to their criminal record.[112]

The *Chetcuti* and *Falzon* cases raise a number of issues in relation to identity and belonging in Australia: the practice of banishing permanent resident non-citizens who commit serious crimes; the retrospective alteration of the law in a way that is inconsistent with the country's history; and further implications of the legacy of White Australia, this time for inhabitants of Maltese origin.

---

110 *Chetcuti v. Commonwealth of Australia* [2021] HCA 25.
111 *Falzon v. Minister for Immigration and Border Protection* [2018] HCA 2.
112 Mr Chetcuti's absorbed persons visa was, in fact, cancelled three times by the minister after twice being set aside by the Federal Court. *Chetcuti v. Commonwealth of Australia* [2021] HCA 25, [9]–[10].

Australia's Banishment Policy

In 2014, Australia introduced mandatory cancellation of visas under the Migration Act if a non-citizen was convicted and given a prison term of 12 months or more.[113] As Justice Gageler and Justice Gordon explained in the *Falzon* case:

> The purpose of cancelling a visa pursuant to s 501(3A) is to exclude from the Australian community a class of persons who, in the view of the Parliament, should not be permitted to remain in Australia.[114]

The idea that people can be disqualified from belonging to the Australian community because they commit crimes conflicts with the reality that all communities contain those who engage in anti-social and/or criminal behaviour. Neither Mr Chetcuti nor Mr Falzon applied for a formal document stating that they were Australian citizens; however, for well over half a century, both men were full members of – in other words, they 'belonged to' – the Australian community in a practical sense. Mr Falzon had 'two sisters and four brothers, four adult children and 10 grandchildren in Australia as well as nieces, nephews and other minor family members'.[115] As Justice Nettle later acknowledged:

> All of his kin had either been born here or come here years before and remained here ever since. As a result of living almost all of his life in Australia, and of all of his kin being here, the man was deeply connected to the Australian community and without any sense of connection to any other country. *On any view, Mr Falzon had been 'absorbed' into the community.*[116]

The discretionary power to cancel a permanent residency or 'absorbed persons' visa on 'character grounds' has existed since 1992.[117] However, a change in 2014 to mandatory cancellation after conviction for serious crime means that no account can now be taken of the range of reasons a person might, nevertheless, be allowed to remain as part of the Australian community. As the *Age* noted in relation to an earlier 'banishment' case:

---

113 *Migration Amendment (Character and General Visa Cancellation) Act 2014*; Henry Sherrell, 'Australia, New Zealand and the "Corrosive" Character Test', *Interpreter*, 19 July 2019, www.lowyinstitute.org/the-interpreter/australia-new-zealand-corrosive-character-test.
114 *Falzon* [2018] HCA 2, [89].
115 Ibid., [7].
116 *Love & Thoms* (2020) 94 ALJR 198, 249–50, [261]. Emphasis added.
117 *Migration (Offences and Undesirable Persons) Amendment Act 1992*.

> In the case of convicted criminals who, but for attention to bureaucratic detail, are in all other respects Australian, the idea of sending them 'home' to countries with which they have no more than a nominal relationship seems neither reasonable nor fair … the fact that these people have committed crimes does not justify the authorities using the citizenship laws to 'dispose' of a social problem any more than transportation to the colonies was a solution to the social ills of late 18th century England.[118]

Although the prime minister of Australia, Anthony Albanese, has foreshadowed a more commonsense approach in the case of New Zealand citizens brought up in Australia,[119] the law as it currently stands compares unfavourably with the situation even at the height of the White Australia policy 120 years ago. Michael Williams points out that, in the 1900s, application of the infamous dictation test under the *Immigration Restriction Act 1901*, which sought to prevent 'undesirables', primarily non-Europeans, from entering or remaining in Australia, was a matter of discretion; each case was dealt with on its merits, including for those convicted of violent crime. For example, Atlee Hunt, secretary of the Department of External Affairs (responsible for administration of the dictation test) asked for further information to help him decide if prisoners due to be released should be given the test and thus deemed to be 'prohibited immigrants':

> In particular, Hunt wished to know such potentially modifying factors as, how long a person had been in the Commonwealth, their marriage status and if the family were in Australia, if the offence was a first one, a report of their character in general, and of course if the 'man is coloured'.[120]

Retrospective Alteration of Legal Belonging

Until well after WWII, the Australia of the white Anglo-Celtic colonisers was proudly 'British'. In his famous welcome to Queen Elizabeth II and the Duke of Edinburgh in 1963, Prime Minister (Sir) Robert Menzies placed great emphasis on the Australian people's allegiance as subjects of the British Crown:

---

118 'Cherish the Right to be a Citizen', *Age*, 11 December 2003, 12.
119 See Chapter 1 (this volume).
120 Michael Williams, *Australia's Dictation Test. The Test It Was a Crime to Fail* (Boston: Brill, 2021), 225, doi.org/10.1163/9789004471108.

> When we see you, we see you as our Queen. We see you as our
> Sovereign Lady ... We are proud to think that so far from abrogating
> any of our liberties because we are your subjects, we know that we add
> to our liberty because we are your subjects. It is a proud thought for
> us to have you here, to remind ourselves that in this great structure
> of government which has evolved, you ... are the living and lovely
> centre of our enduring allegiance.[121]

Australian governments over many generations were eager to accept
British migrants as full members of the Australian political community.
British subjects living in Australia were entitled to vote in federal and state
elections,[122] could be employed in the public service, were liable for jury
service and (like Mr Chetcuti) were obliged to perform national military
service. Before 1976, a person's nationality was recorded in the Australian
census as either 'British' or 'foreign'.[123] Until 1984, Australian passports could
be issued to British subjects who were not Australian citizens. Perhaps most
significantly, British subjects without Australian citizenship were eligible to
become members of the Australian Parliament. According to the Australian
Constitution, 'until Parliament otherwise provides', members of parliament
'must be a subject of the Queen' and meet residency requirements.[124] After
Australian citizenship was created in 1949,[125] the Australian Parliament had
the opportunity to specify citizenship as a requirement,[126] but it did not do
so until 1981.[127] Before then, it was impossible for British subjects living in
Australia who had not become citizens to contravene section 44(i) of the
Constitution,[128] the (now infamous) section that prohibits any person 'under
any acknowledgement of allegiance, obedience, or adherence to a foreign

---

121 Robert Menzies, '18 February 1963', in *Well May We Say ... The Speeches That Made Australia*, ed.
Sally Warhaft (Melbourne: Black Inc, 2004), 547.
122 And can still vote if enrolled before 26 January 1984. Commonwealth Electoral Act 1918, section
93(1)(b)(ii).
123 *Chetcuti* [2020] HCA 42, [110] (Justice Steward).
124 Australian Constitution, sections 16, 34.
125 *Nationality and Citizenship Act 1948* (Cth).
126 In 1949, the Commonwealth Electoral Act 1918 was amended to require British subject status but
not Australian citizenship itself for a person to be nominated as a senator or member of the House of
Representatives. *Commonwealth Electoral Act (Amendment) Act 1948* (No. 10 of 1949), section 5.
127 The requirement to be an Australian citizen to nominate for federal parliament was inserted into
the Commonwealth Electoral Act by section 34 of the *Statute Law (Miscellaneous Amendments) Act 1981*
(No. 176 of 1981).
128 See recent decisions by the High Court (sitting as the Court of Disputed Returns) on section
44(i) of the Constitution, which held that the election of several federal parliamentarians was invalid
because they were 'citizens or subjects of a foreign power' at the time of their nomination. For example,
Re Gallagher (2018) 355 ALR 1; *Re Canavan, Re Ludlam, Re Waters, Re Roberts* [No. 2], *Re Joyce, Re Nash,
Re Xenophon* [2017] HCA 45 (2017) 349 ALR 534. For a good discussion of this issue, see Kyriaco
Nikias, 'Dual Citizens in the Federal Parliament', *Adelaide Law Review*, 39 (2018), 479.

power … or a subject or a citizen of a foreign power' from standing for federal parliament.[129] Until the mid-1980s, therefore, British subjects living in Australia who had not become citizens could not have been regarded as 'aliens' in a constitutional sense.

But, in 2003, in the *Shaw* case,[130] the High Court retrospectively decreed that all British subjects who arrived after 'Australian citizenship' was formally created in 1949 could be regarded as 'aliens' from the time of their arrival unless they were subsequently naturalised as Australian citizens, no matter how many decades they had lived in Australia. In the *Chetcuti* case in 2021, the High Court extended this further, stating that 'the aliens power reached all those persons who entered this country *before* 26 January 1949 who did not become Australian citizens'.[131] This affects hundreds of thousands of settlers from the United Kingdom[132] as well as arrivals from British colonies like Malta, such as Mr Falzon and Mr Chetcuti.

As in *Love & Thoms*, the High Court's retrospective pronouncement of what, in its view, the law should have been does not accord with the actual legal treatment of such people in Australia. As Justice Kirby remarked in his dissenting judgment in *Shaw*, arrivals from the United Kingdom 'were immediately welcomed into full membership of the Australian community. Nor did they see themselves as aliens.'[133] Nevertheless, under Australian law as currently interpreted by the High Court, settlers from Britain and its former colonies such as Malta who have not become citizens – even those like Mr Chetcuti and Mr Falzon who came to Australia as young children and made Australia their home for well over half a century – are deemed to be 'aliens'; for such people, the right to remain freely in Australia has been lost. They are now subject to laws made under the 'aliens power' in the Constitution, including cancellation of their resident visas under the Migration Act and banishment if convicted of a serious crime.

---

129 *Chetcuti v. Commonwealth of Australia*, M122/2020, Appellant's submissions, 5 March 2021, 17; Appellant's reply, 29 April 2021, 6.
130 *Shaw v. Minister for Immigration and Multicultural Affairs* (2003) 218 CLR 28.
131 *Chetcuti v. Commonwealth of Australia* [2021] HCA 25, [15]. Emphasis added.
132 Peter Prince, 'Deporting British Settlers' (the *Shaw* case), Parliamentary Library, *Research Note*, no. 33 (2003–4).
133 (2003) 218 CLR 28, 62 [97].

The decisions in *Falzon* and *Chetcuti* exemplify the separation of the law on 'belonging' in Australia from historical and social reality. This concerns at least some members of the High Court. In 2022, Justice Edelman (backed by Justice Steward and with some support also from Justice Gordon)[134] stated that, since the 1980s, High Court cases had seen:

> an imperial march of the application of the aliens power, extending it far beyond any ordinary understanding, capturing more and more members of the permanent population of the Commonwealth of Australia ... [C]ase by case, the application of the essential meaning of 'alien' – a foreigner to the Australian political community – was extended further and further to apply to persons who had less and less foreign connection.[135]

Justice Edelman criticised the outcomes in *Shaw*, *Falzon* and *Chetcuti*, declaring 'an overly broad application of the aliens power was adopted in decisions of this Court that, described politely, would strike an ordinary person as very curious'.[136] Although part of the majority in the last two cases, Justice Edelman indicated that he believed the High Court's labelling of Mr Falzon and Mr Chetcuti as 'aliens' who could be expelled despite having spent their lives in Australia was flawed:

> it is very hard to see how those conclusions can be supported by any ordinary application, with regard to today's morals and standards, of the essential meaning of 'alien' as a foreigner or outsider to the Australian political community.[137]

Justice Edelman suggested a new approach, arguing that the test for non-alien status should be the same as for moving beyond the category of 'immigrant' under the Constitution. If a person lacked formal citizenship, he or she should nevertheless be accepted as a full legal member if 'unconditionally absorbed' into the Australian community.[138] This would allow a return to the type of discretionary approach in place even when the White Australia policy was at its zenith. As Sangeetha Pillai observes, such comments 'may foreshadow future change with wide ranging implications for migration law, especially since Edelman J is guaranteed a place on the High Court until 2044'.[139]

---

134 See *Alexander v. Minister for Home Affairs* [2022] HCA 19, [182]–[184], [200]–[201] (Edelman); [291] (Steward); [144] (Gordon).
135 Ibid., [183]–[184].
136 Ibid., [218].
137 Ibid., [219].
138 Ibid., [209]–[210].
139 Sangeetha Pillai, 'Judicial Agreements and Disagreements in Alexander v Minister for Home Affairs', *AUSPUBLAW*, 21 September 2022, www.auspublaw.org/blog/2022/09/judicial-agreements-and-disagreements-in-alexander-v-minister-for-home-affairs.

More Echoes of White Australia: Maltese 'White Aliens'

The labelling of Mr Chetcuti and Mr Falzon as 'aliens' who did not 'belong' despite living almost their entire lives in Australia would not have surprised Maltese settlers from earlier generations. Notwithstanding their equal legal membership status as British subjects, Maltese migrants in the 1920s and 1930s were labelled, along with other southern Europeans, as 'white aliens'.[140] Barry York notes that Maltese settlers 'suffered discrimination whenever they were excluded from "British preference" systems of employment'. The Australian Workers' Union 'refused to count the Maltese as British'.[141]

In 1925, Queensland appointed a Royal Commission to *Inquire into and Report on the Social and Economic Effect of Increase in Number of Aliens in North Queensland*. As the *Brisbane Courier* reported:

> Representatives of the Australian Workers' Union have called on the Premier and urged upon him the need for State action in respect of the large arrivals in the North of *Southern Europeans*. They maintained that the arrival of hundreds of *aliens* in the North would mean starvation and misery either for them or for those whose employment they would take.[142]

Maltese settlers in north Queensland, along with Sicilians and Greeks, were a focus of the royal commission. Commissioner T. A. Ferry lauded the efficiency of workers from Britain and northern Italy, but lamented 'that, unfortunately, the majority of the new arrivals in Queensland happened to be of the Southern Italian and Mediterranean type':

> There is sufficient evidence to show that many of the new arrivals are of the latter type here referred to. Their behaviour in the trains in crowding out the carriages and jostling women and children is adding to the objection to foreigners generally, and their standard of living is obviously very low. According to the evidence of one witness, the principal offenders in this respect are Maltese, Sicilians, and Greeks.[143]

---

140 Michele Langfield, '"White Aliens": The Control of European Immigration to Australia 1920–1930', *Journal of Intercultural Studies* 12, no. 2 (1999): doi.org/10.1080/07256868.1991.9963375.
141 Barry York, *The Maltese in Australia* (Melbourne: AE Press, 1986), 68.
142 'Italian Influx', *Brisbane Courier*, 1 April 1925, 7. Emphasis added.
143 'Anti-Foreign Feeling', *Brisbane Courier*, 3 June 1925, 7; Queensland, Alien Immigration Commission, *Report of the Royal Commission Appointed to Inquire into and Report on the Social and Economic Effect of Increase in Number of Aliens in North Queensland* (Brisbane: Qld GPO, 1925), 9–10.

Ferry said the Maltese were:

> hard-working and honest, but uneducated and their standard of living is inferior to the British or Italian … I inspected a Maltese lodging-house in Innisfail and found about twenty (20) men living in one room. Every room was crowded with bunks with just enough space between to enable the occupants to move about.[144]

Ferry visited a number of townships in north Queensland but interviewed only 39 witnesses.[145] His cursory 26-page report relied heavily on hearsay and rumour and concluded that:

> It is certain that the growing animosity against all foreigners is due to the different and inferior types arriving … Workers who for years have sacrificed much to obtain favourable industrial conditions naturally resent the intrusion into their midst of large numbers of immigrants, many of whom are of a hopelessly inferior type.[146]

Michelle Langfield argues that Australian inhabitants of Maltese descent 'objected to the principle of British subjects of "white race" being treated as "aliens"'.[147] According to York:

> The number of Maltese immigrants would have been greater were it not for the Australian government's introduction, in 1931, of a Landing Permit requirement for them. In effect, this placed them in exactly the same category as non-British 'aliens'.[148]

In 1938, Malta's high commissioner complained that settlers from the British colony were 'citizens' who belonged in Australia:

> the Commissioner for Malta in Australia (Captain Henri Curmi), in an address to the Constitutional Club yesterday, said that the 10,000 Maltese in this country had proved valuable citizens. Their combined assets, according to a recent census, had a total value of £4,000,000. Maltese had been coming to Australia for 80 years, but many of their descendants, over about three generations, had passed out of the classification of Maltese.[149]

---

144 Ibid., 10–11.
145 Ibid., 2.
146 Ibid., 16–17.
147 Langfield, 'White Aliens', 6.
148 York, *Maltese in Australia*, 106. Intending Maltese settlers could also be excluded using the infamous dictation test. As Michael Williams notes, in 1917, 'Prime Minister Billy Hughes ordered 200 Maltese labourers – all British subjects – to be tested in Dutch'. In 1920, a limit of 200 Maltese settlers per year was imposed. Williams, *Australia's Dictation* Test, 141, 214.
149 '10,000 Maltese in Australia', *Argus* (Melbourne), 1 March 1938, 3. See also Barry York's discussion of Curmi, *Maltese in Australia*, 83–85.

Conclusion: The High Court's History Matters

As Helen Irving has observed in relation to the High Court's use of the 1890s constitutional convention debates: 'how well did the justices perform as historians? … [T]he respectful answer must be: not brilliantly.'[150] This was also true in the case studies above. This chapter contends that the High Court has put forward an idealised version of Australian history – one that disregards or ignores the shameful legal treatment of First Nations peoples; the deliberate exclusion of Papuan Australians because of their dark skin; and the unquestioned past acceptance of British settlers as 'belongers', along with the gifting to such people of all the rights of 'citizenship' denied to First Nations peoples whose ancestors had 'belonged' on the lands of Australia for tens of thousands of years. As Irving explains, 'it would appear, indeed, that the "history" done by judges occupies a different hermeneutical space from the "history" done by historians'.[151]

As the case studies show, the adjudication by the High Court on issues of identity and belonging determines, in a very real way, whether people can remain part of the Australian community. But the history presented by the court also matters, not just the decisions themselves. As Galarrwuy Yunupingu said in relation to the Uluru Statement:

> Let us be who we are – Aboriginal people in a modern world – and be proud of us. Acknowledge that we have survived the worst that the past had thrown at us, and we are here with our songs, our ceremonies, our land, our language and our people – our full identity. What a gift this is that we can give you if you choose to accept us in a meaningful way.[152]

How can Australia acknowledge that First Nations peoples 'have survived the worst that the past had thrown at' them if the legal history portrayed by the highest court in the land inaccurately describes the citizenship or subject status of Aboriginal people as having always been equal to whites?

---

150 Helen Irving, 'Constitutional Interpretation, the High Court and the Discipline of History', *Federal Law Review* 41 (2013): 95, 109, doi.org/10.22145/flr.41.1.4.
151 Ibid., 97. 'Hermeneutics' is the science of interpretation.
152 Cited in Department of the Prime Minister and Cabinet, *Final Report of the Referendum Council* (Australian Government, 2017), iii; see Kim Rubenstein, 'Power, Control and Citizenship. The Uluru Statement from the Heart as Active Citizenship', *Bond Law Review* 30, no. 1 (2018): 19, 20, doi.org/10.53300/001c.5659.

As *Love & Thoms* makes clear, it is not only the Australian Constitution but also the High Court that should properly reflect Australia's history in relation to First Nations peoples by acknowledging their past exclusion and disempowerment from the Australian community.

Curthoys, Genovese and Reilly argue that:

> law cannot avoid history, nor, we argue, should it do so. What is called for is not for law to escape the dilemma of historiography but, fully recognising it, to respond appropriately. One alternative to maintaining the separation of law and history is to embrace history in judgment.[153]

It should be automatic that legal precedents from the era of White Australia that adjudicated on elements of that policy are now treated with caution. Regrettably, it must be concluded that the High Court has been deficient in this regard. Chapter 1 notes the shameful *Robtelmes* case from 1906, in which the High Court authorised the mass deportation of Australia's South Sea Islander community on the basis of their race. Remarkably, almost 120 years later, it is still being cited by the High Court as foundational authority for sweeping use of the 'aliens power' in the Constitution.[154] Despite that case approving a key legislative element of the White Australia policy, until 2020 no High Court judge had considered its validity against this historical context, let alone tested the perfunctory labelling by Chief Justice Griffith of the entire Islander community as 'indisputably alien'. Even though Justice Edelman agreed in *Love & Thoms* that *Robtelmes* was decided on racial grounds, the case continues to be relied on by Edelman and his fellow judges in the High Court's jurisprudence.[155] As Irving suggests, the High Court has some distance to go both in its portrayal of the history of identity and belonging in Australia, and in properly applying that history in its decisions in this area.

---

153 Curthoys, Genovese and Reilly, *Rights and Redemption*, 5:2.
154 See Chapter 1 (this volume).
155 *Love & Thoms* (2020) 94 ALJR 198, [415]; *Commonwealth v. AJL20* [2021] HCA 21 at [21] (Chief Justice Kiefel, Justice Gageler, Justice Keane, Justice Steward); *Alexander v. Minister for Home Affairs* [2022] HCA 19 at [138], [150] (Justice Gordon), [208] (Justice Edelman).

Contributors

Margaret Allen is professor emerita in gender studies at the University of Adelaide. She is interested in transnational, postcolonial and feminist histories and whiteness. For 20 years she has been researching India–Australia relationships with a particular emphasis upon Indians living in Australia and their negotiation of the restrictive White Australia policy in the period c. 1880–1940. She has published widely in this field. She is a member of the Fay Gale Centre for Research on Gender.

Kate Bagnall is a social historian whose research focuses on the intersections of migration, family and the law in the British settler colonial world. Kate is best known for her work in Chinese Australian history, particularly the history of women, children and families in Australia's early Chinese communities, and her recent publications include the groundbreaking edited collection, *Locating Chinese Women: Historical Mobility between China and Australia* (Hong Kong University Press, 2021), co-edited with Julia Martínez. Before becoming a senior lecturer in humanities (history) at University of Tasmania in 2019, Kate was an ARC DECRA research fellow at the University of Wollongong (2016–19).

Emma Bellino is a PhD candidate at the University of Wollongong examining marriage, women's nationality and Australia's Asian communities in the early twentieth century. Her research interests include women's histories, marital and reproductive histories, and the historical connections between law, society and lived experiences.

Sophie Couchman is a professional historian and curator who works closely with communities to tell their stories. She has researched and published in the field of Chinese Australian history for many years and has been involved in the development of a wide variety of historical projects including exhibitions, walking tours, oral histories and online resources.

Jane McCabe is the author of *Race, Tea and Colonial Resettlement* (Bloomsbury, 2017) and *Kalimpong Kids: The New Zealand Story, in Pictures* (Otago University Press, 2020). She completed her PhD at the University of Otago in 2014, where she taught history for the next six years. Jane's research has critically examined the relationship between colonial bureaucracies and family history-making. Her doctorate explored the intergenerational legacies of a Presbyterian migration scheme that permanently relocated mixed-race children of tea planters from north-east India to New Zealand. From 2017 to 2020 she conducted a cross-cultural study of rural land ownership and inheritance, funded by a Royal Society of New Zealand Marsden Fast-Start Grant.

Peter Prince has been writing about legal identity and belonging in nineteenth- and twentieth-century Australia for the last two decades. He has published articles, papers and blogs on the implications of this history for the right to belong in modern Australia. His work has been cited by the High Court of Australia in critical 'aliens' cases including *Singh* (2004), *Love & Thoms* (2020) and *Chetcuti* (2021). His PhD thesis, 'Aliens in Their Own Land. "Alien" and the Rule of Law in Colonial and Post-Federation Australia', is available online.[1] He is an affiliate of the University of Sydney Law School.

Kim Rubenstein is Australia's leading expert on citizenship, both in relation to legal status and to participation in government and society. This has led to her scholarship on gender and public law, including her legal work and oral histories of women lawyers' contributions in the public sphere. Currently a professor in the Faculty of Business, Government and Law at the University of Canberra, Kim was director of the Centre for International and Public Law at The Australian National University from 2006 to 2015 and inaugural convener of the Gender Institute from 2011 to 2012. She is a fellow of the Australian Academy of Law and the Academy of the Social Sciences in Australia.

---

1   hdl.handle.net/1885/101778.

Table of Authorities

Cases

Statutes

Index

www.ingramcontent.com/pod-product-compliance
Lightning Source LLC
Chambersburg PA
CBHW040137270326
41927CB00020B/3421